ATLA Monograph Series
edited by Dr. Kenneth E. Rowe

1. Ronald L. Grimes. *The Divine Imagination: William Blake's Major Prophetic Visions.* 1972.
2. George D. Kelsey. *Social Ethics Among Southern Baptists, 1917-1969.* 1973.
3. Hilda Adam Kring. *The Harmonists: A Folk-Cultural Approach.* 1973.
4. J. Steven O'Malley, *Pilgrimage of Faith: The Legacy of the Otterbeins.* 1973.
5. Charles Edwin Jones. *Perfectionist Persuasion: The Holiness Movement and American Methodism, 1867-1936.* 1974.
6. Donald E. Byrne, Jr. *No Foot of Land: Folklore of American Methodist Itinerants.* 1975.
7. Milton C. Sernett. *Black Religion and American Evangelicalism: White Protestants, Plantation Missions, and the Flowering of Negro Christianity, 1787-1865.* 1975.
8. Eva Fleischner. *Judaism in German Christian Theology Since 1945: Christianity and Israel Considered in Terms of Mission.* 1975.
9. Walter James Lowe. *Mystery & The Unconscious: A Study in the Thought of Paul Ricoeur.* 1977.
10. Norris Magnuson. *Salvation in the Slums: Evangelical Social Work, 1865-1920.* 1977.
11. William Sherman Minor. *Creativity in Henry Nelson Wieman.* 1977.
12. Thomas Virgil Peterson. *Ham and Japheth: The Mythic World of Whites in the Antebellum South.* 1978.
13. Randall K. Burkett. *Garveyism as a Religious Movement: The Institutionalization of a Black Civil Religion.* 1978.
14. Roger G. Betsworth. *The Radical Movement of the 1960's.* 1980.
15. Alice Cowan Cochran. *Miners, Merchants, and Missionaries: The Roles of Missionaries and Pioneer Churches in the Colorado Gold Rush and Its Aftermath, 1858-1870.* 1980.
16. Irene Lawrence. *Linguistics and Theology: The Significance of Noam Chomsky for Theological Construction.* 1980.
17. Richard E. Williams. *Called and Chosen: The Story of Mother Rebecca Jackson and the Philadelphia Shakers.* 1981.
18. Arthur C. Repp, Sr. *Luther's Catechism Comes to America: Theological Effects on the Issues of the Small Catechism Prepared In or For America Prior to 1850.* 1982.
19. Lewis V. Baldwin. *"Invisible" Strands in African Methodism.* 1983.
20. David W. Gill. *The Word of God in the Ethics of Jacques Ellul.* 1984.
21. Robert Booth Fowler. *Religion and Politics in America.* 1985.
22. Page Putnam Miller. *A Claim to New Roles.* 1985.
23. C. Howard Smith. *Scandinavian Hymnody from the Reformation to the Present.* 1987.
24. Bernard T. Adeney. *Just War, Political Realism, and Faith.* 1988.
25. Paul Wesley Chilcote. *John Wesley and the Women Preachers of Early Methodism.* 1991.
26. Samuel J. Rogal. *A General Introduction to Hymnody and Congregational Song.* 1991.
27. Howard A. Barnes. *Horace Bushnell and the Virtuous Republic.* 1991.

A General Introduction to Hymnody and Congregational Song

by
SAMUEL J. ROGAL

ATLA Monograph Series, No. 26

The American Theological
Library Association
and
The Scarecrow Press, Inc.
Metuchen, N.J., & London
1991

British Library Cataloguing-in-Publication data available

Library of Congress Cataloging-in-Publication Data

Rogal, Samuel J.
    A general introduction to hymnody and congregational
song / by Samuel J. Rogal.
        p.   cm. — (ATLA monograph series ; no. 26)
    Includes bibliographical references and index.
    ISBN 0-8108-2416-7   (alk. paper)
    1. Hymns, English—History and criticism.   2. Hymns,
English—United States—History and criticism.   I. Title.
II. Series.
BV312.R64   1991
264'.2—dc20   91-16693

CONTENTS

LIST OF TABLES

EDITOR'S FOREWORD

SINCE 1972 THE American Theological Library Association has undertaken responsibility for a modest monograph series in the field of religious studies. Our aim in this series is to publish two dissertations of quality each year at reasonable cost. Titles are selected from studies in a wide range of religious and theological disciplines. We are pleased to publish Samuel J. Rogal's introduction to hymnody and congregational song as number twenty-six in our series.

Following undergraduate studies at Clarion State College (PA), Mr. Rogal took an M.A. in English from the University of Pittsburgh. Mr. Rogal has taught at Waynesburg College, Iowa State University, State University of New York at Oswego, Mary Holmes College, and Illinois State University. He currently chairs the Division of Humanities and Fine Arts at Illinois Valley Community College in Oglesby, Illinois. Mr. Rogal is a prolific author, having published fourteen books and pamphlets, and more than fifty scholarly articles.

KENNETH E. ROWE
Series Editor
Drew University Library
Madison, New Jersey 07940

PREFACE

A General Introduction to Hymnody and Congregational Song has come forth, principally, as an attempt to serve the interests and the needs (both actual and anticipated) of those who labor, regularly and willingly, to provide music and song for the worship service. By the term *laborers* I refer to those who sing (in the pews and from the choir lofts) and those who select hymns for public worship. Thus, I would hope sincerely that the contents of this volume will accommodate all of those concerned with text and music that they, with equal sincerity, dedicate to the glory of God. I have specifically directed the ideas and the observations contained herein to those clerics, musicians, singers, and worshipers who wish to pursue the study of the hymn on a serious (though not necessarily formal) level—who wish to read, evaluate, analyze, and even debate the historical and theological issues relating to hymnody. To initiate active, intellectual exchange on the subject, I have attempted to direct my own efforts toward a readership of diverse interests and purposes, believing that the discussion will become meaningful for all persons concerned with and involved in congregational song.

I would further declare my intention to place this discussion of hymnody and congregational song firmly within the framework (or system, in specific instances) of the existing religious establishment, where hymnody is a principal concern. That intention does not mean to imply the denigration or the denunciation of hymnody associated with past or current cults, folk communities, or even societies and organizations directed by self-appointed clerics. However, hymnody representative of such organizations and institutions does indeed require methods of research, description, and presentation too ambitious for the confines of the present volume. Similarly, I have found it necessary to restrict the scope, both historical and geographical, of this particular project to the hymnody of the Western world. Such cultural, geographical, and political divisions as Asia, India, Africa, and the Middle East certainly ought to be seriously surveyed and analyzed in terms of congregational singing. In fact, few will argue against the notion that the contributions to the general history and development of hymnody in those areas of the world have been rich, permanent, and vital. Nonetheless, the subject of the hymn outside the Western world—outside the English-speaking Western world, to be accurate—needs to be developed and discussed in a separate volume, perhaps to complement and to expand the present study.

I would, simply but directly, dedicate this volume to all who give of their time, their love, and their voices to advance the notion and the purpose of congregational singing. For the singers especially reflect the spirit of that classic statement with which, long ago, a poet of the Church, Henry Francis Lyte, identified the role of song within the context of divine service and worship:

> Strings and voices, hands and hearts,
> In the service bear your parts:
> All that breathe, your Lord adore;
> Praise Him, praise Him, evermore.

Samuel J. Rogal
Illinois Valley Community College
Oglesby, Illinois 61348

Chapter One
SOME DEFINITIONS

IN THE BROADEST OF DEFINITIONS and in the most traditional of applications, the *hymn* exists, fundamentally, as a lyric poem expressing religious emotion—or perhaps religious faith and commitment. It is intended usually to be sung by a chorus that may or may not be identified as a congregation of worshipers. Strictly as a poem (for hymnody belongs as much to poetry as it does to theology or music), the hymn originally referred to almost any song of praise directed to gods, goddesses, or even to earthly beings of noteworthy position and accomplishment. However, there exists some danger (mostly of a spiritual sort) in embracing such a broad definition, for it can easily yield something as unconventional as this:

> The hosts were sandalled and their wings were fire!
> (Are you washed in the blood of the Lamb?)
> But their noise played havoc with the angel-choir.
> (Are you washed in the blood of the Lamb?)
> Oh, shout Salvation! It was good to see
> Kings and Princes by the Lamb set free.
> The banjos rattled and the tambourines
> Jing-jing-jingled in the hands of Queens.
>
> And when Booth halted by the curb for prayer
> He saw his Master thro' the flag-filled air.
> Christ came gently with a robe and crown
> For Booth the soldier, while the throng knelt down.
> He saw King Jesus. They were face to face,
> And he knelt a-weeping in that holy place.
> Are you washed in the blood of the Lamb?
>   (lines 42–56)

Certainly Vachel Lindsay's poem, "General William Booth Enters into Heaven" (1913)—in part or in total—constitutes a song of praise. It even carries with it a specific tune ("The Blood of the Lamb"), and the poet went so far as to match certain stanzas with appropriate musical instruments, noting instructions to that effect in the margins. And his subject, William Booth (1829–1912), the founder of the Salvation Army, can be identified as both noteworthy and accomplished.

Nevertheless, as tempting as it may be to recite, chant, or even attempt to sing Lindsay's lines, the piece has nothing to do with *hymnody*. That term has come to rest firmly within the context of church, synagogue, and theological doctrine; it resides most assuredly within the environment of sacred worship. Still, in focusing attention upon the general subjects of sacred worship and sacred music, one needs to spend at least a few moments in considering those forms closely related to the congregational hymn—such as the pious poem, the lyric of social or political protest, and the commemorative ode. Simply, the comparison-contrast exercise helps one to understand the uniqueness of what has come to be known as the *congregational* hymn. That same exercise will also be of help for determining in the future what does and does not constitute a legitimate congregational hymn.

Anyone who has surveyed or studied British and American literature ought to recall a number of poems in which the word *hymn* formed an important part of the title: Edmund Spenser's "Fowre Hymnes" (1596); John Donne's "Hymne to Christ" (1619), "Hymne to God the Father" (1623), and "Hymne to God My God" (1631); Percy Bysshe Shelley's "Hymn to Intellectual Beauty" (1816); Ralph Waldo Emerson's "Boston Hymn" (1863) and "Concord Hymn" (1837); Algeron Charles Swinburne's "Hymn to Proserpine" (1866); Elinor Wylie's "Hymn to Earth" (1929); and Geoffrey Hill's "Mercian Hymns" (1971).

Despite their titles, however, each poem or group of poems lies even further outside congregational concern than Lindsay's piece on William Booth. The briefest of glimpses at Hill's effort tells one not to place much faith in titles.

> He swayed in sunlight, in mild dreams. He tested the
> little pears. He smeared catmint on his palm for
> his cat Smut to lick. He wept, attempting to mas-
> ter *ancilla* and *servus.*

In terms of the conventions and the concerns of worship, the "hymns" of Hill, Wylie, Swinburne, Emerson, Shelley, Donne, and Spenser belong almost totally to the literary historian and the critical commentator upon belles lettres. They hold no interest for the hymnologist. Nonetheless, a legitimate question arises regarding such poetic pieces: Aside from the obvious fact that the poets wrote them for purposes other than singing, chanting, or uttering by congregations at worship, how do such works actually differ from those poetical pieces found upon the pages of church and synagogue hymnals?

Consider, for the sake of brevity, just the "hymns" by Donne and Emerson—all of which may be identified as occasional pieces of poetry—productions of specific personal or historical moment. Two of the three pieces by Donne concern the poet's serious illness during the winter of 1623, and thus reflect his personal reservations and fears prior to entering "that Holy roome, / Where, with thy Quire of Saints for evermore, / I shall be made Thy Musique." The third poem anticipates Donne's journey to Germany in May of 1619 as part of Lord Doncaster's ambassadorial staff. Again, the motifs of personal fear and concern present themselves, specifically in terms of an ocean voyage to an unknown land.

> As the tree's sap doth seek the root below
> In winter, in my winter now I go
> Where none but Thee, th' eternal root

Of true love, I may know.
("A Hymne to Christ, at the Author's Last
Going into Germany," lines 13–16)

Aside from the strong echoes of Donne's personal conflicts
and anxieties, his three "Hymnes" contain an abundance
of dark imagery while lacking the orthodox poetical
conventions and properties of his own early seventeenth
century. Such qualities may have been responsible for
Samuel Taylor Coleridge's epigrammatic labeling of
Donne as "Rhyme's sturdy cripple." Nonetheless, although
few persons of any sensitivity would attack John Donne on
pure poetic ground, few congregations (if indeed any)
would be able to universalize his profound sentiments or
sing his rasping candences.

At first glance, Emerson's "hymns" might appear
capable of passing the congregational litmus test, but one
must not be misled by the poet's regular rhythm or clear
poetic diction and form. He, as did Donne, clings steadfastly to specific occasions—the principal difference between the two being that Emerson addresses national and
political deities to underscore the patriarchal image of his
commonwealth. In the "Boston Hymn," for example, God
comes to the Pilgrims for the purpose of denouncing
human suffering and political tyranny.

My angel, —his name is Freedom,—
Choose him to be your king;
He shall cut pathways east and west
And fend you with his wing.
(lines 13–16)

He read that piece during the height of the Civil War,
which served to intensify both its tone and its substance. In
the most widely known "Concord Hymn" (1837), which
almost every American schoolchild used to commit to
memory (during the days when school children memo-
rized—or at least read—poetry), the poet homes on that

flash of historical significance when "once the embattled farmers stood / And fired the shot heard round the world" (lines 2–3). Certainly Emerson captures the imagination of his readers and even fires their national pride; however, he places himself in a context similar to Donne's, for his flame lights an extremely small and narrow surface. Notice what results in this short, relatively little known piece, "The Bohemian Hymn" (written about 1840):

> In many form we try
> To utter God's infinity,
> But the boundless hath no form,
> And the Universal Friend
> Doth as far transcend
> An angel as a worm
>
> The great Idea baffles wit,
> Language falters under it,
> It leaves the learned in the lurch;
> Nor star, nor power, nor toil can find
> The measure of the eternal Mind,
> Nor hymn, nor prayer, nor church.

No one can argue Emerson does not offer his readers some opportunities for individual and collective song, but he wrote for every day of the week but the sabbath.

One may safely assume, then, that certain pieces from such poets as Emerson, Donne, Spenser, Shelley, Swinburne, Wylie, and even Hill can in a technical sense qualify as hymns. But if those particular occasional odes cannot serve congregational needs within the context of a worship service, then what, specifically, constitutes a *congregational* hymn? Or from another point of view, must all congregational hymns—those pieces found in hymnals for public worship—need to have been written intentionally and specifically as such? At least one answer to both questions may be found in a well-known hymn by a minister of the Congregationalist communion, Washington Gladden (1836–1918). During the Reverend Mr.

Gladden's tenure as pastor of North Church, in Springfield, Massachusetts, he edited a magazine entitled *Sunday
Afternoon.* In 1879, he inserted into that periodical one of
his own poems under the title "Walking with God"; the
opening stanza reads:

> O Master, let me walk with Thee
> In lowly paths of service free;
> Tell me Thy secret, help me bear
> The strain of toil, the fret of care.
>
> (lines 1–4)

The poem belongs to the same general period as a number
of other pieces that would eventually become standard
fixtures of American congregational hymnody: Phillips
Brooks's "O little town of Bethlehem" (1868); Daniel C.
Roberts's "God of our Fathers, whose almighty Hand"
(1876); Ernest W. Shurtleff's "Lead on, O King eternal"
(1887); and Katharine Lee Bates's "O beautiful for spacious skies" (1893).

At any rate, Charles H. Richards discovered Gladden's
"O Master, let me walk with Thee," almost immediately after
its publication, set it to a contemporary tune by H. Percy
Smith entitled "Maryton," and included it in his 1880
American Collection, *The Manual of Christian Praise,* a
Congregationalist hymnal published in Oberlin, Ohio (reprinted in his *New Manual of Christian Praise,* New York,
1901). No doubt Richards recognized, in "Walking with
God" (or "O Master, let me walk with Thee") the same
hymnodic and theological qualities that, more than a century
later, continue to attract participants in the worship service:
it is personal, yet universal; biblical, yet without denominational specificity; poetic, yet rhetorically clear; emotional, yet
respectfully quiet. To sing the combination of Gladden's
poem and Smith's hymn tune is to achieve a balance between
the language of poetry and the conventions of congregational song. Upon the vehicle of that balance, a collection of
people engaged in public worship may convey their praise

both of and to their God. "Be filled with the Spirit," declared Paul to the Ephesians (5:18–20), "addressing one another in psalms, and hymns, and spiritual songs, singing and making melody to the Lord with all your heart, always and for everything giving thanks."

Chapter Two
FROM THE BEGINNING

IN EXTENDING THE CONVENTIONS AND definitions of hymnody to a discussion of the historical development of the hymn form, the name of Ambrose of Milan (340–397)—perhaps the most significant bishop of his day in the Western Church—comes immediately to mind in terms of a beginning. The son of a prefect of Gaul, Ambrose studied law, after which he received an appointment as governor of the district of northern Italy (including Milan). In the conflict between Catholics and Arians, he displayed both boldness and wisdom; thus, on the death of the bishop of Milan in 374, the relatively young Ambrose found himself elected bishop by acclamation. Although a mere catechumen—a convert to Christianity who had not yet received baptism, but only doctrine and discipline—his baptism and consecration proceeded quickly after election. During his tenure as bishop, he demonstrated a rare combination of gentleness and firmness, as seen in his long and ultimately victorious conflict with the Arian empress Justina and in his refusal to permit the emperor Theodosius to enter the church until that monarch had done penance for the massacre at Thessalonica.

Although his prose tracts and sermons achieved popular acceptance, Ambrose's most significant contribution to the Western Church focused upon his efforts to improve the musical service, for which he embraced the concept of antiphonal singing. At its simplest level, the antiphonal style assumes a combination of psalmody with the antiphon sung as an alternating chant between two choirs, sometimes at the octave. (See examples on page 9.)

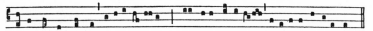

Veni sponsa Christi, accipe coronam, quam tibi Dominus præparavit in æternum.

Ve - ni spon - sa Chri - sti, ac - ci - pe co - ro - nam,

quam ti - bi Do - mi - nus præ-pa - ra-vit in æ -ter - num.

O Rex gloriæ, Domine virtutum, qui triumphator hodie super omnes cœlos

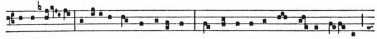

ascen-di - sti, ne derelinquas nos orphanos : sed mitte promissum Patris in nos,

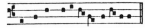

Spiritum veritatis, alleluia.

(Transposed a fifth upwards)

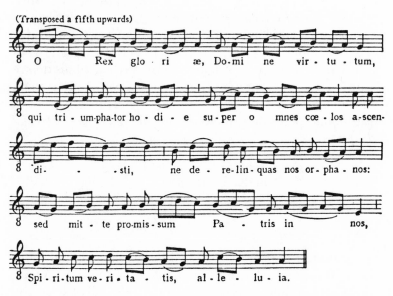

O Rex glo - ri æ, Do-mi ne vir - tu - tum,

qui tri - um-pha-tor ho - di - e su - per o mnes cœ - los a-scen-

di - - sti, ne de - re-lin-quas nos or - pha - nos:

sed mit - te pro-mis - sum Pa - tris in nos,

Spi - ri-tum ve - ri - ta - tis, al - le - lu - ia.

(Hughes, *Early Medieval Music*, pp. 114–115)

Ambrose became indirectly responsible for the spread of antiphonal singing to the Church at Rome during the papacy of Celestine I (422–432). Not only did the bishop offer a concise definition of the liturgical hymn, but—with an equal degree of conciseness—he identified what did not constitute that form. "If you praise God, without singing," maintained Ambrose, "you do not have a hymn. If you praise anything, but not to the glory of God, even if you sing it, it is not a hymn." Then, having dispensed with all of the negative concepts, Ambrose proceeded to the positive qualities: "A hymn . . . contains three elements: song, and praise, it being praise of God" (quoted in Julian, *Dictionary of Hymnology*, 1:56).

Fortunately for succeeding ages, Ambrose actually practiced what he had preached. Of a dozen or so hymns that have been attributed to his authorship, five pieces have been identified with scholarly confidence as his: "Aeterna rerum Conditor" (Framer of earth and sky); "Deus Creator omnium" (Maker of all things, God most high); "Iam surgit hora tertia" (Now appears the third hour); "Veni Redemptor gentium" (Come Thou Saviour of our race); and "Splendor paternae gloriae" (O splendor of God's glory bright). The poet Robert Bridges (1844–1930), poet laureate of England from 1913 until his death, translated "Splendor paternae gloriae" into four stanzas and included it (the tune being a Sarum form of a traditional plainsong melody) in his *Yattendon Hymnal* (1899) as

> O Splendor of God's glory bright,
> O Thou that bringest light from light;
> O Light of light, light's living spring.
> O Day, all days illumining.
>
> (lines 1–4)

Even though the translator has filtered the original Latin through the language and the imagery of another tongue, the modern reader/singer/worshiper can easily observe the characteristics of Ambrosian hymnody: simple but always dignified, relying upon careful repetition, common imagery, and uncomplicated rhythm. In fact, the Ambrosian hymn became the basis for what evolved into the *long meter* hymn form—four eight-syllable lines.

> Weary of all this wordy strife,
> These notions, forms, and modes and names,
> To Thee, the Way, the Truth, the Life,
> Whose love my simple heart inflames.
> (Charles Wesley)

That same Ambrosian hymn further emerged as the model for the Protestant church (or Lutheran) chorale—characterized by sober, elegant, but nonetheless bouyant melody that made little or no distinction between religious and human qualities.

To illustrate the degree to which the idea of hymnody may be variously applied, consider the word *hymnos* in the context of the Septuagint (the pre-Christian Greek version of the Hebrew Scriptures). In that text, the term refers specifically to psalms representative of the Israelites' songs of praise to Jehovah, as for example in Psalms 98:4–6.

> Make a joyful noise to the Lord, all the earth;
>   break forth into joyous song and sing praises!
> Sing praises to the Lord with the lyre,
>   with the lyre and the sound of melody!
> With trumpets and the sound of the horn
>   make a joyful noise before the King, the Lord!
> (RSV)

On two occasions within the New Testament, however, Paul refers to psalms *and* hymns *and* spiritual songs, clearly meaning to distinguish one form from another, to identify the hymn as appropriate to the time of the Gospels and beyond as applicable to singing, as well as to offering thanks in the name of Jesus Christ. Paul practically demands that the Ephesians (5:18–19) "do not get drunk with wine, for that is debauchery; but be filled with the Spirit, addressing one another in psalms and hymns and spiritual songs, singing and making melody to the Lord with all your heart." To the Colossians, the apostle suggests strongly (3:16) that they "let the word of Christ dwell in you richly, as you teach and admonish one another in all wisdom, and as you sing psalms and hymns and spiritual songs with thankfulness in your hearts to God."

Direct references and allusions to hymns and songs abound throughout the Old and New Testaments; in fact, it would require close consultation with a biblical concordance to locate all references and to perceive the extent to which hymnody occurs through the Scriptures. However, in order to pay at least some small service to specificity, the summaries in Table 1 identify the major references.

Table 1. Principal Hymn References in Scripture

Exodus 15:1–18. Moses' Song of Deliverance:

> I will sing to the Lord, for he has triumphed gloriously;
> The horse and the rider he has thrown into the sea.
> The Lord is my strength and my song,
> And he has become my salvation.

Deuteronomy 32:1–43. Moses' Song of Deliverance:

> Give ear, O heavens, and I will speak;
> And let the earth hear the words of my mouth.
> May my teaching drop as the rain,
> My speech distil as the dew.

Judges 5:1–31. Deborah's Song:

> That the leaders took the lead in Israel,
> That the people offered themselves willingly,
> Bless the Lord!

Samuel 1:19–27. David's Lamentation over Saul:

> Thy glory, O Israel, is slain upon thy high places!
> How are the mighty fallen!
> Tell it not in Gath, publish it not in the streets of Ashkelon;
> Lest the daughters of the Philistines rejoice,
> Lest the daughters of the uncircumcised exult.

2 Samuel 22:1–51. David's Song of Deliverance:

> The Lord is my rock and my fortress and my deliverer,
> My God, my rock, in whom I take refuge,
> My shield and the horn of my salvation,
> My stronghold and my refuge.

1 Chronicles 16:7–36. David's Psalm of Thanksgiving:

> O give thanks to the Lord, call on his name,
> Make known his deeds among the peoples!
> Sing to him, sing praises to him,
> Tell of all his wonderful works!

Psalms 1:1–6. The Happiness of the Godly:

> He is like a tree
>   Planted by streams of water,
> That yields its fruit in its season
>   And its leaf does not wither.
> In all that he does, he prospers.

Psalms 19:1–14. The Heavens Declare the Glory of God:

> The heavens are telling the glory of God;
> And the firmament proclaims his handiwork.
> Day to day pours forth speech,
> And night to night declares knowledge.

Psalms 33:1–22. Rejoice in the Lord:

> Rejoice in the Lord, O ye righteous!
> Praise befits the upright.
> Praise the Lord with the lyre,
> Make melodies to him with the harp of ten strings!

Psalms 46:1–11. God Is Our Refuge and Strength:

> God is our refuge and strength,
> A very present help in trouble.
> Therefore, we will not fear, though the earth should change,
> Though the mountains shake in the heart of the sea.

Psalms 84:1–12. My Soul Longs for the Courts:

> How lovely is thy dwelling place, O Lord of hosts!
> My soul longs, yea faints, for the courts of the Lord;
> My heart and flesh sing for joy to the living God.

Psalms 139:1–24. Whither Shall I Go from Thy Spirit?

> Whither shall I go from thy Spirit?
> Or whither shall I flee from thy presence?
> If I ascend to heaven, thou art there!
> If I make my bed in Sheol, thou art there!

Matthew 21:1–11. Christ's Entry into Jerusalem:

> Tell the daughter of Zion,
> Behold, your king is coming to you,
> Humble, and mounted on an ass,
> And on a colt, the foal of an ass.

Matthew 21:14–17. Hosannah to the Son of David:

> Yes, have you ever read,
> Out of the mouths of babes and sucklings
> Thou has brought perfect praise?

Mark 11:1–11. Christ's Entry into Jersusalem:

> Hosanna! Blessed is he who comes in the name of the Lord!
> Blessed is the kingdom of our father, David, that is coming!
> Hosanna in the highest!

Matthew 26:26–30. After the Last Supper:

> And when they had sung a hymn, they went out to the Mount of Olives.

Mark 14:22–26. After the Last Supper:

> And when they had sung a hymn, they went out to the Mount of Olives.

Luke 19:29–44. Christ Enters Jerusalem:

> Blessed is the King who comes in the name of the Lord!
> Peace in heaven and glory in the highest!

Luke 2:8–20. The Angels' Song:

> Glory to God in the highest,
> And on earth peace among men with whom he is pleased!

John 12:12–19. Christ Enters Jerusalem:

> Fear not, daughter of Zion;
> ·Behold your king is coming,
> Sitting on an ass's colt!

Acts 16:19–40. Paul and Silas in Prison:

> But about midnight, Paul and Silas were praying and singing hymns to God, and the prisoners were listening to them, and suddenly there was a great earthquake, so that the foundations of the prison were shaken.

Returning for a moment to the Ambrosian strain of hymnody, one needs to take some notice of the venerated Augustine of Hippo (345–430), a Manichaean converted to Christianity after hearing the sermons of Bishop Ambrose.

Enthralled with the new metrical strains of his friend and teacher (the same Ambrose of Milan), Augustine saw both Christ and the Church as essential to the entire composition of psalmody and hymnody; in fact, the ninth book of Augustine's celebrated *Confessions* contains an emotional appeal in behalf of the antiphonal chant. The philosopher then arrived at a conclusion that eventually emerged as the recognized Church definition of the hymn. In reality, however, that conclusion simply extended the one that had been set forth by Ambrose. For Augustine, then, metrical strains without praise could not serve as hymns. And if both poetry and music praised only earthly or natural objects—including noted and even highly respected personages—they, too, could not be considered as hymns for the purpose of public or private worship.

The Ambrosian-Augustinian concept of hymnody, in combination with Ambrose's actual hymnodic compositions, helped the form—principally by arousing the interest of some rather competent Latin poets, not all of whom can be identified with certainty. And to increase the theological and aesthetic value of the Latin poems for those who worship in English, the pieces have undergone translation by versifiers whose religious commitment and poetic competence rise at least to the level of the originals. For example, a classic hymn (classic in both the chronological and artistic senses) that generally goes by the title "Of the Father's love begotten" came originally from the fourth-century poet Aurelius Clemens Prudentius by way of the "Hymnus omis horae," in his *Liber Cathermerinon* (or hymns for the twelve hours of the day). The Reverend John Mason Neale, warden of Sackville College, East Grimstead, translated Prudentius's Latin original, "Corde natus ex parentis," for the musical edition of *The Hymnal Noted* (1854), wherein the Reverend Thomas Helmore, master of the choristers of the Chapel Royal, set it to a version of a thirteenth-century plainsong, "Divinum Mysterium." Then, ten years later, Sir Henry Williams Baker, vicar of Monkland, penned another translation for the celebrated *Hymns Ancient and Modern* (1861), a volume for which he served as chairman of the editorial committee. Both Neale and Baker captured the broad theological application and the overall timelessness of Prudentius's lines. Neale wrote of "the things that are, that have been, /And that future years shall see"; Baker implored, "Let no tongue on earth be silent, / Every voice in concert ring." Both translators ended their various stanzas with the original intent of Prudentius's own chorus—"Evermore and evermore!"

The same general period as that represented by Prudentius yielded three other hymns of note—pieces that, with alterations, have found their way into a number of British and American hymnals of the nineteenth and twentieth centuries and have become fixtures in the worship service. The Reverend John Cosin—prebendary of Durham, archdeacon of the East Riding of Yorkshire, chancellor of the University of Cambridge, and dean of Peterborough—translated for his *Collection of Private Devotions in the Practice of the Ancient Church, Called the House of Prayer* (1627), a ninth-century Latin hymn ("Veni Creator Spiritus") into a piece that begins, "Come, Holy Ghost, our souls inspire." The Christmas hymn, "O come, O come, Emmanuel, / And ransom captive Israel," derives from John Mason Neale's translation of another anonymous ninth-century Latin hymn—this one found in the *Psalteriolum Cantionum Catholicarum* (1710). Finally, for the purpose of unity, one should take note of a piece beginning "Welcome, happy morning! age to age shall say"—a translation by the Reverend John Ellerton (1826–1893), vicar of Crewe Green and domestic chaplain to Lord Crew, of "Tempora florigero rutilant distincta sereno," written originally by Venantius Honorius Clementianus Fortunatus, bishop of Poitiers in the sixth century. The "Tempora florigero" constituted a section for Easter of a long poem by Fortunatus, addressed to his friend Felix, bishop of Nantes, emphasizing the beauty of spring coming to greet the risen Lord. All three of the preceding pieces (original and translations) underscore the congregational voice in appeals to God and to godly action. Further, each contains a short refrain (a chorus, if you will) to reinforce the choral appeal.

> Praise to Thy eternal merit,
> Father, Son, and Holy Spirit.
>> (Cosin translation)

> Welcome, happy morning! age to age shall say.
>> (Fortunatus)

> Rejoice! Rejoice! Emmanuel
> Shall come to Thee, O Israel!
>> (Neale translation)

Despite the interest of Latin poets of the ninth and tenth centuries in hymnody—as well as in the high quality of secular poetry that they produced—the Roman Church did not officially recognize the hymn as part of its service until the twelfth century. The Council of Laodicea, that synod of bishops which met some time between 341 and 381, set the tone for the Church's attitude toward congregational song. The bishops permitted only appointed singers to sing from the book, referring to the priest's part or those sentences allotted to him. In other words, psalms or hymns composed by those outside of the Church could not be read in the Church. The participation of the congregation would be restricted to responses—or, at best, recitations or chants of verses that related to the antiphons of the Roman Office. Further, only Scriptures could form the basis for anything to be sung (or chanted) by choirs or worship leaders. However, once hymnody assumed legitimacy in the eyes of Church officers, a number of poets emerged, during the twelfth through fourteenth centuries, to provide a small but significant body of Latin hymnic literature, the most noteworthy pieces of which are in common congregational use to this day. Four individuals from that period come immediately to mind.

Peter Abelard (1079–1142) was born at Pailais, Brittany. He was a philosopher, theologian, and priest; married Heloise, the niece of the canon of the Cathedral of Paris; and was condemned for heresy by the Council of Soissons (1121) and by the Council of Sens (1140).

Bernard of Clairvaux (1091–1153) was born near Dijon, Burgundy. He entered the Cistercian monastery at Cîteaux, was abbot of Clairvaux, was in the service of Pope Innocent II, and campaigned in favor of the Second Crusade.

Bernard of Cluny (or of Morlaix) (fl. twelfth century) was born in England and spent practically his entire adult life at the luxurious abbey of Cluny. He was the author of social satires, as well as of hymns.

Francis of Assisi (1182–1226) was the self-indulgent son of an Italian trader. A severe illness at the age of twenty-five caused him to change his attitude and concerns to self-sacrifice and the welfare of others. He formed an order of men sworn to poverty and the renunciation of all worldly goods, and he went forward to preach the Gospel and to relieve distress.

At some point prior to the middle of the twelfth century, Peter Abelard prepared a hymn collection for the Abbey of the Paraclete entitled *Hymnarius Paraclitensis,* from which the twentieth-century American hymnodist, Francis Bland Tucker, extracted a piece and in 1940 translated it as "Alone Thou goest forth, O Lord, / In sacrifice to die" for the 1940 revised *Hymnal* of the Protestant Episcopal Church in America. To discuss the contribution to the hymnody of the Latin world (and later to the hymnody of the entire Western world) of Bernard of Clairvaux requires an essay unto itself. Hymns translated from and based upon his poetry still appear in almost every major hymnal published in Great Britain and North America, while an equal number have fallen from common use. For the sake of both brevity and specificity, mention must be made of certain of those poetic pieces of Bernard of Clairvaux, particularly "Jesu, dulcis memoria" (a long poem on the Name-of-Jesus theme and generally known as the Jubilus of Saint Bernard or the "Rosy Hymn"); "Salve mundi Salutare" (a 350-line poetic address to the various limbs of Christ on the Cross); "Laetabundus, exultet fidelis chorus: Alleluia" (a popular sequence, in common use throughout France and England, particularly in the mass at daybreak on Christmas); "Cum sit omnis homo foenoum," "Ut jucundas cervas undas" (a sacred poem of 68 lines); "Eheu, Eheu, mundi vita" (also known as "Heu, Heu, mala mundi vita," 400 lines in length, but actually only attributed to Bernard of Clairvaux); and "O miranda vanitas" (included in several editions of the poet's works, but still only attributed to him).

The major difficulty surrounding both authorship and chronology of Bernard's hymns concerns the tendency to ascribe to him practically any poem of quality belonging to the twelfth century and having no clear sign of authorship. Nonetheless, most twentieth-century hymnals contain at least one or two translations from Bernard's longer pieces, as well as combinations and variations thereof. His niche in the general history of hymnody seems secure.

The hymnodic reputation of Bernard of Cluny (or, more correctly, Bernard de Morlaix, monk of Cluny) appears equally secure, if for no other reason than those well-known lines translated into English almost a century and a half ago by John Mason Neale:

> Jerusalem the golden, with milk and honey blest,
> Beneath thy contemplation sink heart and voice oppressed.
> I know not, O I know not, what joys await us there,
> What radiancy of glory, what bliss beyond compare!

Neale extracted his text from Bernard's monumental poem of some three thousand lines, *De Contemptu Mundi* (c.

1145)—the title of the selection being "Urbs Sion aurea, patria Lactea." In those lines, the French monk explicated such biblical themes as the apprehension of heaven, the enormity of sin, and the terrors of hell. In the preface to his *Hymns, Chiefly Medieval, on the Joys and Glories of Paradise* (1865), Neale informs readers and worshipers that "the greater part of *De Contemptu Mundi* is a bitter satire on the fearful corruption of the age. But as a contrast to the misery and pollution of earth, the poem opens with a description of the peace and glory of heaven, of such rare beauty, as not easily to be matched by any medieval composition on the same subject" (p. 68). In one sense, Neale's translation may have been the instrument that plucked Bernard's epic poem from literary oblivion, even though for purposes of congregational worship the nineteenth-century English hymnodist had to severely alter the sense of the twelfth-century Latin original.

In considering the hymnodic contributions of Francis of Assisi, one must allow historical and intellectual prominence to compensate for a lack of literary output. The thirteenth-century Italian friar receives little attention from hymnologists; however, his small service to the development of the English hymn cannot be totally ignored. In 1926 the Reverend William Henry Draper, rural dean of Shrewsbury, produced a rhymed version of Francis's "Cantico di fratre sole, laude della creature"—known generally as the "Sun Song" or the "Song about Creatures." The familiar opening of Draper's Paraphrase reads, "All creatures of our God and King, / Lift up your voice and with us sing." The "Cantico di fratre sole" dates from approximately 1225, when Francis, then at San Damiano, lay in a state of severe spiritual depression and physical suffering: tortured by his failing sight and the unbearable heat, unable to endure any light upon his sensitive and weak eyes, plagued by swarms of vermin and rodents that gave him no opportunity for rest or for sleep. As John Mason Neale had done with the *De Contemptu*

Mundi of Bernard of Cluny, Draper attempted to inject a high level of positivism into the relatively dark background of the original text. Specifically, Draper sought to prepare a meaningful hymn for a schoolboy's festival at Adel, near Leeds. In so doing, he managed to capture the essence of praise found both in Francis's song and in Psalms 145:11 ("They shall speak of the glory of thy kingdom, and talk of thy power"). Clearly, translators of the nineteenth and twentieth centuries sought, through their own poetic thought and language, the means to achieve meaningful transition from the poetry of the early Church to the hearts and minds of modern congregational worshipers.

Chapter Three
LUTHER AND OTHERS

IN HIS LECTURE-ESSAY, "The Hero as Priest" (1840), Thomas Carlyle pointed to Martin Luther's classic conclusion to his address before the Diet of Worms on 17 April 1521: "Here stand I; I can do no other: God assist me!" For Carlyle—the Scottish-born contemporary of both Romantics and early Victorians—Luther's appearance on that spring day constituted the most significant scene in the history of modern Europe. Thus he viewed the two-hour oration as "the greatest moment in the Modern history of Men. English Puritanism, England and its Parliament, Americas, and the vast work of these two centuries; French Revolution, Europe and its work everywhere at present: the germ of it all lay there: had Luther in that moment done other, it had all been otherwise!" ("On Heroes, Hero-Worship, and the Heroic in History," 1841). Indeed, the same sentiments may be echoed, although not quite so dramatically or rhetorically, concerning the effects of Luther upon church hymnody, for as the Reformation introduced the language of the people into public worship, it also provided worshipers with the opportunity to express themselves through congregational song in the language of the common people. Such action in turn brought about the eventual unification of Christians in singing praises to their God.

Luther's actual contribution to hymnody focused upon the fact that he initiated the radical shift away from emphasis upon choral chanting by priests and choirs. In a sense, he passed the vocal torch from the officers of the service to the participants, thus elevating congregational singing to a significant place in the worship service. Indeed, Martin Luther has received recognition from hymnologists as the first *evangelical* hymnodist: in 1524 he gave to his own countrymen (and subsequently, by way of a group of sensitive nineteenth-century translators, to the entire Western world) their own hymnal in their own language—*Etlich Christliche Lieder* (the *Achtliederbuch*). He followed that volume with nine additional collections published between 1524 and 1545: *Eyn Enchiridion oder Handbuchlein*, 1524, (twenty-five hymns, eighteen by Luther); *Geystliche Gesangk Buchleyn*, 1524, (thirty-two hymns, twenty-four by Luther); *Geistliche Lieder auffs neu gebessert*, 1529, (fifty hymns, twenty-nine by Luther); *Geistliche Lieder auffs neu gebessert*, 1531, (a reprint of the 1529 volume); *Geistliche Lieder auffs neu gebessert*, 1539, (sixty-eight hymns, twenty-nine by Luther); *Christliche Gesang, Lateinisch und Deudsch, zum Begrebnis*, 1542; *Geistliche Lieder*, 1543, (sixty-one hymns, thirty-five by Luther); and *Geistliche Lieder*, 1545, (one hundred forty-one hymns, thirty-five by Luther).

Luther's thirty-eight original hymn compositions (twenty-one of which date from 1524) may be arranged into five distinct classifications: translations from the Latin works of other poets, revisions of earlier popular religious odes, psalm paraphrases, paraphrases from the other books of the Holy Scriptures, and eight pieces that are purely original. For convenience, the hymns are cataloged in Tables 2 through 6.

Table 2. Luther's Latin Translations

Luther's Title	Source	Common English Version
Christum wir sollen loben schon (1524)	Paen Alphabeticus de Christo (5th century)	Praise we Christ, the Holy One (Richard Massie, 1854)

Luther's Title	Source	Common English Version
Der du bist drei Einigkeit (1543)	O Lux beata Trinitas, et Principalis Unitas (Ambrose)	Thou who are Three in Unity, true God (Richard Massie, 1854)
Jesus Christus unser Heiland (1524)	Jesus Christus, nostra salus (c. 1410)	Lord Jesus Christ! to Thee we pray (William Morton Reynolds, 1849)
Komm Gott Schopfer, heiliger Geist (1524)	Veni Creator Spiritus, mentes tuorum visita (10th century)	Creator Spirit, Holy dove (Richard Massie, 1854)
Nun komm der Heidenheiland (1524)	Veni Redemptor gentium (Ambrose)	Come, Thou Saviour of our race (William Morton Reynolds, 1850)
Was furchat du Feind Herodes sehr (1541)	Paean Alphabeticus de Christo (5th century)	Why, Herod, unrelenting foe! (Richard Massie, 1854)
Herr Gott dich loben wir! (1529)	Te Deum laudamus (7th century)	Thee, Lord, our God, we praise (*Ohio Lutheran Hymnal*, 1880)
		Lord God, Thy praise we sing, Lord God (Richard Massie, 1854)
Verleih uns Frieden gnadiglich (1527, 1529)	Da pacem, Domine (7th century)	Lord, in Thy mercy and Thy grace (Caroline Fry Wilson, 1845)
Wir glauben all in einen Gott ('1524)	Nicene Creed	We all one holy God believe (Arthur Tozer Russell, 1851)
Komm, heiliger Geist, Herre Gott (1524)	*Basel Plenarium* (1514) and Veni Sancte Spiritus (11th century)	Come Holy Ghost! Come Lord our God (Johann Christian Jacobi, 1722)
		Come, Holy Ghost! Lord God, fulfill (Richard Massie, 1854)
Mitten wir im Leben sind (1524)	*Basel Plenarium* translation (1514) of Media vita in morte sumus (c. 7th century)	Though in midst of life we be (Richard Massie, 1854)

Table 3. Luther's Revisions of Earlier Popular Religious Odes

Luther's Title	Source	Common English Version
Gelobet seist du Jesus Christ (1524)	German translation (c. 1370) of a Latin sequence (c. 11th century), Hine oportet ut canamus cum angelus septem gloria in excelsis	Jesus! all praise is due to Thee (Charles Kinchen, 1742) O Jesu Christ! all praise to Thee (Arthur Tozer Russell, 1851)
Gott der Vater wohn uns bei (1524)	15th-century litany, Sanctus Petrus, won uns bey	God the Father, with us be (Arthur Tozer Russell, 1851)
Gott sei gelobet und gebenedeiet (1524)	Latin processional, as well as chanted during mass as a post-Communion	God be blessed, and God be praised (Caroline Fry Wilson, 1845)
Nun bitten wir den heiligen Geist (1524)	From a manuscript sermon attributed to Bertholt von Regensberg (d. 1272)	Now pray we all God the Comforter (Arthur Tozer Russell, 1851)

Table 4. Luther's Psalm Paraphrases

Luther's Title	Source	Common English Version
Ach Gott von Himmel sieh darein (1523, 1524)	Psalm 12	O Lord, our God, from heaven look down (Caroline Fry Wilson, 1845)
Aus tiefer Noth schrei ich zu dir (1523, 1524)	Psalm 130	From depths of woe I raise to Thee (Richard Massie, 1854) Out of the depths I cry to Thee to Thee, Lord (Catherine Winkworth, 1863)

Luther's Title	Source	Common English Version
Ein' feste Berg ist unser Gott (1529)	Psalm 41	A mighty fortress is our God, / A bulwark never failing (Frederick Henry Hedge, 1852)
		A safe stronghold our God is still (Thomas Carlyle, 1831)
Es spricht der Unweisen Mund wohl (1524)	Psalm 14	The mouth of fools doth God confess (Richard Massie, 1854)
Es wollt' uns Gott genadig sein (1524)	Psalm 67	May God unto us gracious be (Arthur Tozer Russell, 1851)
War Gott nicht mit uns diese Zeit (1524)	Psalm 124	Had God not come, may Israel say (Richard Massie, 1854)
Wohl dem, der in Gottes Furcht (1524)	Psalm 128	Happy the man who feareth God (Richard Massie, 1854)

Table 5. Luther's Paraphrases from Other Books of Scripture

Luther's Title	Source	Common English Version
Dies sind die heiligen zehn Gebot (1524)	The Ten Commandments (Exodus 20)	That men a godly life might live (Richard Massie, 1854)
Jesaia dem Propheten das geschah (1526)	Isaiah 6:1–4	Unto the seer Isaiah it was given (Arthur Tozer Russell, 1851)
Mensch willt du leben seliglich (1524)	The Ten Commandments (Exodus 20)	Wilt thou, O man, live happily (Richard Massie, 1854)
Mit Fried und Freud ich fahr danin (1524)	Song of Simeon (Luke 2:29–32)	In peace and joy I now depart (Catherine Winkworth, 1863)
Sie is mir lieb die werthe Magd (1524)	Revelation 12:1–6	Dear is to me the Holy Maid (Richard Massie, 1854)

Luther's Title	Source	Common English Version
Vater unser in Himmelreich (1539)	The Lord's Prayer (Matthew 6:9–13)	Our Father in the heav'ns above (Arthur Tozer Russell, 1848)
		Our Father, dear, which art in heaven (Richard Massie, 1854)
		Our Father, Thou in heaven above (Catherine Winkworth, 1863)

Table 6. Luther's Original Hymns

Luther's Title	Source	Common English Version
Christ lag in Todesbanden (1524)		Christ lay awhile in Death's strong bands (Richard Massie, 1854)
Christ unser Herr zum Jordan kam (1541)	Matthew 3:13–17; Mark 16	To Jordan came our Lord the Christ (Richard Massie, 1854)
Ein neues Lied wir haben an (1523, 1524)		Flung to the heedless winds (John Alexander Messenger, 1843)
Erhalt uns, Herr, bei deinem Wort (1541, 1542)		O Lord, uphold us by Thy word (William Morton Reynolds, 1850)
		From all her foes Thy Church, O Lord (Arthur Tozer Russell, 1851)
		Lord, by Thy word deliverance work (Richard Massie, 1854)
		Lord, keep us steadfast in Thy word (Catherine Winkworth, 1863)
Jesus Christus unser Heiland, Der den Tod überwand (1524)		Christ, our Lord, who died to save (John Anderson, 1846)
		Jesus Christ, our great Redeemer (Arthur Tozer Russell, 1851)

Luther's Title	Source	Common English Version
		Jesus Christ to-day is risen (Richard Massie, 1854)
Nun freut euch lieben Christengemein (1523, 1524)		Rejoice, ye ransomed of the Lord (William Morton Reynolds, 1849)
Von Himmel hoch da komm ich her (1535)		From yonder world I come to earth (John Hunt, 1853)
		From heaven above to earth I come (Catherine Winkworth, 1855)
		From heaven high I come to earth (Roland Bainton, 1948)
Von Himmel kam der Engel Schaar (1543)	Luke 2:10–11; Matthew 2:6	To shepherds as they watched by night (Richard Massie, 1854)
Für allen Freuden auf Erden (1538)		Search ye the world— search all round (John Hunt, 1853)
Kyrie eleison (1529)	Setting of the Litany	Good Lord! us deliver (John Anderson, 1846)
		Have mercy on us, Lord we pray (John Hunt, 1853)
		Lord have mercy (Richard Massie, 1854)

Although now not every one of Luther's poetic compositions ·is a standard piece of congregational hymnody, each can certainly be seen to possess high poetic and hymnodic quality. Consider for example the original hymn entitled "Christ lag in Todesbanden," wherein Luther provided a poem of seven stanzas in which part 1 (lines 1–25) explicates the message of Easter; part 2 (lines 26–49) indicates the application of that message; and each stanza contains six lines of seven syllables, with line seven extended to eight syllables. Notice how one nineteenth-century translator captured the essence of that structure in the third stanza:

> Jesus Christ, God's only Son,
> Into our place descending,
> Away with all our sins hath done,
> And therewith from death rending.
> Right and might, made him a jape,
> Left him nothing but death's shape:
> His ancient sting—he has lost it. Alleluia!

This translation comes to us by way of the Scottish theologian, hymnodist, and writer of fiction (*David Elginbrod*, 1863; *Alec Forbes*, 1865; *Robert Falconer*, 1868), George MacDonald (1824–1905), who ministered to the Congregational church at Arundel, Sussex; left there because of the displeasure of his congregation and his attraction toward the Church of England; lectured on English literature at King's College, London; and finally devoted himself entirely to literary labors. In 1876 MacDonald published his *Exotics: A Translation of the Spiritual Songs of Novalis, the Hymn-Book of Luther, and Other Poems from the German and Italian.* That volume contains his translations of all of Luther's hymns. Those may now be found (for readers who seek a single translation of all of Luther's hymns) in *Luther's Works,* edited by Leupold and Lehmann.

Luther grasped quickly the principles of writing popular sacred poetry—the need for easy but mature rhymes, clear and accurate language, and strong style and tone to attract musical settings that would, in turn, inspire singers engaged in worship. He apparently possessed a natural inclination toward hymnody, which emerged as a manifestation of his urge to comfort and to encourage those who sought God. During the very period that the Roman Catholic Church stood in strong opposition to hymns sung in the vernacular, Luther found a central role for such activity within the service. In "Ein nues Lied wir haben an," for example, he not only celebrated the death and the martyrdom of two young Augustinian monks, but he also created a stirring narrative to underscore the meaning of the Reformation and the early evangelical movement in the Western world. Luther saw, at the end of his poem, a new beginning for the Christian world, a poetic moment accurately captured by Richard Massie.

> Summer is even at our door,
> The Winter now hath vanished,
> The tender flowerets spring once more,
> And He, who Winter banished,
> Will send a happy Summer.

The reasons for the continued popularity of Massie's translations as congregational songs may be readily observed by contrasting these lines to George MacDonald's 1876 version.

> Even at the door is summer nigh,
> The winter now is ended,
> The tender flowers come out and spy;
> His hand when once extended
> Withdraws not till he's finished.

Each version has its own particular virtue: MacDonald, in his attempt to represent Martin Luther's original design, emphasized the folk ballad form and tone of the piece that begins, characteristically, with "A new song here shall be begun— / The Lord God help our singing!" Summer, for MacDonald, is "nigh"; his winter has "ended," rather than "vanished"; his flowers "come out and spy"; his creator (in the last two lines) appears thoroughly involved in the seasonal process. Richard Massie, on the other hand, concerned himself with adapting the poem to the requirements of congregational worship. His language, though accurate in terms of Luther's intent, emphasizes the subtle, spiritual aspects of the seasonal transition. The singer-worshiper realizes the differences between the hymnodist (Massie) and the poet (MacDonald).

Interestingly enough, the extent of Luther's hymnodic influence upon the German Protestant church may best be understood in terms of what did not follow him. The Reverend Erik Reginald Routley (1917–1982)—a British-born clergyman, hymnodist, hymnologist, and professor of church history at Westminster Choir College, Princeton, New Jersey—began his survey of the hymn form (*A Panorama of Christian Hymnody*) with a discussion of four hymns by Luther. Upon completing that brief section, however, he did not return to the issue of German hymns until he had surveyed through to the end of the sixteenth century. Then Routley considered Philipp Nicolai's "Wacht auff, rufft uns die Stimme." That piece has reached the English-speaking world in two popular translations: Francis Crawford Burkitt's "Wake, O wake! with tidings trilling" (1906), and the more popular "Wake, awake! for night is flying" (1855), by Catherine Winkworth. Few students of hymnody would argue with Routley's contention that a truly great hymn writer, who at the same time contributed significantly to the overall history of the Western world, may well have intimidated the hymnic activity of future generations. Such a conclusion, however, must await an extensive survey and analysis of both religious and hymnic development in Germany during the sixteenth century.

Nonetheless, Routley's reasoning may be seen in a clearer light following a discussion of the Anabaptists—that branch of the Reformation which began in Switzerland in the first quarter of the sixteenth century. It spread to southern Germany, the Austrian Alpine region, and Moravia. At the risk of oversimplification, that sect can be defined in terms of its opposition to infant baptism, which it held as unscriptural. Further, historians of religion

divide the membership into two groups: sober Anabaptists
and fanatical Anabaptists.

The Anabaptists published the *Ausband* in 1583, a
collection of extremely long hymns and poetic narratives.
The 1969 American *Mennonite Hymnal*, as one example,
contains fifteen lines from a twenty-seven stanza original
by Jorg Wagner (translated by David Augsburger). The
opening lines read:

> He who would follow Christ in life
> must scorn the world's insult and strife
>   and bear his cross each day.
> For this alone leads to the throne;
>   Christ is the only way.

The *Ausband* contained the hymns and long narratives of
the early Anabaptist martyrs. Wagner, for instance, per-
ished at the stake in 1527, while others suffered similar
fates: Felix Mans, by drowning (1527); Michael Sattler,
burning (1527); Leonhart Schiemer, Hans Schlaffer, and
Ludwig Hatzer, all beheaded in 1528; and Balthasar
Hubmaier by burning in 1528. The notes of suffering and
persecution that permeate early Anabaptist history and
influenced its hymnody may well have been responsible for
the limited acceptability for congregational song of pieces
from the *Ausband*.

A more successful offshoot of Lutheranism, the
United Brethren of Bohemia (and later of Moravia)
contributed significantly to the development of hymnody
throughout the English-speaking world. As early as 1531,
Michael Weisse—priest, monk at Breslau, and an occupant
of the Bohemian Brethren's house at Leutomischl—edited
the Brethren's first hymn book in German, *Ein Neu
Gesangbuchlein*. The volume contained 155 hymns—all
either written or translated by Weisse. Table 7 summarizes
his contribution to hymnody, as well as identifies the
principal translations into English.

Weisse's Originals, 1531	English Versions
Christus is erstanden, Von des Todes Banden	Christ the Lord is risen again! (Catherine Winkworth, 1858)
	Christ—and 'tis no wonder (*Moravian Hymn Book*, 1754)
	Christ our Lord is risen (Henry Mills, 1856)
Es geht daher des Tages Schein	The light of day again we see (Henry James Buckoll, 1842)
	Great God, eternal Lord of heaven— stanzas 3, 4, 6, 7 (Henry James Buckoll, 1843)
	Once more the daylight shines abroad (Catherine Winkworth, 1858)
Gelobt sei Gott im höchsten Thron	Praise God upon his heavenly throne (Arthur Tozer Russell, 1851)
	Glory to God upon his throne (Harriet Reynolds Spaeth, 1883)
Gott sah zu seiner Zeit	When the due time has taken place (Charles Kinchen, 1742)
	Ah, come, Lord Jesus, hear our prayer—stanza 10 (*Moravian Hymn Book*, 1886)
Lob sei dem allmachtigen Gott	Praise be to that almighty God (John Gambold, 1754)
	To God we render thanks and praise (*Moravian Hymn Book*, 1789, 1886)
	O come, th' Almighty's praise declare (Arthur Tozer Russell, 1851)
O Herre Jesu Christ, der du erschienen bist	Christ Jesus, Lord most dear (*Moravian Hymn Book*, 1754)
	Lord Jesus, we come to Thee (Catherine Winkworth, 1863)
Den Vater dort oben	Father, Lord of Mercy (John Christian Jacobi, 1722)
Die Sonne wird mit ihrem Schein	Soon from our wishful eyes awhile (Henry James Buckoll, 1842)

Weisse's Originals, 1531	English Versions
Komm, heiliger Geist, wahrer Gott	Come, Holy Ghost, Lord God, indeed (*Moravian Hymn Book*, 1754)
	Thou, great Teacher, who instructest (*Moravian Hymn Book*, 1801, 1849)
Lob und Ehr mit stettem Dankopfer	Praise, glory, thanks, be ever paid (Catherine Winkworth, 1869)
O Jesu Christ, der Heiden Licht	O Jesus Christ, the Gentiles' light (*Moravian Hymn Book*, 1754)
Singet lieben Leut	Sing, be glad, ye happy sheep (Christian Gottfried Clemens, 1789)
	O rejoice, Christ's happy sheep (*Moravian Hymn Book*, 1801, 1849)

The Bohemian Brethren issued a number of hymnals between 1541 and 1544 besides Weisse's *Ein Neu Gesangbuchlein*. However, the denomination's most meaningful and lasting collection came in June 1561: the *Kirchengesange*, published at Eibenschutz, Moravia, containing 744 hymns. A translation of the colophon of that volume reads, "This Cancional was printed and finished by Alexander of Aujzed [or of Pilsen], at Samter [Poland], at the castle of his Grace Lucas, Count of Gorka, Waywode of Lancic, Starost of Bus" (Julian, *Dictionary of Hymnology*, 1:56). Although the Brethren continued to produce hymnals throughout the remainder of the sixteenth century and well into the seventeenth, further discussion of their contribution to sacred and congregational song must be postponed until the end of Chapter 5, when I consider the work of Count Nicholas von Zinzendorf's Moravians and their influence upon British and American hymnody.

Chapter Four
PSALTER AND PSALM PARAPHRASE

IN SURVEYING, WITH BOTH conciseness and specificity, the
development of the congregational hymn from its begin-
nings, a smooth and clear transition from the first half of
the sixteenth century (the period of Luther) to the last
quarter of the seventeenth century (the introduction of
hymn singing by the English Baptists) proves not alto-
gether an easy task to complete. There exists between
Martin Luther and the English Baptists a relatively short
but significant chronological gap. I refer, of course, to the
metrical psalm paraphrase, and to that subject I turn
before continuing to chart the course of hymnodic history.

Historically, the metrical psalm paraphrase lies as a
middle ground between the medieval *office hymn* (versified
devotions inserted into the prose psalms of the daily office)
and the *modern hymn* (a divine ode set to music). The office
hymn was never really intended for congregational singing, while the hymn as we know it was (and still is) intended
for a large but not necessarily skilled group of singers. In
terms of transition and clarity, psalmody grew out of a
need for a form less artistic than the office hymn, while
hymnody provided the means for breaking away from the
poetic and textual limitations of Hebrew psalmody and
later from Christian paraphrases of Hebrew psalmody.
Because the entire history of congregational song has been
viewed by hymnologists in light of such transition, the pure
metrical psalm paraphrase, although no longer a popular
form of congregational expression in the majority of
denominations, remains important because of its tradition

and its influence upon current hymnological tastes, trends, and forms.

The textual development of metrical psalmody begins, naturally enough, with the *psalter*—the Old Testament Book of Psalms as translated into a particular language and then adapted to public or private worship. The Christian Church found its initial book of praise readily available in the Hebrew psalter, essentially the product of three centuries (from c. 400 to c. 100 B.C.) and representing literature after the Exile. As a complete text, the Hebrew psalter represents the poetry of a number of persons from a large historic period; it is an anthology of praise and devotion to the faith of Israel. The Hebrew psalm extends its application to the entire area of man's relationship with God. The Old Testament Jehovah emerges principally as a living God, and the psalmists praise God's power, tenderness, and mercy. Further, the sound and the sense of the complete psalter capture the effect upon human beings of the holy and personal God, a divine Providence active throughout the world and cognizant of godly and thankful people.

During the first three centuries following the birth of Christ, the psalter became the primary source of liturgical and devotional literature for the earliest Christians. Jesus certainly relied for guidance upon the Hebrew psalms, and those pieces formed the pattern for the fundamentally Christian hymns that began to emerge at the time of the apostles. The devotional and liturgical functions of the psalter in Christian worship soon became evident. Such early Church fathers as Jerome and Ambrose recognized its significance and adaptability as a devotional vehicle, while Augustine envisioned Christ and the Church throughout the various sections of the psalter. Then with the development of a truly Christian set of structures and patterns for worship, the psalter developed as an essential ingredient of the Church service. In other words, as the structure of Christian worship became outwardly eucharistic, the celebration leaned heavily upon the psalter, the devotional manifestation of Christ's spiritual existence.

Following the Reformation (that is, beginning with the seventeenth century), metrical psalmody began to develop into a tradition that would last through the next four centuries. In fact, by the middle of the sixteenth century, an entire body of metrical psalm paraphrases had become an essential ingredient of common public and private worship. The psalms of David, or *psalter,* became the center of a spiritual, emotional, and creative revival—a rediscovery, as it were, of biblical literature. Since the appearance in 1539 at Strasbourg of one of the earliest public renderings of vernacular psalms in rhymed verse, the voices of millions of people have been raised in expressing their understanding of and praise to God.

Table 8, an annotated listing of selected and representative psalters (both with and without music), as well as musical collections to accompany such books, provides a general idea of the scope and variety of activity in the area. A complete listing of psalters published in Great Britain, America, and on the European Continent would undoubtedly fill a significant number of pages—and certainly scholars have attempted to do so. For example, in 1898 James Warrington published *Short Titles of Books Relating to or Illustrating the History and Practice of Psalmody in the United States, 1620–1820* (privately printed in Philadelphia; reprinted Pittsburgh: Pittsburgh Theological Seminary, 1970). However, Warrington's title proves inaccurate (he begins with Miles Coverdale's *Goostly Psalmes* and all of those British and European volumes that preceded the American Bay Psalm Book); his dates tend to confuse; his entries lack the necessary bibliographical completeness; and the entire volume is difficult to follow. For a more complete listing of psalters published throughout the Western world, from the earliest periods until the beginning of the twentieth century, John Julian's *Dictionary of Hymnology* continues to provide valuable data. In consulting that work, readers must be prepared to wend their way through a number of separate entries: "English Psalters," "French Psalters," "German Psalters," and the like.

Again, the titles set forth in Table 8 constitute simply a bibliographical survey, done more for the sake of establishing familiarity with the subject than for any form of scholarly immersion. A discussion of actual psalmists and psalm paraphrases appears later in this chapter. For now, the entries in Table 8 appear in chronological order (date of publication to the left) with places of publication indicated.

Table 8. Selected and Representative Psalters
(* = musical collection)

1525. *Kirchenampt* (Strasbourg): Not a psalter in the complete sense of the term, but a collection that does contain a significant number of metrical versions of the psalms.

1526. *Psalmen, Gebett und Kirchenubung* (Strasbourg).

1533. Clement Marot. *Miroir de Treschrestienne Princesse Marguerite de France* (Paris): A collection of poems dedicated to Marot's patroness that includes a version of Psalm 6.

1539. *Alcuns Psaumes* (Strasbourg): The first of the "Strasbourg psalters"; superintended by John Calvin.

Miles Coverdale. *Goostly Psalmes and Spirituall Songes drawn out of the Holy Scripture* (Oxford).

1540. *Souterliedekins* (Amsterdam): A Dutch translation of psalms, set to popular Netherlandish folk melodies.

1542. John Calvin. *The Genevan Psalter* (Geneva): Includes thirty psalm translations by Clement Marot.

1547. Louis Bourgeois. *Premier Liure des Pseaulmes de David* (Lyon): Contains four-part settings of the psalm tunes.

Thomas Sternhold. *Certayne Psalmes chose out of the Psalter of David and drawen into Englishe metre* . . . (London): Contains nineteen psalms.

1549. Richard Crowley. *The Psalter of David* (London).

Thomas Sternhold. *Certayne Psalmes* . . . *of David* . . . , 2d ed. (London): Contains thirty psalms; see above, 1547.

1550. John Marbecke. *The Booke of Church Song* (London).

1551. John Calvin. *The Genevan Psalter* (Geneva): Includes forty-nine psalm translations by Clement Marot and thirty-four by Theodore de Beze; see above, 1542.

Thomas Sternhold. *Certayne Psalmes* . . . *of David* . . . , 3d ed. (London): John Hopkins added seven new psalm versions to the thirty versions of the 1549 edition; see above, 1547, 1549.

1553. Francis Seagar. *Certayne Psalmes, in four partes* . . . (London).

1554. John Calvin. *The Genevan Psalter* (Geneva): Includes forty-one psalm translations by Theodore de Beze; see above, 1542, 1551.
1556. *One and Fiftie Psalmes of David in Englishe Metre* . . . (Geneva): Known as the Anglo-Genevan Psalter; contains psalms by Sternhold (thirty-seven), Hopkins, and William Whittingham (seven).
1557. Thomas Sternhold. *Certayne Psalmes* . . . *of David* . . . , 4th ed. (London): Thirty-seven psalms by Sternhold and seven by John Hopkins; see above, 1547, 1549, 1551.
1558. *The Psalmes of David in Englishe Metre* . . . (Geneva): An enlargement of the 1556 Anglo-Genevan Psalter; contains sixty-two Psalms—forty-four by Sternhold and Hopkins, sixteen by Whittingham, and two by John Pullain.
1560. *Psalmes of David in Englishe Metre by Thomas Sterneholde and Others* . . . (London): The English version of the Anglo-Genevan Psalter.
1561. John Hopkins. *Four Score and Seven Psalmes of David in English Metre* . . . (London): A revision of and additions to Sternhold's *Certayne Psalmes.*
       William Kethe. *The Psalmes of David in Englishe Metre* . . . (Geneva): An enlargement of the Anglo-Genevan Psalter of 1556 and 1558; contains forty-four psalms by Sternhold and Hopkins, sixteen by Whittingham, two by Pullain, and twenty-five by Kethe.
1562. John Calvin. *The Genevan Psalter* (Geneva): The complete edition.
       Thomas Sternhold and John Hopkins. *The Whole Booke of Psalmes, Collected into Englishe Meetre* . . . (London): Known as the Olde Version or simply as Sternhold and Hopkins; writers include Sternhold, Hopkins, Whittingham, Kethe, and Thomas Norton.
1563. William Parsons et al. *The Whole Psalmes in Foure Partes* . . . (London:): The 1562 Sternhold and Hopkins with sixty-five tunes.
1564. *Claude Goudimel. *Les Cent Cinquante Pseaumes de David, Nouvellement mis en Musique a Quatre Parties* (Geneva): A harmonization of the psalter of 1562.
       John Knox and John Pont. *The Whole Psalmes of David* (Edinburgh): Issued as part of the Presbyterian *Book of Common Order;* texts by Sternhold, Hopkins, Kethe, Whittingham, Norton, Pullain, John Marckand, John Craig, and John Pont.
1566. Peter Datheen. *The Genevan Psalter* (Amsterdam): A Dutch translation of the 1562 Geneva edition; the version brought to America in 1620 by the Pilgrims.
       Psalmen der Propheten David's (Amsterdam): Reprints at Amsterdam in 1599 and 1670.
1567. Matthew Parker. *The Whole Psalter Translated into English Metre* . . . (London): Printed for private circulation.
1573. Ambrosius Lobwasser. *The Genevan Psalter* (Leipzig): A German translation of the 1562 Geneva edition.
1579. William Damon. *The Whole Psalmes* (London).
1585. *John Cosyn. *Musike of Six and Five Partes Made upon the Common Tunes in Singing of the Psalmes.* (London).
1586. Lucas Osiander. *Funfftzig Geistliche Lieder und Psalmen* (Nuremberg).
1591. William Damon. *The Whole Psalmes* (London): An expanded version of the 1579 edition.
1592. Thomas Estes. *The Whole Booke of Psalmes* . . . (London): The first psalter to provide four-part harmony for the tunes and to place them on

opposite pages from texts (previously, harmonized tunes were published in separate part-books); the Jamestown, Virginia, settlers brought this volume with them to America in 1607.

1594. John Mundy. *Songs and Psalmes composed into 3. 4. and 5. parts* . . . (London): Mundy served as organist of Saint George's Chapel, Windsor Castle.

1599. Richard Allison. *The Psalmes of David in Meter, the Plaine Song being the Common Tune to be Sung* . . . (London).

1606. Claude LeJeune. *Le Pseaumes de Marot et Beza* (Geneva).

1612. Henry Ainsworth. *The Whole Booke of Psalms* (Amsterdam): Prepared especially for the Pilgrims and brought by them to Plymouth, Massachusetts.

1615. *The CL. Psalmes of David in Prose and Meeter with their whole usual Tunes newly corrected and amended* (Edinburgh): The so-called Scottish Psalter.

1621. William Prys. *Lylfr y Psalmau* (London): Contains a Welsh version for each psalm.

Thomas Ravenscroft. *The Whole Booke of Psalmes* (London): Contains almost all of the psalm tunes that had appeared in previously published English psalters; Ravenscroft systematically named tunes after places.

1627. John Cosyn. *Collection of Private Devotions in the Practice of the Ancient Church called the Houres of Prayer* (London).

1632. *All the French Psalm Tunes with English Words* (London).

1635. *The Psalmes of David in Prose and Meeter with their whole Tunes in foure or more parts, and some Psalmes in Reports* . . . (Edinburgh): Another version of the Scottish Psalter of 1615.

1636. George Sandys. *Paraphrase upon the Psalms of David* (London): Henry Lawes composed tunes for twenty-four of Sandys's psalm paraphrases.

1638. George Sandys. *A Paraphrase upon the Divine Poems* (London): An enlarged edition of the 1636 *Paraphrase*.

1640. *The Whole Booke of Psalmes Faithfully Translated into English Metre* (Cambridge, Mass.): Known as the Bay Psalm Book; editions and revisions continued through 1800.

1643. William Slatyer. *The Psalmes of David in Fower Languages, Hebrew, Greeke, Latin and English, and in 4 parts Set in the Tunes of our Church* (London): Dedicated (for reasons not clear) to the University of Oxford.

1648. *Henry Lawes. Choice Psalmes put to Musick for Three Voices* (London).

1650. *All the French Psalm Tunes with English Words* (London): The second edition of the 1632 title.

The Psalmes of David in Prose and Meeter . . . (Edinburgh): Another edition of the 1615 Scottish Psalter.

1651. Henry Dunster and Richard Lyon. *The Psalms, Hymns, and Spiritual Songs of the Old and New Testament, faithfully translated into English Metre* (Cambridge, Mass.): Twenty-seven editions through 1762; the third edition of the Bay Psalm Book that became known as the New England Psalm Book.

1654. William Barton. *Book of Psalms in Metre* (London).

1661. John Eliot. *Wame Ketoohomae Uketookomsongash David* (Cambridge, Mass.): Metrical songs in the language of the Algonquin Indians; translated into that language by Eliot, who became known as the Apostle to the Indians.

1666. **A Collection of Tunes for Use with the Scottish Psalter* (Aberdeen).
1668. John Austin. *Devotions, in the Ancient Way of Offices: With Psalms, Hymns, and Prayers* (Paris): A Roman Catholic psalter.
1671. John Playford. *Psalms and Hymns in Solemn Musick* (London): In the preface, Playford discusses the origin of metrical psalmody and laments the decay into which the singing of it has fallen.
1677. John Playford. *The Whole Booke of Psalmes: with Usual Hymns and Spiritual Songs* (London): Became a standard work, from its publication to the end of the eighteenth century.
1679. John Patrick. *A Century of Select Psalms and Portions of the Psalms of David* . . . (London).
1688. *The Psalms and Hymns usually sung in the Churches and Tabernacles of St. Martin's in the Fields and St. James's Westminster* (London): Contains twenty-four select psalms and two morning hymns.
1692. Richard Baxter. *Paraphrases of the Psalms of David in Metre* . . . (London).
1696. Nahum Tate and Nicholas Brady. *A New Version of the Psalmes of David, Fitted to the Tunes used in Churches* (London): Known as the New Version to supplant Sternhold and Hopkins; also referred to simply as Tate and Brady; no tunes in this edition.
1697. *Select Psalmes and Hymns for the Use of St. James's Westminster* (London): Successor to the 1688 *Psalms and Hymns.*
1698. **John Bishop. *A Sett of New Psalm Tunes in Four Parts* . . . (London): A second edition in 1700; Bishop served as organist for the College at Winton.
Henry Hunt. *A Collection of Psalms* (London).
1699. *The Psalm-Singers Necessary Companion* (Standish, Lancs.): A second edition in 1700.
1700. Nahum Tate and Nicholas Brady. *A Supplement to a New Version of the Psalms of David* . . . (London): Further editions in 1702, 1704, 1708; tunes included in these editions.
1701. **Henry Playford. *The Divine Companion, or David's Harp New Tun'd, being a Choice Collection of New and Easy Psalms and Anthems* (London): Intended to be bound with John Playford's psalters of 1671 and 1677; a second edition in 1709.
1706. Elias Hall. *The Psalm-Singers Compleat Companion* (London).
1708. William Croft. *Supplement to a New Version of the Psalms of David* . . . *by N. Tate and N. Brady* (London): The sixth edition of the 1700 *Supplement.*
Lyra Davidica (London): Translations of German and Latin Psalm versions.
1711. **John Bishop. *A Set of New Psalm-Tunes in Four Parts* (London).
*A Collection of Psalm Tunes in Four Parts fitted to the Old or New Version (London): All new tunes.
1713. **Philip Hart. *Melodies Proper to be sung to any of the Versions of the Psalms* (London).
1715. **John Green and James Green. *A Collection of Choice Psalm Tunes,* 3d ed. (Nottingham).
1717. **David Purcell. *The Psalms set full for the Organ or Harpsichord* (London).
1718. **John Chetham. *A New Book of Psalmody* (London): Contains chanting tunes, anthems, and psalm tunes.
Cotton Mather. *Psalterium Americanum* (Boston): Contains psalm versions in blank verse so as not to distort the original Hebrew meanings; failed to gain wide acceptance or recognition.

1719. *William Lawrence. *A Collection of Tunes suited to the various Metres in Mr.
Watts's Imitation of the Psalms of David* . . . (London): Lawrence taught
psalmody at the Presbyterian meetinghouse in Eastcheap; the
volume sold for one shilling.

Isaac Watts. *The Psalms of David Imitated* (London): Remains to this day one
of the finest examples of the relationship between English poetry
and metrical paraphrase (or imitation) of the Hebrew psalms; for
Watts, these were the Hebrew psalms Christianized.

1722. Johann Christian Jacobi. *Psalmodia Germanica* (London): Not completed
until 1765; Jacobi served as keeper of the German chapel in Saint
James's Palace.

1723. Richard Barber and James Barber. *Book of Psalmody* (London).

John Church. *Introduction to Psalmody* (London).

1724. *Het Nieuw Testament;* [and] *De CL Psalmen Des Propheten Davids, met Eenige
andere Lof Sanged* (Dordrecht).

1730. *Nathaniel Gawthorne. *Harmonia Perfecta* (London): The successor to
Lawrence's 1719 *Collection*.

Matthew Wilkins. *Book of Psalmody* (London).

1734. *William Tans'ur. *A Compleat Harmony of Syon* (London).

1738. *William Knapp. *Sett of New Psalm Tunes and Anthems* (London).

1739. Magnus Falconer. *A Choice Collection of Psalms* (Philadelphia).

1741. John Arnold. *The Compleat Psalmodist* (London): Another edition in 1749;
fourth edition in 1756.

1745. *A Collection of Tunes in Three Parts That are now us'd in the dissenting
Congregations in London, fit to bind up with Dr. Watts's Psalms* . . .
(London).

1752. John Barnard. *A New Version of the Psalms* (Boston).

1756. Thomas Cradock. *A New Version of the Psalms of David* (Annapolis).

Johann Christian Jacobi. *Psalmodia Germanica* (New York): An American
edition of Jacobi's 1722 *Psalmodia Germanica*.

1762. *William Riley. *Parochial Harmony, consisting of a Collection of Psalm-tunes in
three and four parts* (London).

1763. Aaron Williams. *The Universal Psalmodist* (London).

1764. *Joshia Flagg. *A Collection of the Best Psalm Tunes* (Boston).

1765. James Merrick. *The Psalms of David, Translated or Paraphrased* (London).

William Riley. *Psalms and Hymns for the Chapel of the Asylum or House of
Refuge for Female Orphans* (London).

1767. Francis Hopkinson. *The Psalms of David, with the Ten Commandments, Creed,
Lord's Prayer* . . . (New York): A translation from the Dutch for the
Reformed Protestant Dutch Church in New York City.

1770. *William Billings. *The New-England Psalm-Singer* (Boston).

*Isaac Smith. *A Collection of Psalm Tunes in Three Parts* (London).

1775. William Romaine. *A Collection out of the Book of Psalms* (London): An "Essay
on Psalmody" prefaces the collection; Romaine served as rector of
Saint Anne's, Blackfriars.

1780. *Stephen Addington. *A Collection of Psalm Tunes* (London).

Henry Gardner. *Select Portions of the Psalms of David* (London).

*Thomas Jackson. *Twelve Psalm Tunes* (London): Jackson served as
organist and master of the song school at Newark-on-Trent, Notts.

1781. *William Billings. *The Psalm-Singer's Amusement* (Boston).

*Andrew Law. *Select Number of Plain Tunes Adapted for Congregational
Singing* (Philadelphia): Provided music for the complete psalter.

The Scottish Paraphrases (Edinburgh).

1783. *Andrew Law. *Rudiments of Music* (Philadelphia): Contains the rules of psalmody.
1785. Joel Barlow. *Doctor Watts's Imitation of the Psalms of David Corrected* (Hartford, Conn.).
Joel Barlow. *A Translation of Sundry Psalms* (Hartford, Conn.).
Richard Cecil. *Psalms of David* (London).
1786. Newcome Cappe. *A Selection of Psalms for Social Worship* (York).
1787. *Psalms, Carefully Suited to the Christian Worship in the United States . . . Allowed by the Reverend Synod of New York and Philadelphia* (Philadelphia).
1789. Thomas Williams. *Psalmodia Evangelica* (London): Intended for churches, chapels, and Dissenting meetinghouses in England, Ireland, and Scotland.
1790. Edward Miller. *The Psalms of David* (London).
1791. William Tattersall. *Psalms* (London).
1793. Jacob French. *The Psalmodist's Companion* (Worcester, Mass.).
1794. William Tattersall. *Improved Psalmody* (London): Another edition in 1795.
Basil Woodd. *The Psalms of David . . . Arranged according to the Order of the Church of England* (London).
1796. *Dutch Reformed Psalms* (New York).
1797. Joel Barlow. *Psalms, Carefully Suited to the Christian Worship of the United States of America* (Wilmington, Del.).
*Richard Merrill. *The Musical Practitioner; or, American Psalmody* (Newburyport, Mass.).
1799. *David Merrill. *The Psalmodist's Best Companion* (Exeter, N.H.).
1802. William Palfray. *The Evangelical Psalmodist* (Salem, Mass.).
1806. Adam Forbush. *The Psalmodist's Assistant* (Boston): Second edition, Boston, 1806.
1808. Isaac Evans. *David's Companion* (Baltimore and New York).
1811. Henry Mason and Samuel Palmer. *The Psalms of David* (Dedham, Mass.).
1812. Richard Davidson. *A New Metrical Version of the Psalms* (Carlisle, Pa.).
1813. Samuel Worcester. *Christian Psalmody* (Boston).
1815. Samuel Worcester. *Christian Psalmody* (Boston).
1818. *William Cross. *Collection of Psalm Tunes for the Use of the Church of England* (Oxford): Cross served as organist of Christ Church Cathedral, Oxford.
1819. * Abraham Clifton. *Original Psalm Tunes* (Baltimore).
1825. James Montgomery. *Christian Psalmist* (London): The introductory essay to this volume may well constitute the first formal English work on hymnology.
1829. Lowell Mason. *The Juvenile Psalmist; or, The Child's Introduction to Sacred Music* (Boston).
1833. Vincent Novello. *The Psalmist*, 4 vols. (London): Continued until 1843.
1843. Baron Stowe and Samuel F. Smith. *The Psalmist* (Boston).
1847. William Henry Havergal. *Old Church Psalmody* (London).
Henry Parr. *Church of England Psalmody* (London).
1858. J. R. Graves and J. M. Pendleton. *The Southern Psalmist* (Nashville).
1872. *The Northern Psalter* (Aberdeen).
Samuel Sebastian Wesley. *The European Psalmist* (London).
1873. J. R. Graves. *The New Baptist Psalmist* (Memphis).
1874. *The Cathedral Psalter* (London).
1880. *The Psalter in Metre: A Revised Version, prepared and published by Authority of the Presbyterian Church in Ireland, with Tunes* (Dublin).
1903. Rowland E. Prothero. *The Psalms of Human Life* (London).

1912. *The Psalter* (Grand Rapids, Mich.): Published for the Protestant Reformed Church.
1913. Walter Marshall. *The Barless Psalter* (London):
1925. Robert Bridges and Walter Marshall. *The Psalter Newly Pointed* (London). *The English Psalter* (London).
1928. *A Collection of Psalms and Hymns* (Richmond, Va.): Published for the Old Order Mennonites; words only.
1929. *The Oxford Psalter* (London).
      The Scottish Psalter (Edinburgh): A new music edition.
      The Scottish Psalter: Authorized Version Pointed with Chants (Edinburgh).
1930. *The American Psalter* (New York).
1932. *The Parish Psalter* (London).
      Richard R. Terry. *Calvin's First Psalter, 1539* (London).
1934. *The St. Paul's Cathedral Psalter* (London).
1939. *Waldo Seldon Pratt. *The Music of the French Psalter* (New York).
1949. Ray F. Brown. *The Oxford American Psalter* (New York).
1950. Millar Patrick. *Four Centuries of Scottish Psalmody* (London).
1953. *Maurice Frost. *English and Scottish Psalm and Hymn Tunes* (London).
1962. Pierre Pidoux. *Le psautier huguenot du XVIe siècle,* 2 vols. (Basel).
1968. Joseph Gelineau. *Psalms: A Singing Version* (Mahwah, N.J.).
1973. *Psalter: Book of Psalms for Singing* (Wilkinsburg, Pa.): Published for the Reformed Presbyterian Church.
1976. *Psalter Hymnal and Psalter Hymnal Supplement* (Grand Rapids, Mich.): Published for the Christian Reformed Church.
1980. Charles L. Towler. *Psalms, Hymns, and Spriritual Songs* (Cleveland, Tenn.): Published for the Church of God.
1982. James E. Barrett. *Psalmnary: Gradual Psalms for Cantor and Congregation.* (Missoula, Mont.).
      Mary Jo Tully. *Psalms: Faith Songs for the Faith Filled* (Dubuque, Iowa).
1983. *Gradual Psalms in Three Volumes, Year A, B, C* (New York): A performing edition of psalmody.
1984. *Book of Praise: Anglo-Genevan Psalter* (Winnipeg): Prepared by the Canadian Dutch Reformed Church.
      Gary Chamberlain. *Psalms for Singing: Twenty-Six Psalms with Musical Settings for Congregations and Choir* (Nashville).
      Richard A. Crawford. *The Core Repertory of Early American Psalmody.* (Madison, Wis.): A reprint of 100 sacred pieces most often printed in America between 1698 and 1810.
      Robin A. Leaver, David Mann, and David Parkes. *Ways of Singing the Psalms* (London): Designed within the context of Anglican worship.
1986. Robert E. Kreutz. *Psalms* (Portland, Oreg.).

The literary and liturgical aspects of the psalm paraphrase, as they relate to congregational song, merit consideration. In terms of its history in the English-speaking world, psalmody arose from the natural inclination (instinct, perhaps) to engrave the very words of Scripture upon the form and the setting of the worship

service. The well-known older versions of psalms—
Sternhold and Hopkins, Tate and Brady, and their
immediate seventeenth- and eighteenth-century successors—suffered from a general lack of poetic merit, most
probably because psalm paraphrases of the sixteenth and
seventeenth centuries were from the outset intimidated by
their source. When Samuel H. Cox and his editorial
associates noted, in the preface to their 1843 *Church
Psalmist* (New York: Mark H. Newman and Company),
that "the harp of David yet hangs heavy on the willow,
disdaining the touch of any hand less skilfull than his own,"
they echoed a then fairly widespread sentiment about the
state of the form. Although the creators of older versions
had managed to grasp on to the language and the meter of
the Old Testament psalmist, they had—universally and
uniformly—failed to consider the spirit of the Davidic
harp, a shortcoming that most directly accounted for the
lack of poetic merit. In other words, the worshiper has
always needed and has always profited from the poet's
ability to fire the spirit and to motivate the heart and the
mind.

As illustration of this, consider some attempts at
metrical paraphrasing of Psalm 47, "A Psalm for the sons
of Korah" directed "To the chief Musician" (or choirmas-
ter). Table 9, by placing the King James (or Authorized)
Version of 1611 beside the Revised Standard Version of
1952 shows the major shifts in tone and language from the
model text to the subsequent psalm paraphrase.

Table 9. Metrical Psalm Paraphrase: Psalm 47

King James Version	Revised Standard Version
1. O clap your hands, all ye people; shout unto God with the voice of triumph.	1. Clap your hands, all peoples! Shout to God with loud songs of joy!
2. For the Lord most high is terrible; He is a great King over all the earth.	2. For the Lord, the Most High, is terrible, a great King over all the earth.

King James Version	Revised Standard Version
3. He shall subdue the people under us, and the nations under our feet.	3. He subdued peoples under us, and nations under our feet.
4. He shall choose our inheritance for us, the excellency of Jacob whom He loved.	4. He chose our inheritance for us, the pride of Jacob whom He loves.
5. God is gone up with a shout, the Lord with the sound of a trumpet.	5. God has gone up with a shout, the Lord with the sound of a trumpet.
6. Sing praises to God, sing praises: sing praises unto our King, sing praises.	6. Sing praises to God, sing praises! Sing praises to our King, sing praises.
7. For God is the King of all the earth: sing ye praises with understanding.	7. For God is the King of all the earth; sing praises with a psalm.
8. God reigneth over the heathen: God sitteth upon the throne of His holiness.	8. God reigns over the nations; God sits on His holy throne.
9. The princes of the people are gathered together, even the people of the God of Abraham: for the shields of the earth belong unto God: He is greatly exalted.	9. The princes of the peoples gather as the people of the God of Abraham. For the shields of the earth belong to God; He is highly exalted.

From a strictly literary viewpoint, Psalm 47 contains uncomplicated themes of praise and awareness: the Israelites' adoration of their God and their recognition of His supremacy over them. The principal images within the two versions support the notion of distance between the Old Testament Jehovah and His chosen people, a sense of distance underscored by allusions to God's theological, political, and even genealogical control over all of the people upon the earth. In terms of metrical psalm paraphrase, succeeding versifiers have attempted not so much to alter the theological emphasis or intent of the Old Testament poem, but rather to provide the means by which individuals may, collectively and rhythmically, express its sentiments in public worship. The exact means, of course, have varied according to denominational intent.

The least observable distance between the original Old Testament psalm and the psalm paraphrase continues in a form known as the *Anglican chant*. Simply defined, the psalm chant (whether Anglican or Gregorian) constitutes a short, simple, and flexible piece of music intended for the singing of short, unmetrical poetry—particularly (and naturally) an Old Testament psalm. The intent specifically focuses upon the preservation of the irregular rhythm of the words in the singing. Thus, in *The Oxford American Psalter* (Brown, 1949), Psalm 47 assumes this form:

1. O clap your hands together, all ye peoples:
   O sing unto God with the voice of melody.
2. For the Lord is high and to be feared;
   He is the great King upon all the earth.
3. He shall subdue the peoples under us,
   and the nations under our feet.
4. He shall choose out an heritage for us,
   even the excellency of Jacob whom He loved.
5. God is gone up with a merry noise,
   and the Lord with the sound of the trump.
6. O sing praises, sing praises unto our God;
   O sing praises, sing praises unto our King.
7. For God is the King of all the earth:
   sing ye praises with understanding.
8. God reigneth over the nations;
   God sitteth upon His holy seat.
9. The princes of the peoples are joined unto the people of
      the God of Abraham;
   for God, which is very high exalted, doth defend the earth
      as it were with a shield.

Aside from the obvious but minor changes in language and meter, the psalter version of Psalm 47 differs not at all from its biblical model; in fact, that lack of substantive difference alone may prove sufficient to tell us most of what we need to know about psalm chant texts. Psalm singing, as a pure form, strives to preserve the essence of the biblical text; thus poets and musicians involved in such exercise seek to allocate words to notes by means of signs—a technique known as *pointing*. They strive for agreement between proper emphasis of words and normal accentuation in music. At the same time, those poets and musicians attempt to circumvent the problem of distortion of syllable duration, allowing worshipers to chant the words, preserve the natural sound, and elicit the clearest textural meaning.

In more specific terms, one may come closer to understanding the intent of the form by observing certain rules and explanations for psalm chanting, as well as certain examples. For instance, the introductory section (pp. xi-xii) of *The Oxford American Psalter* contains these ten items:

1. Breath is always to be taken at the end of a line, and only at that point.
2. A comma is to be observed only as the sense would require in good reading, and not by a complete break as for breath.
3. An asterisk [*] corresponds in location to the double bar at the end of the first half of a single chant.
4. The dot [•] is used between words, and the hyphen [-] between the syllables of a word, to indicate that the syllable or syllables before it are sung to the first note of a measure, and the syllable or syllables after it to the second note.
5. The bar sign [/] corresponds in location to a single bar line in the music.
    —When a single syllable occurs between two bar signs, it is sung to the two half notes of the measure [*For the Lord is / great / God*]. The *extra space* after the syllable is a reminder of its increased duration.
    —When two syllables occur between two bar signs, each is sung to one of the two half notes of the measure [*let us heartily rejoice in the / strength of / our sal / vation*].
    —When three syllables occur between two bar signs, the general rule is that the first two are

sung to the first note of the measure, and a third
to the second note [*Let us come before His / presence
with / thanksgiving*]. Often, a dot or a hyphen is
placed after the second syllable as a reminder
[*and a great / King a-bove / all / gods—The sea is /
His and • He / made it*]. When an exception to the
general rule occurs, a dot or a hyphen is always
used to indicate that the first syllable is sung to
the first note, and the second and third to the
second note [*The holy Church throughout all the /
world • doth ac / knowledge / Thee*].

—When four or five syllables occur between two
bar signs, a dot or hyphen is always used to
indicate the allocation of the syllables to the two
notes of the measure [*O come, let us / sing un-to
the / Lord—In His hand are all the / corners • of
the earth—The goodly / fellowship • of the Prophets / praise Thee—Blessed art Thou on the glorious /
throne of • Thy kingdom*].

6. An accent [´] is used to indicate a syllable near the
end of a recitation that is stronger than the first
syllable of the inflection following, and which
should be accented accordingly [*Glory be to the
Fáther, and / to the / Son*].

7. The dash [—] indicates that the reciting note of the
chant is to be omitted [*—/ Lord, be / Thou my / helper*].

8. The direction "2nd part" at the beginning of a
verse indicates that the second half of the chant is to
be repeated for that verse.

9. The syllable "-ed" at the end of a word is not to be
pronounced separately except—
   (a) when a hyphen is used,
   (b) in obvious cases like "regarded," and
   (c) in the word "blessed";
when it is intended that "blessed" is to be pronounced as one syllable, it is spelled "blest."

10.   When a verse appears all on one line, it should be
       sung all in one breath without the usual break at the
       asterisk [*Thou sittest at the right / hand of God, * in the
       / glory / of the / Father*].

Now, returning once more to Psalm 47, notice how it
appears on p. 110 in *The Oxford American Psalter* as pointed
and set to an Anglican chant:

DAY 9   **EVENING PRAYER**
                                  PSALM 47

1   O clap your hands together, / all ye / peoples:
      * O sing unto / God • with the / voice of / melody.
2   For the Lord is / high and • to be / feared;
      * he is the great / King up-on / all the / earth.
3   He shall subdue the / peoples / ꞎnder us,
      * and the / nations / under our / feet.
4   He shall choose out an / heri - tage / for us,
      * even the excellency of / Jacob / whom he / loved.
5   God is gone up with a / merry / noise,
      * and the / Lord • with the / sound of • the / trump.
6   O sing praises, sing praises / unto our / God;
      * O sing praises, sing / praises / unto our / King.
7   For God is the King of / all the / earth:
      * sing ye / praises with / under / standing.
8   God reigneth / over the / nations;
      * God sitteth up / on his holy / seat.

9   The princes of the peoples are joined unto the people of
the / God of / Abraham;
 * for God, which is very high exalted, doth defend the
/ earth • as it / were • with a / shield.

GLORIA.

The transition from the psalm chant to the metrical
psalm paraphrase of the sixteenth and seventeenth centuries can now be observed with maximum clarity if one
keeps in mind the importance of the term *meter*. Those who
undertook metrical psalm paraphrases focused upon re-
taining the sense (and in certain instances even the
language) of the Old Testament originals, but they also
concentrated upon developing a recognizable poetic form
and sound. The conversion from chant to poem, of course,
allowed the piece to be sung rather than chanted. For
examples of that transition, Table 10 considers Psalms 23,
82, and 100 from three perspectives—the 1611 Authorized
Version (King James), *The Oxford American Psalter*, and
three poetic paraphrases by (respectively) "Sir Philip
Sidney, John Milton, and William Kethe."

The next step, then, leads from psalm paraphrase to
the congregational hymn—or at least that form of the
hymn which relies heavily upon the substance and the
imagery of Hebrew psalmody without actually paraphrasing the Old Testament meter. John Hopkins—a Suffolk
clergyman and teacher who contributed psalm paraphrases to the third edition (1557) of Thomas Sternhold's
Certayne Psalmes, the 1561 *Anglo-Genevan Psalter*, and the
1562 *English Psalter*—represents well the transitional problems that arose during the literary trek from paraphrase to
hymn. Table 11 considers Psalm 47—specifically Hopkin's
version placed beside those of the King James Bible and
The Oxford American Psalter.

Table 10. Metrical Psalm Paraphrase

Psalm 23

King James	Oxford American Psalter	Sir Philip Sidney (c. 1579)
1 The Lord is my shepherd; I shall not want.	1 The Lord is my shepherd; Therefore can I lack nothing.	The Lord the Lord my shepherd is, And so can never I Taste misery.
2 He maketh me to lie down in green pastures: He leadeth me beside the still waters.	2 He shall feed me in a green pasture, and lead me forth beside the waters of comfort.	He rests me in green pasture his. By waters still and sweet He guides my feet.
3 He restoreth my soul: He leadeth me in the paths of righteousness for His name's sake.	3 He shall convert my soul, and bringeth me forth in the paths of righteousness for his Name's sake.	He me revives, leads me the way Which righteousness doth take, For His name's sake.
4 Yea though I walk through the valley of the shadow of death, I will fear no evil: for Thou art with me; Thy rod and Thy staff they comfort me.	4 Yea, though I walk through the valley of the shadow of death, I will fear no evil; for thou art with me; thy rod and thy staff comfort me.	Yea though I should through valleys stray Of death's dark shade I will No whit fear ill. For Thou dear Lord Thou me beset'st, Thy rod and Thy staff be To comfort me.
5 Thou preparest a table before me in the presence of mine enemies: Thou anointest my head with oil; my cup runneth over.	5 Thou shalt prepare a table before me in the presence of them that trouble me; thou has anointed my head with oil and my cup shall be full.	Before me Thou a table set'st Ev'n when foe's envious eye Doth it espy. With oil Thou dost anoint my head, And so my cup dost fill That it doth spill.
6 Surely goodness and mercy shall follow me all the days of my life: And I shall dwell in the house of the Lord for ever.	6 Surely thy loving-kindness and mercy shall follow me all the days of my life; and I will dwell in the house of the Lord for ever.	Thus shall all my days be fed, This mercy is so sure It shall endure, And long, yea long abide I shall, There where the Lord of all Doth hold His hall.

Psalm 82

King James	Oxford American Psalter	John Milton (1648)
1 God standeth in the congregation of the mighty; He judgeth among the gods.	1 God standeth in the congregation of princes; he is a judge among gods.	1 God in the great assembly stands Of Kings and lordly States, Among the gods on both his hands He judges and debates.
2 How long will ye judge unjustly, and accept the persons of the wicked?	2 How long will ye give wrong judgment, and accept the persons of the ungodly?	2 How long will ye pervert the right With judgment false and wrong, Favouring the wicked by your might, Who thence grow bold and strong?
3 Defend the poor and the fatherless; do justice to the afflicted and needy.	3 Defend the poor and fatherless; see that such as are in need and necessity have right.	3 Regard the weak and fatherless, Dispatch the poor man's cause, And raise the man in deep distress By just and equal Laws.
4 Deliver the poor and needy; rid them out of the land of the wicked.	4 Deliver the outcast and poor; save them from the hand of the ungodly.	4 Defend the poor and desolate, And rescue from the hands Of wicked men the low estate, Of him that help demands.
5 They know not, neither will they understand; they walk on in darkness: all the foundations of the earth are out of course.	5 They know not, neither do they understand, but walk on still in darkness: all the foundations of the earth are out of course.	5 They know not nor will understand, In darkness they walk on, The Earth's foundations all are mov'd And out of order gone.
6 I have said, Ye are gods; and all of you are children of the most high.	6 I have said, Ye are gods, and ye are all the children of the most Highest.	6 I said that ye were gods, ye all The Sons of god most high;
7 But ye shall die like men, and fall like one of the princes.	7 But ye shall die like men, and fall like one of the princes.	7 But ye shall die like men, and fall As other Princes die.
8 Arise, O God, judge the earth: for Thou shalt inherit all nations.	8 Arise, O God, and judge thou the earth; for thou shalt take all nations to thine inheritance.	8 Rise God, judge Thou the earth in might, This wicked earth redress, For Thou art He who shalt by right The Nations all possess.

Psalm 100

King James	*Oxford American Psalter*	William Kethe (c. 1560)
1 Make a joyful noise unto the Lord, all ye lands.	1 O be joyful in the Lord, all ye lands: serve the Lord with gladness, and come before His presence with a song.	1 All people that on earth do dwell, Sing to the Lord with cheerful voice; Him serve with mirth his praise forth tell, Come ye before Him and rejoice.
2 Serve the Lord with gladness: come before His presence with singing.	2 Be ye sure that the Lord He is God; it is He that hath made us, and not we ourselves; we are His people and the sheep of His pasture.	2 The Lord, ye know, is God indeed; Without our aide He did us make. We are His folk, He doth us feed, And for His sheep He doth us take.
3 Know ye that the Lord He is God: it is He that hath made us, and not we ourselves; we are His people, and the sheep of His pasture.	3 O go your way into His gates with thanksgiving, and unto His courts with praise; be thankful unto Him and speak good of His Name.	3 O enter then His gates with praise, Approach with joy His courts unto; Praise, laud, and bless His name always, For it is seemly so to do.
4 Enter into His gates with thanksgiving, and into His courts with praise: be thankful unto Him, and bless His name.	4 For the Lord is gracious, His mercy is everlasting; and His truth endureth from generation to generation.	4 For why? the Lord our God is good, His mercy is for every sure; His truth at all times firmly stood, And shall from age to age endure.
5 For the Lord is good; His mercy is everlasting; and His truth endureth to all generations.		

Table 11. Metrical Abbreviation: Psalm 47

King James	*Oxford American Psalter*	John Hopkins (c. 1562)
1 O clap your hands, all ye people; shout unto God with the voice of triumph.	O clap your hands together, all ye peoples; O sing unto God with the voice of melody.	Ye people all in one accord, Clap hands and eke rejoice;
2 For the Lord most high is terrible: He is a great King over all the earth.	For the Lord is high and to be feared; he is the great King upon all the earth.	Be glad and sing unto the Lord With sweet and pleasant voice.
3 He shall subdue the people under us, and the nations under our feet.	He shall subdue the people under us, and nations under our feet.	Sing praises to our God, Sing praises to our King: For God is King of all the earth,
4 He shall choose our inheritance for us, the excellency of Jacob, whom He loved.	He shall choose out an heritage for us, even the excellency of Jacob whom He loved.	All skilful praises sing.
5 God is gone up with a shout, the Lord with the sound of a trumpet.	God is gone up with a merry noise. and the Lord with the sound of the trump.	
6 Sing praises to God, sing praises: sing praises unto our King, sing praises.	O sing praises, sing praises unto our God;	
7 For God is the King of all the earth: sing ye praises with understanding.	O sing praises, sing praises unto our King. For God is the King of all the earth: sing ye praises with understanding.	
8 God reigneth over the heathen: God sitteth upon the throne of His holiness.	God reigneth over the nations; God sitteth upon His holy seat.	
9 The princes of the people are gathered together, even the people of the God of Abraham: for the shields of the earth belong unto God: He is greatly exalted.	The princes of the people are joined unto the people of God of Abraham; for God, which is very high exalted, doth defend the earth as it were with a shield.	

The low state of the art instantly reveals itself: Hopkins's metrical abbreviation of Psalm 47 seems barren of imagery and goes forward upon a meter that would dull the senses of the most insensitive readers, chanters, or singers. The seventeenth-century historian and Anglican divine, Thomas Fuller, (1608–1661), in his *Church History of Britain* (1655), remarked that the paraphrases of Sternhold and Hopkins—as well as those of their contemporaries William Whittingham, John Pullain, Robert Wisedome, Thomas Norton, Richard Cox, and others—generally failed to achieve even the level of their creators' collective piety: "they had drank more of Jordan than of Helicon" and "have in many verses much poor rhyme that two hammers on a smith's anvil would make better music" (Julian, *Dictionary of Hymnology,* 1:865). Even the often impious John Wilmot, earl of Rochester (1648–1680), could not control himself upon hearing a parish clerk chant from the "Old Version."

> Sternhold and Hopkins had great Qualms,
> When they translated David's Psalms,
>   To make the heart full glad:
> But had it been poor David's Fate
> To hear thee sing, and then Translate,
>   By ———, 'twould have made him mad.

The humor in such a passage cannot, unfortunately obscure the accuracy of its author's observations. Few examples from the early English psalters, either of music or of poetry, have found their way into mid- and late-twentieth-century British or American hymnals; they appear to have more value as museum pieces than as models for current practices in hymnody or metrical psalm paraphrase.

Little wonder, then, considering the relatively low artistic quality of psalm paraphrases found in sixteenth- and seventeenth-century English psalters, that worshipers lost interest in expressing such forms, while poets turned their creativity to different forms. In 1719, Isaac Watts (1674–1748)—the Nonconformist minister of Stoke Newington, London—issued his *Psalms of David: Imitated in the Language of the New Testament, and Applied to the Christian State of Worship*. Principally through that collection, the psalm paraphrase became the congregational hymn—the divine ode, in poetic terms—based upon a specific psalm text (either all of it, its distinct parts or sections, or merely one or two verses). Despite such labels as "Nonconformist divine" and "exponent of Calvinist morality," Watts came forth as a serious and skilled poet whose attempts to Christianize the Hebrew psalms produced poetic and hymnodic models that held forth in England and America for the next two hundred years. In fact, an accurate tribute to his efforts to redirect the form and the function of psalmody came from no less a literary figure than Samuel Johnson (1709–1784). The London sage justified Watts's inclusion in his *Lives of the Poets* (1779–1781)—both biography and selections from his verse—because Johnson wished "to distinguish Watts, a man who never wrote but for a good purpose." One purpose, of course, concerned repairing the damage to psalm paraphrase from the days of Sternhold and Hopkins. Watts set out to restore poetic dignity and meaningful expression to what, for him, remained a significant and necessary part of public worship. The degree to which he accomplished his task may be seen in Table 12, which contrasts his interpretation of Psalm 47 to the version by John Hopkins.

Table 12. Psalm 47: John Hopkins vs. Isaac Watts

Hopkins (1562)	Watts (1719)
Ye people all in one accord, Clap hands and eke rejoice: Be glad and sing unto the Lord, With sweet and pleasant voice.	(1) Oh! for a shout of sacred joy To God, the sovereign King; Let every land their tongues employ, And hymns to triumph sing.

Hopkins (1562)	Watts (1719)
Sing praises to our God, Sing praises to our King: For God is King of all the earth, All skilful praises sing.	(2) Jesus, our God, ascends on high! His heavenly guards around Attend Him rising through the sky, With trumpets' joyful sound.
	(3) While angels shout and praise their King, Let mortals learn their strains; Let all the earth His honour sing,— O'er all the earth He reigns.
	(4) Rehearse His praise with awe profound; Let knowledge lead the song; Nor mock Him with a solemn sound Upon a thoughtless tongue.
	(5) In Israel stood His ancient throne:— He loved that ancient race; But now He calls the world His own, The heathen taste His grace.

In extending four of his five verses beyond the content and certainly the intent of Psalm 47, Watts seemed to have supported the claim set forth in the title of his 1719 volume: the application of Old Testament form to New Testament sentiment. Unlike Hopkins's 1562 version, in which the paraphraser remained within the strictest confines of the Hebrew model, Watts's lines announce a new time for a new world under the rule and influence of God and of Jesus Christ. Nonetheless, Watts did not turn his back entirely upon the language and the imagery of Old Testament poetry; in fact, one can see from the comparison in Table 12 that he, more than Hopkins, demonstrated an awareness of those elements. The latter seemed content merely to direct English worshipers upon a repetitive and circuitous path of singing and clapping. As Hopkins's lines indicate, those worshipers must have tired quickly.

Within the next hundred years or so, three poets demonstrated the degree of Watts's influence upon both hymnody and psalm paraphrase. James Merrick, William Goode, and James Montgomery all tried their hands at Psalm 47 (as well as hundreds of other hymnodic themes) and achieved the results shown in Table 13.

Table 13. Psalm 47: Merrick, Goode, and Montgomery

James Merrick (1765)	William Goode (1811)	James Montgomery (1822)
(1) Arise ye people! and adore,— / Exulting strike the chord: / Let all the earth, from shore to shore, / Confess th' almighty Lord.	(1) Jesus, the Lord, ascends on high; / He reigns in glory o'er the sky: / Let all the earth its offerings bring,	(1) Extol the Lord, the Lord most high, / King over all the earth; / Exalt His triumph to the sky, / In songs of sacred mirth.
(2) Glad shouts aloud, wide echoing round, / Th' ascending God proclaim; / Th' angelic choir respond the sound, / And shake creation's frame.	(2) Wide through the world He spreads His sway, / And bids the heathen lands obey, / His church, with willing offerings, greet, / And bend submissive at her feet.	(2) God is gone up with loud acclaim, / And trumpets' tuneful voice; / Sing praise, sing praises to His name, / Sing praises, and rejoice.
(3) They sing of death and hell o'erthrown / In that triumphant hour; / And God exalts His conquering Son / To His right hand of power.	(3) His reign the heathen lands shall own; / His holiness secures His throne; / And earthly princes gather round, / Where Christ, the mighty God, is found.	(3) Sing praises to our God; sing praise / To every creature's King: / His wondrous works, His glorious ways, / All tongues! all kindred! sing.
(4) Oh! shout, ye people! an adore, / Exulting strike the chord: / Let all the earth, from shore to shore, / Confess th' almighty Lord.	(4) Princes by Him their power extend, / Earth's mightiest kings to Jesus bend; / He bids them rule, He bids them die, / Himself o'er all exalted high.	(4) God sits upon His holy throne, / God o'er the heathen reigns; / His truth through all the world is known,— / That truth His throne sustains.
		(5) Princes round His footstool throng, / Kings in the dust adore; / Earth and her shields to God belong;— / Sing praises evermore.

Of the three versions, Montgomery's appears the closest to the style, language, and even organization of the Old Testament psalm. Indeed, he accomplished what Sternhold, Hopkins, and their contemporaries had seemed unwilling or unable to do: produce a fairly close paraphrase of the English translation of psalms, yet also create odes that could be sung in public worship with such feeling and meaning that worshipers might find common ground between the Davidic intent and their own religious commitments. Given his reputation as a transitional figure from the Wesleyan and evangelical hymnody of the eighteenth century to the emergence of a new Anglican hymnody during the century following, Montgomery certainly would not have produced an unexpected interpretation of Psalm 47. Merrick and Goode, however, willingly retrieved the gauntlet cast down by Isaac Watts. Goode, especially, transferred Psalm 47 to a Christian context: beginning with the ascent of Christ, he moved to develop the idea of discipleship ("Wide through the world he spreads His sway") and to announce the formation of the Holy Church. Merrick, on the other hand, focused on the single image of the angelic choir announcing "that triumphant hour" when "God exalts His conquering Son / To His right hand of power." Both of those poets, however, continued to emphasize the joint supremacy of God and Christ over all the earth, that point being clear reflection from Watts's earlier scheme.

Although the composition of psalm paraphrases tends to be identified principally with the sixteenth, seventeenth, and eighteenth centuries (both in England and in America), one should not think that production of the form has ground to a halt in the late twentieth century. Two examples will serve to reveal the present state of the art. In 1936 T. C. Chao published in a Shanghai collection entitled *P'u T'ien Sung Tsan* (Hymns of Universal Praise), a paraphrase of Psalm 19; ten years later, Bliss Wiant (b. 1895) translated the piece and set it to an arrangement of a Christian folk melody. Table 14 compares the result with the King James Version and with Isaac Watts.

Table 14. Psalm 19: King James, Isaac Watts, and Bliss Wiant

King James	Isaac Watts (1719)	Bliss Wiant (1946)
1 The heavens declare the glory of God; and the firmament showeth His handiwork.	(1) The heavens declare Thy glory, Lord; In every star Thy wisdom shines; But, when our eyes behold Thy word, We read Thy name in fairer lines.	(1) Rise to greet the sun Red in the eastern sky, Like a glorious groom His joyous race to run. Flying birds in heavens high, Fragrant flowers a-bloom Tell the gracious Father's nigh, Now His work assume.
2 Day unto day uttereth speech, and night unto night sheweth knowledge.	(2) The rolling sun, the changing light, And nights and days Thy power confess; But the blest volume Thou has writ Reveals Thy justice and Thy grace.	(2) May this day be blest, Trusting in Jesus' care, Heart and mind illumined By heaven's radiance fair. Thanks for raiment unadorned, Rice and wholesome food; These the Lord in mercy gives, Never failing good.
3 There is no speech nor language, where their voice is not heard.	(3) Sun, moon, and stars convey Thy praise, Round the whole earth, and never stand; So, when Thy truth began its race, It touched and glanced on every land.	
4 Their line is gone out through all the earth, and their words to the end of the world. In them hath He set a tabernacle for the sun,	(4) Nor shall Thy spreading gospel rest, Till through the world Thy truth has run, Till Christ has all the nations blest, That see the light or feel the sun.	
5 Which is as a bridegroom coming out of his chamber, and rejoiceth as a strong man to run a race.	(5) Great Sun of Righteousness! arise; Bless the dark world with heavenly light; Thy gospel makes the simple wise, Thy laws are pure, Thy judgments right.	
6 His going forth is from the end of the heaven, and His circuit unto the ends of it: and there is nothing hid from the heat thereof.	(6) Thy noblest wonders here we view, In souls renewed, and sins forgiven: Lord! cleanse my sins, my soul renew, And make Thy word my guide to heaven.	

The differences between the Watts text and the Wiant translation from the Chinese readily reveal themselves, especially in terms of the eastern flavor of the imagery and meter of the latter. The "red sun" provides a radiant background for the "flying birds" and "fragrant flowers"— all of which underscore nicely the third verse of the King James psalm: "There is no speech nor language, where their voice is not heard." The Chao/Wiant version of Psalm 19 provides worshipers with a different tone or shade from that with which they have been familiar; for Western minds and voices, complete discoloration has been avoided.

For the second example of psalmody in the late twentieth century, Table 15 considers a version of Psalm 113 by Heinz Werner Zimmerman and Marjorie Jillson entitled "Praise the Lord," which appeared in Zimmerman's *Five Hymns*. Once again, the similarities and differences can be seen when the contemporary version rests beside the biblical text and a traditional interpretation by James Montgomery. Interestingly enough, the Zimmerman/Jillson paraphrase does not stray too far from the sentiment and the sound of the Hebrew psalmist; in fact, it appears even closer to both the form and the purpose of the psalm paraphrases prevalent during the sixteenth and seventeenth centuries. Thus, although the Zimmerman/Jillson text is a contemporary piece, it shows clearly that hymnodists of the present have not shut themselves off from their historical sources, that the metrical psalm paraphrase will continue to convey meaning and inspiration to future generations of both congregational poets and congregational singers.

Before departing entirely from the area of psalmody and the metrical psalm paraphrase, one may wish to consider a means for locating and comparing paraphrases of and hymns based upon the Old Testament Book of Psalms. The restrictions of space impose obvious limits to such a project, particularly given the total of 150 psalms. Thus, Table 16 is illustrative of the sound and sense of the

Table 15. Psalm 113: King James, James Montgomery, and Zimmerman/Jillson

	King James		James Montgomery (1819)		Zimmerman/Jillson (1973)
1	Praise ye the Lord. Praise, O ye servants of the Lord, praise the name of the Lord.	(1)	Servants of God! in joyful lays, Sing ye the Lord Jehovah's praise; His glorious name let all adore, From age to age, for evermore.	(1)	Praise the Lord! Praise, O servants of the Lord! Praise the name of the Lord! Blessed be the name of the Lord! Blessed be the name of the Lord
2	Blessed be the name of the Lord from this time forth and for evermore.	(2)	Blest be that name, supremely blest, From sun's rising to its rest: Above the heavens His power is known; Through all the earth His goodness shown.		From this time forth and for evermore! Praise the Lord! Praise the Lord!
3	From the rising of the sun unto the going down of the same, the Lord's name is to be praised.			(2)	Praise the Lord! Thanks and praises sing to God! Day by day to the Lord! High above the nations is God, High above the nations is God, His glory high over earth and sky! Praise the Lord! Praise the Lord!
4	The Lord is high above all nations, and His glory above the heavens.	(3)	Who is like God?—so great, so high, He bows Himself to view the sky; And yet, with condescending grace, Looks down upon the human race.	(3)	Praise the Lord! Praise and glory give to God! Who is like unto Him?
5	Who is like unto the Lord our God, who dwelleth on high,	(4)	He hears the uncomplaining moan Of those, who sit and weep alone; He lifts the mourner from the dust, And saves the poor in Him who trust.		Raising up the poor from the dust, Raising up the poor from the dust, He makes them dwell in His heart and home. Praise the Lord! Praise the Lord!
6	Who humbleth himself to behold the things that are in heaven, and in the earth!	(5)	Servants of God! in joyful lays, Sing ye the Lord Jehovah's praise; His saving name let all adore, From age to age, for evermore.	(4)	Praise the Lord! Praise, O servants of the Lord! Praise the love of the Lord:
7	He raiseth up the poor out of the dust, and lifteth the needy out of the dunghill:				Giving to the homeless a home, Giving to the homeless a home, He fills their hearts with new hope and joy! Praise the Lord! Praise the Lord!
8	That He may set him with princes, even with the princes of His people.				
9	He maketh the barren woman to keep house, and to be a joyful mother of children. Praise ye the Lord.				

Old Testament originals in English. Indeed, the sheer quantity of verses, paraphrases, and hymns based upon psalms and intended for public worship almost defies attempts at concise statistical summary or bibliographical notation, therefore forcing the most skeletal of descriptions and examples. The very nature and state of the form incline one toward preceding centuries; examples from those periods are easy to locate and to identify, and they generally come close to the thought and the language of the psalms in English. However, one must also realize that later examples do exist (see particularly Psalms 19 and 113 in Table 16), and a number of those may even parallel the style and the sentiments of the Hebrew psalmist or his seventeenth-, eighteenth-, and nineteenth-century imitators.

Table 16. A Reference Guide to Select Verse Paraphrases of Psalms

Psalm	Date	Author	Opening Lines of Paraphrase	Scripture Reference (and Verse Number)
1	1719	Isaac Watts (1674–1748)	Happy the man whose cautious feet Shun the broad way that sinners go	Blessed is the man that walketh not in the counsel of the ungodly, nor standeth in the way of sinners (1)
2	1769	Thomas Gibbons (1720–1785)	Father, is not Thy promise pledged To Thine exalted Son	I will declare the decree: the Lord hath said unto me, Thou art my Son (7)
3	1822	James Montgomery (1771–1854)	The tempter to my soul hath said,— "There is no help in God for thee"	Many there be which say of my soul, There is no help for him in God (2)
4	1695	Thomas Ken (1637–1710)	Glory to Thee, my God! this night, For all the blessings of the light	There be many that say, who will shew us any good? Lord, lift Thou up the light of Thy countenance upon us (6)
5	1829	William Wrangham (d. 1832)	Soon as the morning-rays appear, I'll lift mine eyes above	My voice shalt Thou hear in the morning, O Lord; in the morning I will direct my prayer unto Thee, and will look up (3)
6	1779	John Newton (1725–1807)	In mercy, not in wrath, rebuke Thy feeble worm, my God	O Lord, rebuke me not in Thine anger, neither chasten me in Thy hot displeasure (1)
7	1719	Isaac Watts	My trust is in my heavenly friend My hope is in Thee my God	O Lord, my God, in Thee do I put my trust: save me from all them that persecute me, and deliver me (1)
8	1811	William Goode (1762–1816)	O Lord, our Lord! in power divine, How great is Thy illustrious name!	O Lord, our Lord, how excellent is Thy name in all the earth! who hast set Thy glory above the heavens (1)
9	1719	Isaac Watts	When the great Judge, supreme and just, Shall once inquire for blood	When He maketh inquisition for blood, He remembereth them: He forgetteth not the cry of the humble (12)
10	1779	William Cowper (1731–1800)	Hear, Lord! the song of praise and prayer, In heaven, Thy dwelling-place	Why standest Thou afar off, O Lord? why hidest Thou Thyself in times of trouble? (1)

Psalm	Date	Author	Opening Lines of Paraphrase	Scripture Reference (and Verse Number)
11	1719	Isaac Watts	My refuge is the God of love: Why do my foes insult, and cry—	In the Lord put I my trust: how say ye to my soul, Flee as a bird to your mountain? (1)
12	1719	Isaac Watts	Help, Lord! for men of virtue fail, Religion loses ground	Help, Lord; for the godly man ceaseth; for the faithful fail from among the children of men (1)
13	1811	William Goode	Lord of mercy, just and kind! Wilt Thou ne'er my guilt forgive?	How long wilt Thou forget me, O Lord? for ever? how long wilt Thou hide Thy face from me? (1)
14	1834	Henry Francis Lyte (1793–1847)	Oh! that the Lord's salvation Were out of Zion come	Oh that the salvation of Israel were come out of Zion! when the Lord bringeth back the captivity of His people, Jacob shall rejoice, and Israel shall be glad (7)
15	1765	James Merrick (1720–1769)	Who, O Lord! when life is o'er, Shall to heaven's blest mansions soar?	Lord, who shall abide in Thy tabernacle? who shall dwell in Thy holy hill? (1)
16	1719	Isaac Watts	I set the Lord before my face, He bears my courage up	I have set the Lord always before me: because He is at my right hand, I shall not be moved (8)
17	1719	Isaac Watts	Arise, my gracious God! And make the wicked flee	Arise, O Lord, disappoint him, cast him down; deliver my soul from the wicked (13)
18	1560	Sternhold and Hopkins (Old Version)	The Lord descended from above, And bowed the heavens most high	He bowed the heavens also, and came down: and darkness was under His feet (9)
19	1946	Bliss Wiant (b. 1895); (trans. from T. C. Chao)	Rise to greet the Sun Red in the eastern sky Like a glorious bridegroom His joyous race to run	Which is as a bridegroom coming out of his chamber, and rejoiceth as a strong man to run a race (5)
20	1829	William Wrangham	The Lord unto thy prayer attend, In trouble's darksome hour	The Lord hear Thee in the day of trouble; the name of the God of Jacob defend thee (1)
21	1786	Joel Barlow (1754–1812)	In Thee, great God! with songs of praise, Our favored realms rejoice	Be Thou exalted, Lord, in Thine own strength: so will we sing and praise thy power (13)

Psalm	Date	Author	Opening Lines of Paraphrase	Scripture Reference (and Verse Number)
22	1719	Isaac Watts	Now let our mournful songs record / The dying sorrows of our Lord	O my God, I cry in the daytime, but Thou hearest not; and in the night season, and am not silent (2)
23	1712	Joseph Addison (1672–1719)	The Lord my pasture shall prepare, / And feed me with a shepherd's care	He maketh me to lie down in green pastures . . . Thou preparest a table before me (2, 5)
24	1719	Isaac Watts	The earth for ever is the Lord's, / With Adam's numerous race	The earth is the Lord's, and the fulness thereof; the world, and they that dwell therein (1)
25	1547	Thomas Sternhold (d. 1549)	I lift my heart to Thee, my God and guide most just: / For suffer me to take no shame, for in Thee I do trust	Unto Thee, O Lord, do I lift up my soul. O my God, I trust in Thee: let me not be ashamed, let not mine enemies triumph over me (1)
26	1829	William Wrangham	Search my heart, my actions prove, / Try my thoughts, as they arise	Examine me, O Lord, and prove me; try my reins and my heart (2)
27	1822	James Montgomery	Grant me within Thy courts a place, / Among Thy saints a rest	One thing have I desired of the Lord, that I will seek after; that I may dwell in the house of the Lord all the days of my life, to behold the beauty of the Lord (4)
28	1786	Joel Barlow	To Thee, O Lord, I raise my cries, / My fervent prayer in mercy hear	Unto Thee will I cry, O Lord . . . Hear the voice of my supplications, when I cry unto Thee, when I lift up my hands toward the holy oracle (1–2)
29	1719	Isaac Watts	Give to the Lord, ye sons of fame! / Give to the Lord renown and power	Give unto the Lord, O ye mighty, give unto the Lord glory and strength (1)
30	1719	Isaac Watts	I will extol Thee, Lord! on high; / At Thy command diseases fly	I will extol Thee, O Lord . . . I cried unto Thee, and Thou hast healed me (1–2)
31	1760	Anne Steele (1716–1778)	My God! my Father! blissful name! / Oh! may I call Thee mine?	But I trusted in Thee, O Lord: I said Thou art my God (14)
32	1719	Isaac Watts	Oh! blessed souls are they, / Whose sins are covered o'er	Blessed is he whose transgression is forgiven, whose sin is covered (1)

Psalm	Date	Author	Opening Lines of Paraphrase	Scripture Reference (and Verse Number)
33	1719	Isaac Watts	Ye holy souls! in God rejoice; / Your Maker's praise becomes your voice	Rejoice in the Lord, O ye righteous: for praise is comely for the upright (1)
34	1696	Tate and Brady (New Version)	Through all the changing scenes of life, / In trouble and in joy	I will bless the Lord at all times . . . My soul shall make her boast in the Lord: the humble shall hear thereof, and be glad (1–2)
35	1811	William Goode	Lo! the Lord, the mighty Saviour, / Quits the grave, the throne to claim	Let them be confounded and put to shame that seek after my soul; let them be turned back and brought to confusion that desire my hurt (4)
36	1719	Isaac Watts	High in the heavens, eternal God! / Thy goodness in full glory shines	Thy mercy, O Lord, is in the heavens; and Thy faithfulness reacheth unto the clouds (5)
37	1719	Isaac Watts	Now let me make the Lord my trust, / And practice all that's good	Trust in the Lord, and do good; so shalt thou dwell in the land, and verily thou shalt be fed (3)
38	1719	Isaac Watts	Amidst Thy wrath, remember, love, / Restore Thy servant, Lord	O Lord, rebuke me not in Thy wrath; neither chastise me in Thy hot displeasure (1)
39	1765	James Merrick	Oh! let me, gracious Lord! extend / My view, to life's approaching end	Lord, make me to know mine end, and the measure of my days, what it is; that I may know how frail I am (4)
40	1765	James Merrick	O Lord! how infinite Thy love! / How wondrous are Thy ways	Many, O Lord my God, are Thy wonderful works which Thou hast done and Thy thoughts which are to us-ward: they cannot be reckoned up in order (5)
41	1719	Isaac Watts	Blest is the man whose bowels move, / And melt with pity to the poor	Blest is he that considereth the poor: the Lord will deliver him in time of trouble (1)
42	1696	Tate and Brady	As pants the hart for cooling streams, / When heated in the chase	As the hart panteth after the water brooks, so panteth my soul after Thee, O God (1)
43	1786	Joel Barlow	Judge me, O God! and plead my cause / Against a sinful race	Judge me, O God, and plead my cause against an ungodly nation: O deliver me from the deceitful and unjust man (1)

Psalm	Date	Author	Opening Lines of Paraphrase	Scripture Reference (and Verse Number)
44	1719	Isaac Watts	Lord! we have heard Thy works of old, Thy works of power and grace	We have heard with our ears, O God, our fathers have told us, what work Thou didst in their days in the times of old (1)
45	1755	Philip Doddridge (1702–1751)	Gird on Thy conquering sword, Ascend Thy shining car	Gird Thy sword upon Thy thigh, O most mighty, with Thy glory and Thy majesty. And in Thy majesty ride prosperously (3–4)
46	1834	Henry Francis Lyte	God is our refuge, tried and proved, Amid a stormy world	God is our refuge and strength, a very present help in trouble (1)
47	1822	James Montgomery	Extol the Lord, the Lord most high, King over all the earth	O clap your hands all ye people; shout unto God with the voice of triumph (1)
48	1822	James Montgomery	Oh! great is Jehovah, and great be His praise, In the city of God He is King	Great is the Lord, and greatly to be praised in the city of our God, in the mountain of His holiness (1)
49	1719	Isaac Watts	Ye sons of pride! that hate the just, And trample on the poor	They that trust in their wealth, and boast themselves in the multitude of their riches . . . For when he dieth, he shall carry nothing away: his glory shall not descend after him (6, 17)
50	1811	William Goode	Lo! the mighty God appearing, From on high Jehovah speaks!	The mighty God, even the Lord, hath spoken, and called the earth from the rising of the sun unto the going down thereof (1)
51	1811	William Goode	No offering God requires, Nor victims please His eye	For Thou desirest not sacrifice; else would I give it: Thou delightest not in burnt offering (16)
52	1786	Joel Barlow	Why should the mighty make their boast, And heavenly grace despise?	Why boastest thou thyself in mischief, O mighty man; the goodness of God endureth continually (1)
53	1719	Isaac Watts	Are the foes of Zion fools, Who thus devour her saints?	The fool hath said in his heart, There is no God. Corrupt are they, and have done abominable iniquity: there is none that doeth good (1)

Psalm	Date	Author	Opening Lines of Paraphrase	Scripture Reference (and Verse Number)
54	1800	Timothy Dwight (1752–1817)	My God! preserve my soul; Oh! make my spirit whole	Save me, O God, by Thy name, and judge me by Thy strength (1)
55	1783	Rowland Hill (1744–1833)	Cast thy burden on the Lord, Only lean upon His word	Cast thy burden upon the Lord, and He will sustain thee: He shall never suffer the righteous to be moved (22)
56	1719	Isaac Watts	O Thou! whose justice reigns on high, And makes th' oppressor cease	When I cry unto Thee, then shall my enemies turn back: this I know; for God is for me (9)
57	1829	William Wrangham	Eternal God, celestial King! Exalted by Thy glorious name	Be Thou exalted, O God, above the heavens: let Thy glory be above all the earth (5, 11)
58	1719	Isaac Watts	Judges! who rule the world by laws, Will ye despise the righteous cause	Do ye indeed speak righteousness, O congregation? do ye judge uprightly, O ye sons of men?
59	1800	Timothy Dwight	When God in wrath shall come · To tell the sinner's doom	Thou, therefore, O Lord God of hosts, the God of Israel, awake to visit all the heathen: be not merciful to . . . transgressors (5)
60	1837	Edwin Francis Hatfield (1807–1883)	Why, O God! Thy people spurn? Why permit Thy wrath to burn?	O God, Thou hast cast us off. Thou hast scattered us, Thou hast been displeased; O turn Thyself to us again (1)
61	1719	Isaac Watts	When overwhelmed with grief My heart within me dies	From the end of the earth I will cry unto Thee, when my heart is overwhelmed: lead me to the rock that is higher than I (2)
62	1719	Isaac Watts	My spirit looks to God alone; My rock and refuge is His throne	In God is my salvation and my glory: the rock of my strength and my refuge is in God (7)
63	1822	James Montgomery	O God! Thou art my God alone; Early to Thee my soul shall cry	O God, Thou art my God; early will I seek Thee: my soul thirsteth for Thee, my flesh longeth for Thee (1)
64	1786	Joel Barlow	Great God! attend to my complaint, Nor let my drooping spirit faint	Hear my voice, O God, in my prayer: preserve my life from fear of the enemy (1)

Psalm	Date	Author	Opening Lines of Paraphrase	Scripture Reference (and Verse Number)
65	1836	Josiah Conder (1789–1855)	Praise on Thee, in Zion's gates, Daily, O Jehovah! waits	Praise waiteth for Thee, O God, in Sion: and unto Thee shall the vow be performed (1)
66	1800	Ralph Wardlaw (1779–1853)	Lift up to God the voice of praise, Whose breath our souls inspired	Make a joyful noise unto God, all ye lands: Sing forth the honour of His name: make His praise glorious (1–2)
67	1696	Tate and Brady	To bless Thy chosen race, In mercy, Lord! incline	God be merciful unto us, and bless us; and cause His face to shine upon us (1)
68	1719	Isaac Watts	Kingdoms and thrones to God belong; Crown Him, ye nations! in your song	Sing unto God, ye kingdoms of the earth; O sing praises unto the Lord (32)
69	1719	Isaac Watts	Deep in our hearts, let us record The deeper sorrows of our Lord	Save me, O God; for the waters are come into my soul. I sink in deep mire, where there is no standing I am come into deep waters (1–2)
70	1822	James Montgomery	Hasten, Lord! to my release, Haste to help me, O my God!	Make haste, O God, to deliver me; make haste to help me, O Lord (1)
71	1719	Isaac Watts	The praises of my tongue I offer to the Lord	My tongue also shall talk of Thy righteousness unto the king's son (1)
72	1829	Harriet Auber (1773–1862)	Hasten, Lord! to my release, Haste to help me, O my God!	Give the king Thy judgments, O God, and Thy righteousness unto the king's son (1)
73	1763	Charles Wesley (1707–1788)	O my all-sufficient God, Thou know it my heart's desire	Thus my heart was grieved, and I was pricked in my reins (21)
74	1762	Charles Wesley	O Lord from heaven, on earth bestow'd, Thy goodness makes our blessings sure	For God is my King of old, working salvation in the midst of the earth (12)
75	1719	Isaac Watts	To Thee, most Holy and most High! To Thee we bring our thankful praise	Unto Thee, O God, do we give thanks, unto Thee do we give Thanks: for that Thy name is near Thy wondrous works declare (1)

Psalm	Date	Author	Opening Lines of Paraphrase	Scripture Reference (and Verse Number)
76	1719	Isaac Watts	In Judah, God of old was known; His name in Israel great	In Judah is God known: His name is great in Israel (1)
77	1822	James Montgomery	In time of tribulation, Hear, Lord! my feeble cries	In the day of my trouble I sought the Lord: my sore ran in the night, and ceased not: my soul refused to be comforted (2)
78	1762	Charles Wesley	Lord, I confess Thy judgments just, If left to my own heart's desires	We will not hide them from their children, shewing in the generation to come the praises of the Lord, and His strength, and His wonderful works (4)
79	1765	James Merrick	Arise, great God! and let Thy grace Shed its glad beams on Israel's race	Help us, O God of our salvation, for the glory of Thy name: and deliver us, and purge away our sins, for Thy name's sake (9)
80	1719	Isaac Watts	Great Shepherd of Thine Israel! Who didst between the cherubs dwell	Give ear, O Shepherd of Israel, Thou that leadest Joseph like a flock: Thou that dwellest between the cherubim, shine forth (1)
81	1762	Charles Wesley	Sing we merrily to God, We the creatures of His grace	Sing aloud unto God our strength: make a joyful noise unto the God of Jacob (1)
82	1719	Isaac Watts	Among th' assemblies of the great, A greater ruler takes His seat	God standeth in the congregation of the mighty; He judgeth among the gods (1)
83	1719	Isaac Watts	And will the God of grace Perpetual silence keep?	Keep not Thou silence, O God: hold not Thy peace, and be not still, O God (1)
84	1824	Josiah Conder	How honoured, how dear, That sacred abode	How amiable are Thy tabernacles, O Lord of hosts! (1)
85	1841	Samuel Francis Smith (1808–1895)	Spirit of holiness descend; Thy people wait for Thee	Surely His salvation is nigh them that fear Him; that glory may dwell in our land (9)
86	1843	James Young	O for a shout of joy, Loud as the theme we sing!	Rejoice the soul of Thy servant: for unto Thee, O Lord, do I lift up my soul (4)

Psalm	Date	Author	Opening Lines of Paraphrase	Scripture Reference (and Verse Number)
87	1719	Isaac Watts	God, in His earthly temple, lays Foundation for His heavenly praise	His foundation is in the holy mountains (1)
88	1800	Timothy Dwight	Shall men, O God of light and life! For ever moulder in the grave?	For my soul is full of troubles: and my life draweth nigh unto the grave (3)
89	1834	Henry Francis Lyte	The mercies of my God and King My tongue shall still pursue	I will sing of the mercies of the Lord for ever: with my mouth will I make known Thy faithfulness to all generations (1)
90	1719	Isaac Watts	Through every age, eternal God! Thou art our rest, our safe abode	Lord, Thou hast been our dwelling place in all generations (1)
91	1819	James Montgomery	Call Jehovah thy salvation, Rest beneath th' Almighty's shade	He that dwelleth in the secret place of the most High shall abide under the shadow of the Almighty (1)
92	1829	Harriet Auber	Sweet is the work, O Lord! Thy glorious name to sing	It is a good thing to give thanks unto the Lord, and to sing praises unto Thy name, O most High (1)
93	1760	Anne Steele	The Lord, the God of glory reigns, In robes of majesty arrayed	The Lord reigneth, He is clothed with majesty; the Lord is clothed with strength, wherewith He hath girded himself (1)
94	1840	Richard Vaughan Yates (1785–1856)	O God, to Thee my sinking soul In deep distress doth fly	Unless the Lord had been my help, my soul had almost dwelt in silence (17)
95	1719	Isaac Watts	Come, let our voices join, to raise A sacred song of solemn praise	O come, let us sing unto the Lord: let us make a joyful noise to the rock of our salvation (1)
96	1811	William Goode	Now let our songs arise, In new exalted strains	O sing unto the Lord a new song: sing unto the Lord, all the earth (1)
97	1812	Henry Kirke White (1785–1806)	The Lord our God is clothed with might; The winds obey His will	The Lord reigneth; let the earth rejoice; let the multitude of isles be glad thereof (1)

Psalm	Date	Author	Opening Lines of Paraphrase	Scripture Reference (and Verse Number)
98	1829	Harriet Auber	To God address the joyful psalm, Who wondrous things hath done	O sing unto the Lord a new song; for He hath done marvellous things: His right hand, and His holy arm, hath gotten Him the victory (1)
99	1719	Isaac Watts	Exalt the Lord, our God, And worship at His feet	Exalt ye the Lord our God, and worship at His footstool; for He is holy (5)
100	1840	Edwin Francis Hatfield (1807–1883)	Sing, all ye lands!—with rapture sing, And bless Jehovah's name	Make a joyful noise unto the Lord, all ye lands . . . be thankful unto Him, and bless His name (1, 4)
101	1719	Isaac Watts	Mercy and judgment are my song; And, since they both to Thee belong	I will sing of mercy and judgment: unto Thee, O Lord, will I sing (1)
102	1696	Tate and Brady	Through endless years Thou art the same, O Thou eternal God	But Thou, O Lord, shalt endure for ever; and Thy remembrance unto all generations (12)
103	1819	James Montgomery	Oh! bless the Lord, my soul! His grace to thee proclaim	Bless the Lord, O my soul: and all that is within me, bless His holy name (1)
104	1816	Thomas Moore (1779–1852)	Thou art, O God, the life and light Of all this wondrous world we see	Bless the Lord . . . Who coverest Thyself with light . . . Who laid the foundations of the earth (1, 2, 5)
105	1831	William Hiley Bathurst (1796–1877)	Oh! give thanks unto the Lord; All His wondrous deeds proclaim	O give thanks unto the Lord; call upon His name: make known His deeds among the people (1)
106	1696	Tate and Brady	Oh! render thanks to God above, The fountain of eternal love	Praise ye the Lord. O give thanks unto the Lord; for He is good: for His mercy endureth for ever (1)
107	1712	Joseph Addison	How are Thy servants blessed, O Lord! How sure is their defence	They that go down to sea in ships . . . He blesseth them also (23, 28)
108	1786	Joel Barlow	Awake, my soul! to sound His praise, Awake, my harp! to sing	Awake, psaltery and harp: I myself will awake early. I will praise Thee, O Lord, among the people (2–3)
109	1794	Ottiwell Heginbothom	Yes, I will bless Thee, O my God, Through all my mortal days	I will greatly praise the Lord with my mouth; yea, I will praise Him among the multitude (30)

Psalm	Date	Author	Opening Lines of Paraphrase	Scripture Reference (and Verse Number)
110	1784	Thomas Gibbons	As showers on meadows newly mown, Our God shall send His spirit down	Thy people shall be willing in the day of Thy power, in the beauties of holiness from the womb of the morning (3)
111	1768	John Needham (d. 1786)	Holy and reverend is the name Of our eternal King	He sent redemption unto His people; He hath commanded His covenant for ever: holy and reverend is His name (9)
112	1719	Isaac Watts	Thrice happy man who fears the Lord, Loves His commands, and trusts His word	Praise ye the Lord. Blessed is the man that feareth the Lord, that delighteth greatly in His commandments (1)
113	1973	Heinz Zimmerman and Marjorie Jillson	Praise the Lord! Praise, O servants of the Lord! Praise the name of the Lord	Praise ye the Lord. Praise, O ye servants of the Lord, praise the name of the Lord. Blessed be the name of the Lord from this time forth (1–2)
114	1719	Isaac Watts	When Israel, freed from Pharaoh's hand, Left the proud tyrant and his land	When Israel went out of Egypt, the house of Jacob from a people of strange language (1)
115	1810	Thomas Cotterill (1779–1823)	O'er the realm of pagan darkness Let the eye of pity gaze	Wherefore should the heathen say, Where is now their God? (2)
116	1836	Thomas Hastings (1784–1872)	I love the Lord;—whose gracious ear Was opened to my mournful prayer	I love the Lord, because He hath heard my voice and my supplications. Because He hath inclined His ear unto me (1–2)
117	1836	Josiah Conder	Jehovah's praise sublime Through the wide earth be sung	O praise the Lord all ye nations: praise him all ye people (1)
118	1696	Tate and Brady	Ye boundless realms of joy, Exalt your maker's name	O give thanks unto the Lord; for He is good: because His mercy endureth for ever (1)
119	1779	William Cowper	Oh! how I love Thy holy word, Thy gracious covenant, O Lord!	Thy word have I hid in mine heart, that I might not sin against Thee. Blessed art Thou, O Lord: teach me Thy statutes. O how I love Thy law (11–12, 97)

Psalm	Date	Author	Opening Lines of Paraphrase	Scripture Reference (and Verse Number)
120	1719	Isaac Watts	Thou God of love, Thou ever-blest! Pity my suffering state	In my distress I cried unto the Lord and He heard me (1)
121	1755	Philip Doddridge	Interval of grateful shade! Welcome to my wearied head	The Lord is thy keeper: the Lord thy shade upon thy right hand (5)
122	1829	Harriet Auber	With joy we hail the sacred day, Which God has called His own	Whither the tribes go up, the tribes of the Lord, unto the testimony of Israel, to give thanks unto the name of the Lord (4)
123	1816	John Bowdler (1783–1815)	Lord! before Thy name we bend; Now to Thee our prayers ascend	Unto thee lift I up mine eyes, O Thou that dwellest in the heavens (1)
124	1719	Isaac Watts	Had not the Lord,—may Israel say,— Had not the Lord maintained our side	If it had not been the Lord who was on our side, now may Israel say; If it had not been the Lord who was on our side when men rose up against us (1–2)
125	1802	Thomas Kelly (1769–1854)	Zion stands with hills surrounded,— Zion kept by power divine	As the mountains are round about Jerusalem, so the Lord is round about His people from henceforth even for ever (2)
126	1831	William Hiley Bathurst	Ye servants of the living God! Let praise your hearts employ	He that goeth forth and weepeth, bearing precious seed, shall doubtless come again with rejoicing, bringing his sheaves with him (6)
127	1829	Harriet Auber	Vainly through the night's weary hours, Keep we watch, lest foes alarm	Except the Lord build the house, they labour in vain that build it: except the Lord keep the city, the watchman waketh but in vain (1)
128	1719	Isaac Watts	Oh! happy man, whose soul is filled With zeal and reverend awe	For thou shalt eat the labour of thine hands: happy shalt thou be, and it shall be well with thee (2)
129	1762	Charles Wesley	They are, as wither'd grass, they are, Who hate the Church by Thee beloved	Let them be as the grass upon the housetops, which withereth afore it groweth up (6)

Psalm	Date	Author	Opening Lines of Paraphrase	Scripture Reference (and Verse Number)
130	1696	Tate and Brady	From lowest depths of woe, To God I send my cry	Out of the depths have I cried unto Thee, O Lord (1)
131	1819	James Montgomery	Lord! for ever at Thy side, Let my place and portion be	Let Israel hope in the Lord from henceforth and for ever (1)
132	1819	James Montgomery	Lord! for Thy servant David's sake, Perform Thine oath to David's Son	For Thy servant David's sake turn not away the face of Thine anointed (10)
133	1837	Edwin Francis Hatfield	Behold! how good and sweet For brethren thus to meet	Behold how good and how pleasant it is for brethren to dwell together in unity (1)
134	1719	Isaac Watts	Ye who obey th' immortal King! Attend His holy place	Lift up your heads in the sactuary, and bless the Lord (2)
135	1800	Timothy Dwight	Sing to the Lord most high; Let every land adore	Praise the Lord; for the Lord is good: sing praises unto His name; for it is pleasant (3)
136	1623	John Milton (1608–1674)	Let us with a joyful mind, Praise the Lord, for He is kind	O give thanks unto the Lord; for He is good: for His mercy endureth for ever (1)
137	1696	Tate and Brady	When we our wearied limbs to rest, Sat down by proud Euphrates' stream	By the rivers of Babylon, there we sat down, yea, we wept, when we remembered Zion (1)
138	1782	John Fawcett (1740–1817)	Praise to Thee, Thou great creator; Praise be Thine from every tongue	I will praise Thee with my whole heart: before the gods will I sing praise unto Thee (1)
139	1719	Isaac Watts	Lord, Thou hast searched and seen me through; Thine eye commands, with piercing view	O Lord, Thou hast searched me, and known me . . . Thine eyes did see my substance (1, 16)
140	1800	Timothy Dwight	My God! while impious men, With malice in their heart	Deliver me, O Lord, from the evil man: preserve me from the violent man; Which imagine mischiefs in their heart (1–2)

Psalm	Date	Author	Opening Lines of Paraphrase	Scripture Reference (and Verse Number)
141	1762	Charles Wesley	What cannot the Almighty do? When by the greatness of Thy power	Lord, I cry unto Thee: make haste unto me; give ear unto my voice, when I cry unto Thee (1)
142	1719	Isaac Watts	To God I made my sorrows known, From God I sought relief	I poured out my complaint before Him; I showed before Him my trouble (2)
143	1829	Josiah Pratt	My God, my prayer attend; O bow Thine ear to me	Hear my prayer, O Lord, give ear to my supplications: in Thy faithfulness answer me, and in Thy righteousness (1)
144	1719	Isaac Watts	For ever blessed be the Lord, My Saviour and my shield	Blessed be the Lord my strength, which teacheth my hands to war, and my fingers to fight (1)
145	1822	Henry Moore (1732–1802)	My God, Thy boundless love I praise; How bright, on high, its glories blaze!	I will extol Thee, my God, O King; and I will bless Thy name for ever and ever (1)
146	1794	Ottiwell Heginbothom	My soul shall praise Thee, O my God, Through all my mortal days	Praise ye the Lord. Praise the Lord, O my soul. While I live I will praise the Lord: I will sing praises unto my God while I have any being (1–2)
147	1719	Isaac Watts	Praise ye the Lord!—'tis good to raise Our hearts and voices in His praise	Praise ye the Lord: for it is good to sing praises unto our God; for it is pleasant; and praise is comely (1)
148	1769	John Ogilvie	Begin, my soul! th' exalted lay; Let each enraptured thought obey	Praise ye the Lord. Praise ye the Lord from the heavens: praise Him in the heights (1)
149	1756	Thomas Blacklock (1721–1791)	Come, O my soul, in sacred lays Attempt thy great Creator's praise	Praise ye the Lord. Sing unto the Lord a new song, and His praise in the congregation of saints (1)
150	1800	Timothy Dwight	In Zion's sacred gates, Let hymns of praise begin	Praise ye the Lord. Praise God in His sanctuary: praise Him in the firmament of His power (1)

Chapter Five
ISAAC WATTS: BEFORE AND AFTER

THE NEXT STEP IN THE DISCUSSION of hymnody and congregational song leads to the British Isles and the state of
hymnody in England from the middle of the Restoration
period until the last decades of the eighteenth century.
Although the Restoration of Charles II to the throne of
England in 1660 reestablished the dominance of the
Anglican Church and provided fresh moments of extreme
discomfort for Protestant Dissenters, both groups evi-
denced some inclination toward congregational singing
during public worship. The Church of England sought to
raise the musical and poetical levels of psalm paraphrases
and original devotional odes, while the Presbyterians, both
in England and in their more comfortable Scottish climes,
continued to issue variations upon their psalters and
collections of original pieces based upon psalmodic texts
and themes. However, the laurel for having actually
introduced the singing of hymns by congregations during
worship must go to the Baptists—specifically the Calvinist
congregation of Broadmead Church, Bristol, whose members carried on that activity between 1671 and 1685.

The initial force behind the spread of English congregational hymnody manifested itself in the form of a Baptist
minister and prolific prose writer who endured suffering
and imprisonment for his Nonconformist principles. Benjamin Keach, who began preaching under the Baptist
banner at the age of eighteen, came in 1668 from his native
Buckinghamshire to London as pastor of a Calvinist (or
Particular) Baptist church at Horsleydown, Southwark. His
earliest hymns appeared in narrative prose and poetic

79

tracts, such as *War with the Powers of Darkness* and *Distressed Sion Relieved; or, The Garment of Praise for the Spirit of Heaviness.* Then in 1691 he published *The Breach Repaired in God's Worship; or, Singing of Psalms, Hymns, and Spiritual Songs Proved to be a Holy Ordinance of Jesus Christ*—a collection of three hundred hymns. Although Keach directed his poetic efforts toward his own congregation, other Dissenting sects adopted them. Unfortunately, Keach's hymns found little acceptance after the seventeenth century; in fact, examples are hard to come by, and thus the following lines, based upon Psalm 100, may be observed more for their historical value than their literary or even hymnodic merits.

> Now let all People on the Earth
> Sing to the Lord with chearful voice,
> Whose love was such to bring Thee forth,
> But chiefly, let Thy Saints rejoyce. . . .
> For why the Lord our God is good
> His Covenant it standeth sure,
> 'Tis ratify'd by Christ's own Blood,
> And shall from age to age endure.

A real problem with Keach's poems as congregational hymns, however, concerns his politics—he tended to rely upon the congregational hymn as a propaganda vehicle for promoting his Baptist principles against threats (real or imagined) from papists and nonbelievers.

> Blessed be God that we were born
>   Under the joyful sound,
> And rightly have Baptized been,
>   And bred on English ground. . . .
>
> We might have been dark Pagans all,
>   Or veiled like each a Jew,
> Or cheated with an Alcoran
>   Amongst the Turkish crew.
>
> Dumb Pictures might we all ador'd,
>   Like Papists in Devotion;

> And with Rome's errours so been stor'd,
>   To drink her deadly Potion.

In such instances, Keach sacrificed any potential hymnodic catholicity for little more than amateur doggerel, a form hardly suited to even the most informal conventions of public worship.

Nonetheless, the major contribution of Benjamin Keach to the development of the English hymn appears to have been his understanding of the notion that a hymn could serve the specific liturgical demands of a particular congregation. He therefore viewed the hymnal as a means of meeting congregational needs rather than an anthology of denominational verse. He managed to form a primitive model for what would come early in the eighteenth century—the hymn and the hymnbook as instruments to complement publicly moral and religious expression. That model, not totally appreciated by Baptist congregations whose members found themselves divided by the issue of hymnody, proceeded almost by default directly into the sanctuaries of the so-called Independents. Richard Baxter (1615–1691), a former Anglican and minister to Charles II, published three volumes of import to the development of hymnody among the Nonconformists: *Poetical Fragments* (1681), *Additions to the Poetical Fragments* (1683), and *A Paraphrase on the Psalms, with Other Hymns* (1692). At about the same time, John Mason (d. 1694)—an Anglican sympathetic to the Independents' theological position (Baxter referred to him as "the glory of the Church of England")—issued his *Spiritual Songs; or, Songs of Praise to Almighty God upon Several Occasions* (1683). Both poets demonstrated the degree to which hymnody had matured from the dogged incantation of Keach. First, notice Baxter:

> Ye holy Angels bright,
>   Who wait at God's right hand,

> Or through the realms of light
> Fly at your Lord's command,
> Assist our song,
>   Or else this theme
>   Too high doth seem
> For moral tongue
>
> (1681)

Then observe a sample from Mason:

> Now from the altar of my heart,
> Let incense flames arise;
> Assist me, Lord, to offer up
> Mine evening sacrifice.
>
> (1683)

Baxter and Mason were two of several Independent hymno-dists (at present they would be termed Congregationalists) who flourished at the end of the seventeenth century. Matthew Henry (1662–1714), the eminent divine and biblical commentator; William Barton (1603–1678), Baxter's friend and author of four metrical renderings of the Te Deum; and Thomas Shepherd (1665–1739), whose *Penitential Cries* (1693) continued pieces of the same form and title by Mason—all five prepared the way for Isaac Watts. (1674–1748) The son of an Independent who maintained a boardinghouse at Southampton and who endured imprisonment, Watts eventually became (in 1702) pastor of an Independent congregation in Mark Lane, London. From 1712 until his death, ill-health forced him to lead the life of a semi-invalid in the home of Sir Thomas Abney, where he devoted his time to writing hymns and theological tracts. Isaac Watts may indeed be the first laureate of English hymnody and the developer of a hymn form that became both meaningful and artistic for English-speaking congregations. He fully deserves the name of poet.

If one had to state concisely Isaac Watt's proper niche in the history of the English hymn, the declaration would read, He created it. Such oversimplification requires considerable qualification, for there certainly did exist individuals who deserved the labels *hymnodist* and *modern* prior to Watts. For example, the office hymns (versified parts of the traditional Divine Office) of George Wither (1588–1667), Bishop Thomas Ken (1637–1711), and John Austin (1640–1669) do indeed contain examples of high-quality lyric poetry. Wither, looking toward the celebration of Ascension Day, 1623, proclaimed:

> To God with heart and cheerful voice
>   a triumph song we sing;
> and with true thankful hearts rejoice
>   in our Almighty King;
> yea, to his glory we record
>   (who were but dust and clay)
> what honour he did us afford
>   on his ascending day.

Bishop Ken, perhaps the best poet of the three, published *A Manual of Prayers* (1695), including hymnodic dedications to morning, evening, and midnight. At the start of the day, he issues a self-command:

> Awake, my soul, and with the sun
> thy daily stage of duty run,
> shake off dull sloth, and joyful rise
> to pay thy morning sacrifice.

Austin, in his *Devotions in the Antient Way of Offices* (1668), seemed aware of the true purpose of public worship—and thus equally aware of how hymnody could support that purpose.

> Behold, we come, dear Lord to Thee,
>   and bow before Thy Throne:
> we come to offer on our knees
>   our vows to Thee alone.

The three examples thus demonstrate the degree to which post-Restoration writers of religious verse sought to inject antiquated Office hymnody with a literary freshness. In so doing, created a form that would produce maximum participation on the part of worshipers with varied denominational allegiances.

Isaac Watts surpassed them all in that effort. What he created consistently during the first three decades of the eighteenth century transcended the Office hymn, the metrical psalm, and the paraphrases of Old and New Testament forms. The physically diminutive Nonconformist divine gave to his affluent London parishoners—as well as to the entire island-kingdom and its possessions abroad—freedom of expression combined with innovative yet disciplined (and certainly learned) poetic forms. Watts wrote his hymns in at least six distinct stages:

1. 1694 to 1696: the "juvenile" period, marked by imitations and translations of others' works, prior to his clerical career
2. 1706, 1709: the two major editions of *Horae Lyricae*
3. 1707: first edition of *Hymns and Spiritual Songs*
4. 1712: beginning of the thirty-six-year period of sporadic literary output because of ill health and the periods of confinement resulting therefrom
5. 1715: first edition of *Divine and Moral Songs for Children*
6. 1719: first edition of *Psalms of David Imitated*

Watts published additions to and revisions of those volumes during his lifetime. In fact, well into the twentieth century, his hymns and psalm paraphrases continued to serve English-speaking congregations as illustrations of how poetry could function within the context of divine worship to meet the needs of people at all levels of intellect and at all stations of earthly existence.

Isaac Watts ranks highest among the Nonconformist writers of divine poetry during the eighteenth century. For more than a hundred years his hymns earned the respect of those British and American Nonconformists who sought spiritual uplift in worship services. Above all else, Watts has been considered a hymnodist—a writer of divine odes for congregational purposes. He viewed himself as a poet, albeit one who had renounced poetry for the sake of edification. Thus, in sacrificing art for theological practicality, he also sacrificed his opportunities for recognition as poet of the first rank. Among lower-class Christians, he sought to promote what he called "pious entertainment," which unfortunately prevented him from achieving his potential as a pure poet. Indeed, on more than one occasion he felt the need to apologize for being so easily understood, for having written poetry that could be read without difficulty.

However, in addressing the simple souls of the English-speaking world, Watts managed to fuse poetic image with religious thought and emotion, attaining a level of intensity not often reached by his more cosmopolitan Augustan colleagues. In so doing, he relieved the English hymn of considerable poetic excess—specifically, of complex theology and imagery that religious versifiers of his day regarded as essential. Thus John Milton in 1629 began his "birthday gift to Christ" with

> This is the month, and this the happy morn,
> Wherein the Son of Heaven's eternal King,
> Of wedded maid and Virgin Mother born,
> Our great redemption from above did bring;
> For so the holy sages once did sing,
> That he our deadly forfeit should release,
> And with his Father work us a perpetual peace.

Watts recognized the difference between the high aesthetic level of divine poetry and the practical environment in which congregational song had to function. There was both the business of worship and the necessary moral questions, directed first to the self and then eventually in an upward direction.

> Alas! and did my Saviour bleed!
> And did my Sov'reign die?
> Would he devote that sacred head
> For such a worm as I?

He therefore set out to compose a body of verse representative of the vigorous human spirit; he aimed for poetry and song that stated and applied the Gospel to the various experiences of life. He strove for clarity of language, simplicity of diction, and sympathy of understanding so that thousands of English worshipers—both within and outside of the Establishment—could lean upon his hymns as the natural expressions of their own religious feelings.

Watts conveyed in his hymnody the soul of the poet and the conviction of the conservative preacher, but as minister, he cast aside the theological mantle and bowed in the direction of the humblest of Christians. He beckoned to them to walk with God on the high ground of Christian piety, thus providing the model—for the last half of the eighteenth century—for a group of hymnodists who continued his vitality and his frankness. The key to Watts's legacy was the relationship between hymnody and literature. He was one of the few poets of the Augustan Age who managed to preserve the spiritual enthusiasm of Protestant Dissent and to demonstrate that it could achieve poetic expression. As both preacher and poet, he formed an obvious link between the Calvinist zeal of the late seventeenth century and the evangelical revival within the eighteenth-century Established Church represented by the Wesleys and George Whitefield. Most important, that link—that transition, if you will—was built upon Watts's conviction that poetic and religious inspiration could be harnessed by a learned man, able to draw from tradition certain ideas congenial with his own times, his own temperament, and his own generation of worshipers.

As a writer of religious odes and hymns for congregational worship, Watts stood almost alone in promoting

the spiritual ardor of Protestant Dissent—the only versifier of his day to donate pure poetic expression to that
ardor. No doubt the eighteenth-century reader and worshiper stood in awe at the wide range of that expression.
Watts could, for example, strike fear into the hearts of
children with his graphic descriptions of heaven and hell.

> There is beyond the sky,
>   A heav'n of joy and love;
> And holy children, when they die,
>   Go to that world above.
>
> There is a dreadful hell,
>   And everlasting pains:
> There sinners must with devils dwell
>   In darkness, fire, and chains.
>   (1715)

At the same time, he could lyrically express extreme
tenderness.

> Hush! my dear, lie still and slumber,
>   Holy angels guard thy bed!
> Heavenly blessings, without number,
>   Gently falling on thy head. . . .
>
> I could give thee thousand kisses,
>   Hoping what I most desire;
> Not a mother's fondest wishes
>   Can to greater joys aspire!
>   (1715)

On a more adult level, he could visualize eternity in the
hands of a God who had made all earthly creatures, and
with that vision he arrived at a truly classical English hymn.

> Before the hills, in order stood,
>   Or earth received her frame,
> From everlasting Thou art God,
>   To endless years the Same.
>
> A thousand Ages in Thy sight
>   Are like an evening gone,

Short as the watch that ends the night
Before the rising sun.

(1719)

Questions may well arise concerning the subjects of
Isaac Watts's hymns and psalm paraphrases; after all,
poetry in any age or of any form must have substance.
Versification and diction cannot alone carry the rhythmical
day. With Watts, his congregational hymns focused upon
items that appear as natural, practical, and historical as
they do religious. Although he set out to Christianize the
Old Testament psalms and to make David speak as a
Christian, Watts also needed to consider those eighteenth-
century Britons who would constitute his readers and his
singers. He saw clear parallels between Judaea and Great
Britain; such historical occurrences as the Gunpowder Plot
(1605), the coming of William and Mary to the throne
(1688), the end of the Stuart reign and the accession of the
Hanoverians (1714), and the Jacobite uprisings (1715 and
1745) became occasions to set forth poetically clear lessons,
sound political doctrines, and general notes of thanksgiving—the same types of events embraced by John and
Charles Wesley in the next generation of English hymnodists. Watts had no interest in limited or local occurrences—Charles Wesley differed sharply from him in that
regard. Instead, Watts focused upon the larger issues that
concerned the citizens of a Christian nation politically and
intellectually. Those who criticized him for uniformity of
subject matter may indeed have done so for the right
reasons, for he limited his hymnody to three or four
general areas: man's weakness, the lack of satisfaction with
society, the transience of human existence, and the hopes
and the fears of common creatures. In reality, Watts
proved himself nondenominational as long as he remained
within those perimeters. He could rightfully claim that his
hymns and psalm paraphrases held fast to the common
themes of universal Christianity.

Only later did scholars of hymnody, theology, and poetry come to terms with Isaac Watts's purpose as a hymnodist. In his three major collections—*Horae Lyricae* (1706, 1709), *Hymns and Spiritual Songs* (1707), and *Divine and Moral Songs for Children* (1715)—he developed a complete system of praise, a process by which persons at all stages of life could come together to express their feelings, experiences, and beliefs. Such a system shows both the theological and historical importance of Watts's hymns and psalm paraphrases: to formulate the divine ode as a representation of the individual worshiper's response to the word of God. The *Psalms of David Imitated* (1719) and the *Hymns and Spiritual Songs* became the hymnodic guidebooks by which the denominations of Nonconformity achieved the fullness and the directness of religious and ethical thought. This applies particularly to the eighteenth and nineteenth centuries, when authority lacked clear form. The hymns of Watts accomplished that end by liturgical objectivity, whereby both sound and sense achieved a certain catholicity without vagueness, and personal intensity without the limits usually imposed upon individual religious expression.

Despite the reception of Watts's hymns in both England and America during the eighteenth and nineteenth centuries, the twentieth century appears unwilling or unable to determine their creator's rightful place in the history of English hymnody. Although traditional Evangelical church leaders continue to hold his work in esteem, followers of more contemporary religious institutions and movements may not feel comfortable reciting his words and phrases, but few intelligent and sensitive worshipers will challenge Isaac Watts's capabilities as a hymnodist. All will eventually accept him as an experimenter, a poet willing to challenge the popular poetic forms of his era. Watts was a wise and discriminating theorist who developed rules of hymnody patterned after the brightest lights of the seventeenth century and who wrote hymns that expressed the doctrines of religious Nonconformity. Most important, Isaac Watts applied those doctrines to almost every facet of human experience, and thus his hymnody will continue to be meaningful for future generations of worshipers.

Although Watts's hymns became standard for congregational worship among the Independents, they did not necessarily clear the field of all hymnodic activity. One certainly ought to consult (among others) the hymns of Joseph Addison (1672–1719), as they appeared in various of the *Spectator* essays (1711—1712); Philip Doddridge (1702—1751), another of the Dissenting ministers, whose hymns appeared collectively after his death (first edition, 1755); Thomas Gibbons (1720–1785), who published seven volumes of hymns during his lifetime; Joseph Hart (1712—1768), who published several versions and editions of his *Hymns Composed on Various Subjects* (1759); and Job Orton, a close friend of Doddridge who published and edited the latter's 1755 collection of hymns.

The next step for English hymnody, then, leads to the veritable hymnodic mountain to John (1703–1791) and Charles (1707–1788) Wesley. The path does not proceed directly from Isaac Watts to the hymns of eighteenth-century Methodism, but wends its circuitous path through the environs of the Church of England. Anglican congregations, particularly during the first four decades of the eighteenth century, relied upon the metrical psalter and on church collections containing chanting tunes for psalm reading, psalm tunes for metrical psalms, and anthems. The Anglican worshiper could usually find, at the end of the church book or psalter, one or two general hymns—as in the Supplement to the New Version of Tate and Brady (see Chapter 4, "Psalter and Psalm Paraphrase"). Thus, when John Wesley published his first two hymn books—*A Collection of Psalms and Hymns* (1737) and *A Collection of Psalms and Hymns* (1738)—he contributed more to the hymnody of the Church of England (into which he had been ordained deacon and priest) than he did to Methodist congregational song. At the time that John Wesley compiled the two collections, he had not yet formed a single Methodist society; at that time he still considered himself an active priest of the Church of England (a position that he, as well as his brother Charles, never abandoned). At the time of the publication of the 1737 collection, John Wesley held the official position of parish priest of Savannah, Georgia. Nevertheless, despite both Wesleys' ties to the Established Church, to study the brothers' contributions to eighteenth-century hymnody requires one to observe the origin and development of a truly evangelical form of congregational song.

Shortly after John Wesley returned to England from his unsuccessful mission to the Georgia colony, he became involved with Count Nicholas Zinzendorf's Moravian Brethren—from whom he heard the call of a new conversion and a new purpose. The elder of the two Wesleys embarked upon his attempt to reform the Anglican Church and to evangelize Great Britain. In 1739 John and Charles Wesley issued their *Hymns and Sacred Poems*—the basis of an identifiable Methodist hymnody. Charles Wesley, who had departed from Georgia some months earlier than his brother and who had preceded him in the formation of the London religious societies (*Anglican* groups), followed John's evangelical lead. Unfortunately, ill-health restricted Charles Wesley's itinerancy, but the younger Wesley continued to look hard in the direction of the Church of England, and from that context he emerged as the bard of British Methodism.

The approximately nine thousand extant hymns of Charles Wesley—of which only approximately three hundred can be comfortably adapted to current congregational needs—echo the essence of the Evangelical revival of eighteenth-century England. Certainly, not every poem evidences the same degree of artistic or hymnodic quality, but together the hymns convey the intensity of the poet's

personal feelings. Few subjects or occasions escaped his
notice: his own religious conversion and marriage; domestic
upheavals caused by panics, earthquakes, religious riots, or
rumors of foreign invasion; festivals of the Church and
doctrines of the faith; scenes from specific passages of the
Scriptures; deaths of friends and relatives; the education of
children; the effects of local surroundings and local occurrences. As can easily be observed in the life and writings of
his elder brother, John, Charles Wesley spent little time
contemplating or transmitting abstract themes; instead he
focused directly upon the personal and the concrete.

>   Love divine, all love excelling,
>   Joy of heaven, to earth come down!
>   Fix in us Thy humble dwelling;
>   All Thy faithful mercies crown.
>   Jesus, Thou art all compassion,
>   Pure, unbounded love Thou art:
>   Visit us with Thy salvation;
>   Enter every trembling heart.

His hymnodic lines thus reflect and then universalize the
experiences of thousands of believers and an equal number of souls struggling to believe.

Although Wesley's hymns demonstrate the influence
of a number and variety of British poets upon the
hymnodist—from Shakespeare to Edward Young—the
content and language of Scripture remained his principal
source. Indeed, the Old and New Testaments dominate
the hymnody of Charles Wesley. Therefore, in "Waiting
for the Promise," one observes,

>   Fainting soul, be bold, be strong;
>   Wait the leisure of thy Lord:
>   Though it seem to tarry long,
>   True and faithful is His word.

Wesley's contemporaries (at least the literate Anglicans
among them) would have recognized the words of Psalms

27:16 from Miles Coverdale's prose version of the *Book of Common Prayer:* "O tarry thou the Lord's leisure"—an indication that the bard of British Methodism continued to hold true to his Anglican upbringing and education (at Westminster School and Oxford). No doubt such an indication is proper; yet Charles Wesley must not be relegated to the role of a mere paraphraser of Scripture, a versifier who combined emotionalism with experience and pumped that combination into the liturgy of the Methodist worship service. Instead, he must be remembered as a legitimate devotional poet who established the idea of the congregational hymn existing as a serious piece of poetry.

> Come, Almighty to deliver,
>   Let us all Thy life receive;
> Suddenly return, and never,
>   Never more Thy temples leave.
> Thee we would be always blessing,
>   Serve Thee as Thy hosts above,
> Pray, and praise Thee without ceasing,
>   Glory in Thy perfect love.

John Wesley—who spent considerable time editing his brother's hymns for easy digestion by the Methodist flocks—in his preface to *A Collection of Hymns for the Use of the People Called Methodists* (1780), set forth what still stands as the most accurate assessment of Charles Wesley's hymnody: "In these hymns there is no doggerel, no botches, nothing put in to patch the rhyme, no feeble expletives. . . . Here are . . . both the purity, the strength and the elegance of the ENGLISH language: and at the same time the utmost simplicity and plainness, suited to every capacity." The Methodist patriarch challenged readers and worshipers alike to judge "whether there is not in some of the following verses, the True Spirit of Poetry: such as cannot be acquired by art and labour; but must be the gift of nature." Through pure labor, concluded John Wesley, "a man may become a tolerable imitator. . . . But unless he is born a Poet, he will never attain the genuine SPIRIT OF POETRY." The elder Wesley saw no reason for separating hymnody from poetry.

Despite his brother's exuberance, Charles Wesley met with only limited success outside of his contemporary Methodist following. Today there exists little doubt about the general hymnodic popularity of such pieces as "All praise to Him who dwells in Bliss"; "Christ the Lord is risen to-day"; "Christ, whose glory fills the sky"; "Come, let us join our friends above"; "Come, Thou long-expected Jesus"; "Hail the day that sees Him rise"; "Hark! how all the welkin sings"; "Hark, the herald angels sing"; "Lo! He comes, with clouds descending"; "Love divine, all love excelling"; and "Jesu, Lover of my soul." However, by the middle of the eighteenth century, when Wesley was turning out hymns by the hundreds, English congregational song had become thoroughly saturated with the common meters and the generalized experiences of Protestant Dissent: Watts, Doddridge, Gibbons, and Hart. Charles Wesley's specific experiences, his departures from the simple meters of the old psalmody, his enthusiastic and controversial spirit—all appeared foreign to the tastes of those Britons unfamiliar with Methodism.

Not until the late nineteenth century, when Methodism finally emerged from the abuse and the contempt of rivals of the Wesleys (particularly the Calvinist Methodists), did Charles Wesley's hymnodic poetry achieve the recognition it deserved, and to a certain extent continues to hold. The major hymns reflected the poet's sincere faith arising from his far-ranging loyalties and his desire to interpret Christian experience. The hymns transmit that faith because Wesley relied upon what people knew and felt, upon the essence of their own religious, moral, and ethical values. Culturally superior to the majority of persons whom he addressed, Wesley intentionally placed restraints upon his own knowledge and instead wove his reactions and concerns through Scripture, attempting to enlighten his readers with fundamental theological lessons. He would, for example, begin with a highly personal poetic comment upon his own religious conversion.

> On this glad day the glorious Sun
>   of Righteousness arose;
> On my benighted soul He shone,
>   And fill'd it with repose.

Within the same long poem (eighteen stanzas of four lines each), he then brought forth his own joy to be shared with others.

> O for a thousand tongues to sing
>   My dear Redeemer's praise!
> The glories of my God and King,
>   The triumph of His grace.

In the end, there remained little doubt as to the purpose and the direction of a new voice who led the chorus of eighteenth-century Britons seeking God in times of trouble.

> Jesus, the name that calms our fears,
>   That bids our sorrows cease;
> 'Tis music to the sinner's ears,
>   'Tis life and health and peace!

Small wonder then that, although not everyone realizes the fact, the sound and the sense of Charles Wesley's work remain meaningful today. One should not be surprised that parts of a poem published first in 1740 became the opening hymn of the noted 1780 *Wesleyan Hymn Book* and remained the opening hymn for subsequent versions published in the United States in 1878, 1887, 1889, 1905, 1958, 1964, and 1966.

From a purely practical point of view, any discussion of Wesleyan Methodist hymnody cannot come to a close without recognizing a short document that requires, really, no further discussion or analysis. Music directors and

worshipers of the twentieth century may still follow all or
parts of John Wesley's *Directions for Congregational Singing*,
or they may (if they have not already done so) cast it aside
as merely representative of a past age. However, no matter
what the agreement with or objection to the *Directions*, it
remains worthy of careful consideration. Wesley, concerned that the hymn portions of divine worship be
acceptable to God and profitable to the congregation,
urged his followers "to observe the following directions":

    1.   Sing all. See that you join with the congregation as
frequently as you can. Let not a slight degree of weakness or
weariness hinder you. If it is a cross to you, take it up, and
you will find a blessing.

    2.   Sing lustily, and with good courage. Beware of
singing as if you were half dead, or half asleep; but lift up
your voice with strength. Be no more afraid of your voice
now, nor more ashamed of its being heard, then when you
sing the songs of Satan.

    3.   Sing modestly. Do not bawl, so as to be heard above,
or distinct from, the rest of the congregation, that you may
not destroy the harmony; but strive to unite your voices
together, so as to make one clear melodious sound.

    4.   Sing in tune. Whatever tune is sung, be sure to keep
with it. Do not run before, nor stay behind it; but attend
closely to the leading, and more therewith as exactly as you
can. And take care you sing not too slow. This drawling way
naturally steals on all who are lazy; and it is high time to
drive it out from among us, and sing all our tunes as quick as
we did at first.

    5.   Above all, sing spiritually. Have an eye to God in
every word you sing. Aim at pleasing Him more than
yourself, or any other creature. In order to do this, attend
strictly to the sense of what you sing; and see that your heart
is not carried away with the sound, but offered to God
continually; so shall your singing be such as the Lord will
approve here, and reward when He cometh in the clouds of
Heaven.

    Wesley published those directions (or more accurately,
commands) in 1761, as an appendix to his *Select Hymns with*

Tunes Annexed, designed chiefly for the Use of the People called Methodists. He intended, as the principal purpose of that volume, that singers and choirs should follow the original tunes to hymns, not those revised and altered by "Masters of Music [who] were above following any direction but their own." He revised the book on several occasions (and included the *Directions for Congregational Singing* in each revision) under the titles, *Sacred Melody; or A Choice Collection of Psalm and Hymn Tunes* (1761) and *Sacred Harmony; or, A Choice Collection of Psalm and Hymn Tunes, in Two or Three Parts, for the Voice, Harpsichord, and Organ* (1781).

In the meantime, during the height of Charles Wesley's poetic activity, hymns continued to play an insignificant role within the worship service of the Church of England. Outside of certain charitable institutions in and around London (the Foundling Hospital, the Lock Hospital, Magdalen Hospital, and the House of Refuge for Female Orphans, for example) that published their own hymnals and encouraged congregational singing by inmates, hymnody made little impression upon those who controlled and directed the Anglican establishment. Anglicans resented what they believed to have been the unhealthy atmosphere of Nonconformist enthusiasm and even fanaticism. For example, in 1775 William Romaine, (1714–1795), an ordained Church of England cleric who became a devoted follower of George Whitefield, published an "Essay on Psalmody," which he affixed to his *Collection of the Book of Psalms*—yet another in the long list of eighteenth-century Anglican psalters and psalm books. Romaine complained that he disliked seeing "Christian congregations shut out divinely inspired psalms, and take in Dr. Watts's flights of fancy. " In other words, the prevailing attitude among the Anglican clergy in particular (even among Evangelicals such as Romaine) held that the principal alternative to Nonconformist hymnody (or original poetry intended for congregational song) lay in mod-

ernizing existing psalm paraphrases. Psalmodic reform
that did little beyond updating language and meter
seemed preferable to original hymnody.

Not until four years after the publication of Romaine's
essay did hymnody enter the portals of Anglicanism,
although it did so in an entirely "unofficial" vehicle, one that
lacked authorization or even immediate recognition. Beginning in 1771, the poet William Cowper (1731–1800) and the
curate of Olney (and former participant in the African slave
trade), John Newton (1725–1807), combined their efforts to
design a set of hymns intended partly to promote the faith of
sincere Christians and partly to establish a lasting symbol of
their friendship. Thus came forth, almost eight years later,
the *Olney Hymns in Three Books:* Book 1, *On Select Texts of
Scripture;* Book 2, *On Occasional Subjects;* Book 3, *On the
Progress and Changes of the Spiritual Life.* Newton, who
assumed the burden of compiling the volume because of
Cowper's illness, included 280 of his own highly evangelical
hymns and 68 by Cowper. Modern congregational singers
will certainly recognize three of Cowper's contributions:
"Hark, my soul! it is the Lord"; "There is a fountain filled
with Blood"; and "Oh for a closer walk with God." An equal
number by Newton also remain popular: "Glorious things of
Thee are spoken"; "Come, my soul, thy suit prepare"; and
"How sweet the name of Jesus sounds." But despite its poetic
quality and its ability to rival the poetry of British Nonconformity, *Olney Hymns* failed to convince the Established
Church that hymnody deserved consideration as a complement to psalmody.

If the Church needed proof that its followers stood
ready to embrace hymnody, such evidence did indeed
come during the late eighteenth century, although it
originated from a source not totally acceptable to the
Church hierarchy. Rowland Hill (1744–1833) received
ordination into the Church of England, as had John and
Charles Wesley; initially, he found some merit in the
Calvinism of George Whitefield and that Methodist

leader's principal sponsor, Selina Shirley, countess of Huntingdon. However, after a dozen or so years of itinerant ministry, he turned his back upon both the Calvinist Methodists and the Anglicans and settled in London, where he established the Surrey Chapel. For that evangelically directed religious house, Hill published, *A Collection of Psalms and Hymns, chiefly intended for Public Worship* in 1783. In 1790 he issued *Divine Hymns attempted in Easy Language for the Use of Children,* a collection of 44 hymns that served initially as an appendix to Isaac Watts's 1715 *Divine and Moral Songs* and then for the children of the Southwark Sunday School Society. In 1808 Hill published a larger *Collection of Hymns for Children* (298 hymns), followed by *Hymns for Schools* in 1832.

Although Anglican bishops generally held Hill in contempt, they never challenged his independent ministry—no doubt because of its popularity among lower class Londoners who had not yet been recruited by the Wesleyan Methodists. The Church never approved of his Surrey Chapel, yet its founder remained officially one of the Established Church's own ordained clerics. Thus, as a quasi-independent, Hill could easily inject into his worship services the most attractive aspects of Protestant Nonconformity—principally, the hymn. The importance of Rowland Hill, then, comes to rest in his function as a transitional figure in the history of the English hymn. He embodied the best of Isaac Watts in such pieces as "Cast thy burden on the Lord"; "We sing His love who once was slain"; and "With heavenly power, O Lord, defend." In a sense, he prepared the way for hymnody to take its place within the worship service of the Church of England.

Before leaving the eighteenth century and the state of hymnody therein, some attention must be directed to the English Moravians and their publication at midcentury of an extremely interesting collection. To John Gambold—at one time a member of John and Charles Wesley's Oxford Holy Club and formerly vicar of Stanton Harcourt, Oxford-

shire—the leader of the London Moravian Brethren, fell the
task of compiling an English hymnbook authorized by Count
Nicholas Zinzendorf. The volume appeared in 1754 under
the title, *A Collection of Hymns of the Children of God in all Ages,
from the beginning till now. In Two Parts. Designed chiefly for the
use of the Congregation in Union with the Brethren's Church.* The
length of the volume proved worthy of its comprehensive
title: 804 pages and 1,160 hymns divided into two parts—the
first 695 hymns comprising a historical anthology of general
Protestant hymnody, the second part containing 460 congregational songs under the heading, "Hymns of the Present
Congregation of the Brethen." Unfortunately, the volume
possessed such a distinct Germanic flavor—owing, of course,
to Count Zinzendorf's influence—that it made little headway
among English-speaking Moravians. As but one example of
Gambold's editorial efforts, consider this stanza from Hymn
No. 386:

> O blest Trinity!
> And side's cavity
> Of the Son who bore our torment!
> Take now towards your Contentment,
> This our Cross's Church,
> As a glowing torch.

The uncomfortable rhythm and confusing (although interesting) imagery of such lines did little to advance the cause
of congregational song among Gambold's English followers. That fact, in addition to the deep division between
John Wesley and Nicholas Zinzendorf, negated the earlier
influence of the Brethren upon the hymnody of the
eighteenth-century Evangelical movement. Although later
revisions of hymns from Gambold's 1754 *Collection of
Hymns* improved slightly the adaptability of those pieces to
public worship, Moravian hymnody, after the middle of
the eighteenth century, remained (with but a single
exception) outside the principal sphere of English congregational song.

Chapter Six
ENGLAND IN THE NINETEENTH CENTURY

FROM THE POINT OF VIEW OF chronology, the battle to admit hymnody within the Church of England began late in the eighteenth century. It occurred in the north of England, and its earliest champion proved to be, of all persons, a member of the Moravian Brethren. Here, then, one may find the single exception alluded to at the end of the preceding chapter. James Montgomery (1771–1854)—the son of an Ulster Scot who had qualified for the Moravian ministry—left the Moravian seminary in Yorkshire, worked at a number of menial trades, failed to achieve recognition in London for his poetic efforts, and finally settled in Sheffield. There he waged and won the hymnodic war on purely poetic grounds—as can be proven by his still popular Christmas piece, "Angels from the realms of glory." As a newspaper editor in Sheffield, Montgomery came into contact with the Reverend Thomas Cotterill (1779–1823), the Perpetual curate of Saint Paul's, Sheffield. Cotterill had published, in 1810, his noteworthy *Selection of Psalms and Hymns for Public and Private Use, adapted to the Festivals of the Church of England;* the volume had gone through six editions before its editor moved from the incumbency of Lane End, Staffordshire, to Sheffield. The eighth edition in 1819 was a joint effort between Cotterill and Montgomery, but it met with firm opposition from the communicants of Saint Paul's, the majority of whom retained a Puritan antagonism toward any form of hymnody. At a hearing before the diocesan court, the Reverend William Vernon Harcourt, archbishop of York, settled the issue by forcing the withdrawal of the 1819

Selection and substituting the tenth edition (1820)—
essentially a new work designed and compiled by Cotterill,
but revised by the archbishop himself. Hymnody thus
gained legitimate entrance into the Church of England.

In one sense, the experience of Cotterill's *Selection*
defines the character of Anglican hymnody in the nineteenth century: a smooth transition from psalm to hymn
based upon the notion that the path to modernity began
with a look backward into the traditions of earlier centuries. Or in another sense, hymnodists of the Established
Church determined to rely upon the ancients as contribu-
tors to modern congregational song. Perhaps the most
outstanding proponent of that design came in the person
of Reginald Heber (1783–1826)—rector of Hodnet,
Shropshire; prebendary of Saint Asaph; and bishop of
Calcutta. He became convinced that hymns should underscore the lessons and the plan of the Book of Common
Prayer. Therefore, he proposed a collection of hymns to
represent the New Testament Gospels and Epistles, to be
sung after recitation of the Nicene Creed. Heber initially
relied upon pieces found in older sources: the Sternhold
and Hopkins psalter, Jeremy Taylor, Bishop Thomas Ken,
Isaac Watts, and Joseph Addison. He even proposed to
consider adaptations from such British Poets as John
Dryden, Alexander Pope, and William Cowper; he would
balance those pieces with sixty or so of his own hymnodic
compositions. Further, Bishop Heber sought to suggest
hymns for every Sunday and for principal festival and holy
days—as well as for such varied occasions as public
thanksgivings, times of distress or danger, post-sermon,
pre-Sacrament, morning, evening, funeral, recovery from
illness, and even for the projects sponsored by such official
Church organizations as the Society for the Propagation of
the Gospel.

The results of Heber's grand scheme (completed in
1820 and submitted for Church review and approval
shortly thereafter) did not appear until the year following

his death. In 1827 the bishop's widow published his *Hymns Written and Adapted to the Weekly Church Service of the Year*. Of importance to the history of Anglican hymnody is the dedication of the work to the archbishop of Canterbury, Charles Manners Sutton—perhaps the closest indication that the collection had been authorized (or at least acknowledged) by the Church of England. More important, particularly from a congregational perspective, Heber's *Hymns . . . of the Year* contained such sufficient examples of his own high poetic quality as "Holy, Holy, Holy! Lord God Almighty"; "From Greenland's icy mountains"; "Creator of the rolling flood"; "Hosanna to the Living Lord"; and "There was joy in heav'n." One piece in that 1827 collection, composed by Henry Hart Milman— vicar of Saint Mary's, Reading; professor of poetry at Oxford; Bampton lecturer at Oxford; canon of Westminster; and Dean of Saint Paul's—constitutes a splendid example of the nineteenth-century Anglican ode, and its popularity continues. In celebration of Palm Sunday, Milman focused his attention upon a sentence from Matthew 21:29—"And the multitudes that went before, and that followed, cried, saying, 'Hosanna to the Sons of David.' " Today, British and American congregations sing the opening sentence of that scriptural theme as

> Ride on! ride on in majesty!
> Hark! all the tribes "Hosanna!" cry:
> Thine humble beast pursues his road
> With palms and scatter'd garments strow'd.

Other hymns by Milman that have gained wide acceptance during the past one hundred years include the Lenten ode based on Matthew 15:25 ("Lord, help me"), "O help us, Lord; each hour of need"; and the dedication for the sixteenth Sunday after Trinity, "When our heads are bow'd with woe." Both pieces appeared in Heber's 1827 collection.

Heber's volume of 1827 began a hymnodic trend

within the Church of England that would go on for more
than a quarter-century, swept along by what has become
known as the Oxford Movement, or in other quarters as
the Tractarian Movement. Simply stated, this movement
announced the revival of a higher conception than previously held by churchmen concerning the position and
functions of the Established Church. That very Church,
according to the proponents of the new thinking, should
exist as more than merely a human institution; rather, it
should possess privileges, sacraments, and a ministry
ordained by Christ. In July 1833 John Keble—vicar of
Hursley (near Winchester) and professor of poetry at
Oxford—preached at Oxford before the judges of assize
on the subject of national apostasy. In September 1833
appeared the periodical *Tracts for the Times*, which lasted
until 1841. Its authors (among them Keble, John Henry
Newman, Richard Hurrell Froude, and Edward Bouverie
Pusey) intended to contribute "something towards the
revival of doctrines which, although held by the great
divines of our Church, at present have become obsolete
with the majority of her members. . . . The Apostolic
succession and the Holy Catholic Church were principles
of action in the minds of our predecessors of the seventeenth century. . . . Nothing but these neglected doctrines
faithfully preached . . . will repress the extension of
Popery." Newman's noted Tract XC on the compatability
of the Thirty-nine Articles with Roman Catholic theology
set off a series of hostile arguments against the movement.

Out of the discussions and debates surrounding the
Oxford Movement emerged a number of Anglican translators and original poets who provided hymns of exception-
ally high poetic quality—hymns that nonetheless gained
wide acceptance at all levels of congregational needs. John
Mason Neale—warden of Sackville College, East Grinstead; founder of the sisterhood of Saint Margaret's, East
Grinstead, an orphanage for girls; and founder of a house
at Aldershot for the reclamation of fallen women—

compiled *The Hymnal Noted* (1852, 1854) and *Hymns of the Eastern Church* (1862), as well as an interesting volume of *Hymns, Chiefly Mediaeval, on the Joys and Glories of Paradise.* He gave to the English-speaking world hundreds of translations of Greek and Latin hymn texts, as well as his own original hymnodic compositions. Neale's contribution to English hymnody can never be overstated; his hymns and translations continue to be sung in churches throughout Britain, the Commonwealth nations, and in North America. For both brevity and clarity, his major efforts are summarized in Table 17, so that the reader may both appreciate and take advantage of the full range of his poetic gifts and hymnodic talents.

Table 17. The Major Hymns of John Mason Neale

Occasion	Date	Opening Line(s)	Original	Biblical Text
Morning	1851	Now that the daylight fills the sky	Iam lucis orto orto sidere (5th century)	Psalms 5:3
Morning	1852	O God of truth, O Lord of might	Rector potens, verax Deus (St. Ambrose)	Psalms 55:18
Morning	1852	O God, the world's sustaining force	Rerum Deus tenax vigor (St. Ambrose)	Acts 3:1
Evening	1853	The day is past and over	Late evening service of the Orthodox Church	Psalms 13:3
Saturday	1852	O Trinity, most blessed Light	O Lux beata, Trinitas	Psalms 16:10
Sunday	1854	Again the Lord's own day is here	En dies est dominica (15th century Karlsruhe MS, ascribed to Thomas à Kempis)	Mark 16:9

Occasion	Date	Opening Line(s)	Original	Biblical Text
Advent	1852	Creator of the starry height	Conditor alme siderum (10th century Canterbury hymnal)	Psalms 19:5
Advent	1851	O come, O come, Emmanuel, And ransom captive Israel	Veni, veni, Emmanuel (9th century Roman Antiphones)	Isaiah 59:20
Christmas	1852	Of the Father's love love begotten Ere the world began to be	Corde natus ex Parentus (Prudentius, 4th century)	1 Timothy 3:16
Holy Innocents Day (28 December)	1851	A hymn for martyrs sweetly sing	Hymnum canentes martyrum (Venerable Bede)	Revelation
Epiphany	1852	Why doth that impious Herod fear	Hostis Herodes impie (Caelius Sedulius, 5th century)	1 John 1:2
From the Octave of the Epiphany to Septuagesima	1851	Alleluia, song of sweetness	Alleluia, dulce carmen (prior to 11th century)	Revelation 19:3
Lent	1854	By precepts taught of ages past	Ex mori docti mystico (10th century MS)	Joel 2:12
Lent	1852	Lo! now is our accepted day	Ecce tempus idoneum (10th century France)	2 Corinthians 6:2

Occasion	Date	Opening Line(s)	Original	Biblical Text
Lent	1862	Christian, dost thou see them On the holy ground	*Original*	1 Peter 5:9
Saints' Days: for Apostles	1852	Th' eternal gifts of Christ the King	Aeterna Christi munera (St. Ambrose)	Revelation 21:14
Saints' Days: for Martyrs	1852	O God, Thy soldiers' faithful Lord	Deus, tuorum militum (St. Ambrose)	James 1:12
Saints' Days: for Martyrs	1852	The triumphs of the Saints, The toils they bravely bore	Sanctorum meritus inclyta guadia (anonymous Latin text)	Hebrews 6:12
Saint's Days: for Martyrs	1851	Blessed feasts of blessed martyrs	O Beata beatorum (14th century German)	Hebrews 11:37
Saints' Days: for Martyrs	1862	Let our choir new anthems raise	Greek text of St. Joseph the Hymnographer (9th century)	Matthew 5:10
Saints' Days: for a Virgin	1854	O Jesu, Thou the Virgins' Crown	Iesu corona virginum (ascribed to St. Ambrose)	Song of Solomon 1:3
Blessed Virgin Mary	1854	The God, whom earth, and sea, and sky	Quem terra, pontus, aethera (Venantius Fortunatus, 6th century)	Luke 1:28

Occasion	Date	Opening Line(s)	Original	Biblical Text
St. John the Baptist's Day	1854	The high forerunner of the morn	Praecursor altus luminous (Venerable Bede)	Malachi 3:1
St. Michael and all Angels	1862	Thee, O Christ, the Father's splendour	Tibi, Christe, splendor Patris (sometimes attributed to Rabanus Maurus)	Daniel 12:1
St. Michael and all Angels	1862	Stars of the morning, so gloriously bright	From the Greek text of St. Joseph the Hymnographer	Job 38:7
All Saints' Day	1854	If there be that skills to reckon	Quisquis valet numerare (attributed to Thomas à Kempis)	1 Corinthians 13:12
The Transfiguration	1854	O wondrous type, O vision fair	Caelestis fornam gloriae (15th century)	Matthew 17:2; Mark 9:2
The Name of Jesus	1852	Jesu! the very thought is sweet	Iesu dulcis memoria (11th century Benedictine MS)	Song of Solomon 1:3
Festival of the Dedication of a Church	1851	Blessed city, heav'nly Salem	Urbs beata Ierusalem (prior to 9th century)	Revelation 21:2
Festival of the Dedication of a Church	1851	Christ is made the sure Foundation, Christ the Head and Cornerstone (second part of Urbs beata Ierusalem)	Angularus fundamentum lapis Christus missus est (prior to 9th century)	Revelation 21:2

Occasion	Date	Opening Line(s)	Original	Biblical Text
Laying the Foundation Stone of a Church	1844	O Lord of Hosts, Whose glory fills The bounds of the eternal hills	*Original*	Isaiah 60:13
Holy Communion	1854	The Heav'nly Word proceeding forth	Verbum supernum prodiens (St. Thomas Aquinas)	John 6:57
Passiontide: 5th Sunday in Lent to Wednesday before Easter	1851	The Royal banners forward go	Vexilla regis prodeunt (Venantius Fortunatus, 6th century)	Psalms 96:10
Passiontide	1851	Sing, my tongue, the glorious battle	Pange, lingua, gloriosi (Venantius Fortunatus 6th century)	Wisdom of Solomon 14:7
Passiontide	1851, 1852	All glory, laud and honour, To Thee, Redeemer, King	Gloria, laus, et honor tibi sit, rex (St. Theodulf of Orleans, 9th century)	Matthew 21:16
Passiontide	1851	O sinner, for a little space	Attolle paulum lumina (Latin translation of old German hymn)	Galatians 3:1
Easter	1852	Light's glittering morn bedecks the sky	Aurora lucis rutilat (origin uncertain)	Psalms 93:1

Occasion	Date	Opening Line(s)	Original	Biblical Text
Easter	1851	The Lamb's high banquet call'd to share	Ad cenam Agni providi (origin uncertain)	1 Corinthians 5:7–8
Easter	1851	Alleluia! alleluia! alleluia! O sons and daughters, let us sing!	Alleluia, alleluia, alleluia. O filii et filiae (Jean Tisserand, 15th century)	Psalms 118:24
Easter	1851	Far be sorrow, tears, and sighing!	Cedant iusti signa luctus (original Latin hymn by Heinrich Lindenborn, 18th century)	1 Corinthians 15:57
Easter	1862	The Day of Resurrection! Earth, tell it out abroad	From the Greek text of St. John of Damascus (8th century)	Matthew 28:9
Easter	1862	Come, ye faithful, raise the strain Of triumphant gladness	From the Greek text of St. John of Damascus (8th century)	
Easter	1853	The foe behind, the deep before, Our hosts have dared and passed the sea	*Original*	Revelation 15:3
Ascensiontide	1852	O Thou Eternal King most high	Aeterne rex altissime (Office hymn)	Matthew 28:18

Occasion	Date	Opening Line(s)	Original	Biblical Text
Whitsuntide	1852	Come, thou Holy Paraclete, And from Thy celestial seat	Veni sancte Spiritus (Middle Ages sequence ascribed to Pope Innocent III and Archbishop Stephen Langton)	Matthew 28:18
Holy Communion	1851	Draw nigh and take the Body of the Lord	Sancti, venite, Christi corpus sumite (7th century Irish liturgical MS)	Proverbs 9:5
General Hymn	1852	The strain upraise of joy and praise, Alleluia!	Cantemus cuncei melodum nunc Alleluia (Swiss monastery of St. Gall)	Psalms 145:10
General Hymn	1851	To the name of our salvation	Gloriosi salvatoria (Antwerp Breviary 15th century)	Acts 4:12
General Hymn	1849	Brief life is here our portion	Hic breve vivitur, hic breve plangitur (Bernard of Cluny)	Hebrews 13:14
General Hymn	1849	The world is very evil The times are waxing late	Hora novissima, tempora pessima sunt (Bernard of Cluny)	Revelation 21:14

Occasion	Date	Opening Line(s)	Original	Biblical Text
General Hymn	1849	For thee, O dear, dear country	O bona patria, lumina sobria (Bernard of Cluny)	Hebrews 11:16
General Hymn	1849	Jerusalem the golden, With milk and honey blest	Urbs Sion aurea, patria lactea (Bernard of Cluny)	Revelation 21:18
General Hymn	1854	Light's abode, celestial Salem	Ierusalem luminosa (attributed to Thomas à Kempis)	Isaiah 60:19
General Hymn	1854	Oh, what the joy and the glory must be	O quanta qualia sunt illa Sabata (Hymnarius Paraclitensis, 12th century)	Hebrews 4:9
General Hymn	1843	They whose course on earth is o 'er Think they of their brethren more?	*Original*	1 Thessalonians 5:10
General Hymn	1862	O happy band of pilgrims, If onward ye will tread	*Original*	Philippians 3:10
General Hymn	1862	Art thou weary, art thou languid, Art thou sore distrest?	*Original*	Matthew 11:28
Church Work: Ember Days	1843	Christ is gone up; yet ere He pass'd From earth, in heav'n to reign	*Original*	John 20:21

Occasion	Date	Opening Line(s)	Original	Biblical Text
Church Work: Ember Days	1843	The earth, O Lord, is one wide field Of all thy chosen seed	*Original*	Matthew 9:37
For the Young	1843	Around the throne of God a band Of glorious Angels ever stand	*Original*	John 10:27
Mission Service	1862	Jesu! Name all names above, Jesu, best and dearest	Theoktistus of the Stadium (9th century)	Proverbs 18:10
Mission Service	1862	Those eternal bowers Man hath never trod	*Original*	1 Corinthians 2:9

Perhaps the most emphatic testimony to Neale's art and popularity may be found in the discovery that of the 643 hymns and litanies in the 1909 edition of the *Hymns Ancient and Modern,* 62 (or 9.6 percent) belong to him, either as translations or original compositions. Although that figure had decreased by the publication of *The Church Hymnary* in 1973—22 of Neale's hymns out of a total of 695—the percentage (3.1) reveals that Neale continued to hold a significant degree of influence upon congregational singing within the Church of England.

Greek and Latin texts were not the only sources for hymn translations during the nineteenth century. In the eighteenth century, John Wesley had translated a number of German *kirchenlied* (a church song in German, as distinguished from one in or from Latin), and those remained standard fare from that language until two women applied their linguistic and artistic talents to the production of hymn texts that continue to be popular in England and North America. Catherine Winkworth (1827–1878)—a daughter of Henry Winkworth of Alderley Edge, Cheshire—spent her later years at Clifton, Bristol, where she pursued an active interest in the Clifton Association for the Higher Education of Women. Prior to that she published *Lyra Germanica* (1855), *The Chorale Book for England* (1863, translations with music), and *Christian Singers of Germany* (1869). Her principal translations are: Michael Weisse's "Christus ist erstanden" (1531), translated as "Christ the Lord is risen again"; Albert Knapp's "O Vaterherz, dad Erd und Himmel schuf" (1841), translated as "O Father, Thou Who hast created all"; Johann Wilhelm Meinhold's child's burial hymn, "Guter Hirt, du hast gesstillt" (1835), translated as "Tender Shepherd, Thou has still'd"; Johann Sheffler's "Leibe, Die du mich zum Bilde" (1657), translated as "O Love, who formedst me to wear / The image of Thy Godhead here"; and Johann Franck's "Herr Gott, dich loben wir, Regier" (1653), translated as "Lord God, we worship Thee."

However, two of Winkworth's most noted hymnodic productions—probably because of their easy adaptability from translated verse to congregational song—continue in the hymnals of most Protestant denominations. The first begins

> Praise to the Lord, the Almighty
>   the King of creation;
> O my soul praise Him, for He is thy
>   health and salvation;
>   All ye who hear
>   Now to His temple draw near,
> Joining in glad adoration.

The piece captures the universal commitment to faith and to prayer expressed in the original—Joachim Neander's "Lobe den Herren, den mächtigen König der Ehren"

(1680)—and is underscored by the biblical source: "Thou, even thou, art Lord alone; thou hast made heaven, the heaven of heavens, with all their host, the earth, and all things that are therein, the seas, and all that is therein, and thou preservest them all; and the host of heaven worshippeth Thee" (Nehemiah 9:6). Winkworth repeated that universal commitment, only with considerably more intensity, when she translated Martin Rinkart's poem of 1636, "Nun danket Alle Gott, / Mit Herzen, Mund, und Handen," as

> Now thank we all our God,
>   With heart, and hands, and voices,
> Who wondrous things hath done,
>   In whom His world rejoices;
> Who from our mother's arms,
>   Hath bless'd us on our way
> With countless gifts of love,
>   And still is ours to-day.

Given the accuracy of Catherine Winkworth's translations, as well as their poetic delicacy and discipline, there is little doubt that she more than any of her contemporaries brought about the revival of Britons' reliance upon German hymn texts.

The hymnodic output of Frances Elizabeth Cox (1812–1897) remains worthy of consideration. An extremely competent translator in her own right, Cox came to the German hymn through the influence of Baron Christian Carl Josias Bunsen, who served as Prussion ambassador to England between 1841 and 1854. In 1833 the baron published his *Versuch eines Allgemeinen Evangelischen Gesang-un Gebetbuchs*, containing 934 hymns and 350 prayers. Cox derived considerable guidance from it as to those hymns most worthy for translation into English.

The vast number of Cox's translations appear in two collections: *Sacred Hymns from the German* (1841) and the second series of that volume, entitled *Hymns from the*

German (1864). From the earlier text come such still-popular pieces as "Jesus lives! thy terrors now," from an Easter hymn by Christian Furchtegott Gellert, "Jesus lebt! mit Ihm auch ich" (1757); "Who are these like stars appearing," a translation of Heinrich Theobald Schenck's "Wer sind die vor Gottes Throne?" (1719)—the only hymn written by the Lutheran pastor from Giessen; and "O let him whose sorrow / No relief can find" from the poem of fourteen stanzas written in 1826 by Heinrich Siegmund Oswald, "Wem in Leidenstagen / Aller Trost steht fern." However, the single translation by Cox that has gained the widest acceptance in English-speaking nations appeared in her 1864 *Hymns from the German,* the opening stanza reading,

> Sing praise to Him Who reigns above,
>   The God of all creation,
> The God of power, the God of love,
>   The God of our salvation;
> With healing balm my soul He fills,
> And every faithless murmur stills;
>   To God all praise and glory.

Although not so prolific a poet and translator as Catherine Winkworth, Cox knew the value to a congregation of serious worshipers of carefully controlled rhythm—of repetition and emphasis, of clear address and strong refrain. And her translation of those seven lines cited above—of John Jacob Schutz's "Sei Lob und Ehr' dem höchsten Gut" (1675)—recreates with accuracy a hymn of general praise that also serves as a poetic declaration of strong personal faith.

Do not believe, though, that the emphasis upon classical and German translations caused an absence of original English hymnody during the first half of the nineteenth century. To the contrary, between 1827 and 1861—the latter date marking the publication of *Hymns Ancient and Modern*—several British poets produced new and original hymns that have found fairly broad congregational acceptance: John Keble, Henry Francis Lyte, Frederick William Faber, and Cecil Frances Alexander. Their major hymnodic contributions are summarized in Tables 18 through 21.

Table 18. The Major Hymns of John Keble

Opening Lines	Occasion	Written/ Published	Biblical Source
Now every morning is the love, Our wakening and uprising move	Morning	1822/1827	Lamentations 3:22–23
Oh! timely happy, timely wise, Hearts that with rising morn arise!	Morning	/1827	Revelation 21:5
Hail, gladdening Light of His pure glory pour'd Who is th' immortal Father	Evening	/1834	John 1:9
Sun of my soul, Thou Saviour dear, It is not right if Thou be near	Evening	/1827	Luke 24:29
'Tis gone, that bright and orbed blaze, Fast fading from our wistful gaze	Evening	/1827	Luke 24:29
Word supreme, before creation Horn of God eternally	St. John the Evangelist Day	1856/1857	John 21:20
Lord, in Thy name Thy servants plead And Thou hast sworn to hear	Rogation Days	1856/1859	Psalms 144:15
When God of old came down from heaven, In power and wrath He came	Whitsuntide	/1827	Acts 2:2

Opening Lines	Occasion	Written/ Published	Biblical Source
The voice that breathed o'er Eden, That earliest wedding day	Holy Matrimony	1857/1869	Ecclesiastes 4:12
There is a book, who runs may read, Which heav'nly truth imparts	Septuagesima	1819/1827	Romans 1:20
A living stream, as crystal clear, Welling from out the throne	General Hymn	/1857	Revelation 22:1
Blessed are the pure in heart For they shall see our God	General Hymn	1819/1827	Matthew 5:8
One Thy light, the temple filling, Holy, Holy, Holy Three	Church Work: Theological Colleges	/1856	Isaiah 6:8

John Kebel (1792–1866), one of the proponents of the Oxford Movement, left Oxford in 1823 for a curacy in Gloucestershire; he then became vicar of Hursley, near Winchester in 1833, and his appointment as professor of poetry at Oxford dates from that same year. In 1827 he published anonymously a collection of his poems entitled *The Christian Year; or, Thoughts in Verse for the Sundays and Holy Days throughout the Year.* His *Psalter; or, Psalms of David in English Verse* (1839) gained little acceptance; in 1869 came a collection of his *Miscellaneous Poems.*

Keble heads the list of poet-hymnodists of the nineteenth century, a loose network of writers (most of them Anglican clerics) whose poetry reflected their observations and interpretations of higher nature and the new freedom associated with the human spirit. He wrote, in his most popular evening hymn, of the "Sun of my soul," of "no earth-born cloud," of "the soft dews of kindly sleep." God's love, for John Keble, existed as an "ocean" wherein "We lose ourselves in heav'n above." Time posed no real problem for him, since all actions (marriage, for instance) remain within that "high mysterious union / Which naught on earth may break." The essence of his form of romanticism (though not romanticism in the sense of Wordsworth or Coleridge) comes forth clearly in this stanza for his wedding hymn:

> Be present, Son of Mary,
>   As Thou didst bind two natures
> In Thine eternal bands.

The duality of nature exists because, on one level, the power and the form of God remain mysterious to human-kind; on another level, however, God will continue to endow people with the pleasure of and benefits from His form and His power. Keble's hymn serves as one means for the acknowledgment of that endowment.

Table 19. The Major Hymns of Henry Francis Lyte

Opening Lines	Occasion	Written/Published	Biblical Source
Abide with me; fast falls the eventide; The darkness thickens; Lord abide with me	Evening	1847/1850	Luke 24:29
God of mercy, God of grace, Show the brightness of Thy face	General Hymn	/1834	Psalms 47:1
Pleasant are Thy courts above In the land of light and love	General Hymn	/1834	Psalms 84:1
Praise, my soul, the King of heaven, To His feet thy tribute bring	General Hymn	/1834	Psalms 103:1

Opening Lines	Occasion	Written/ Published	Biblical Source
Far from my heav'nly home, Far from my Father's breast	General Hymn	/1834	Psalms 63:2
When at Thy footstool, Lord, I bend, And plead with Thee for mercy there	Mission Service	/1833	1 John 2:1

Educated at Trinity College, Dublin, principally for the purpose of entering the medical profession, Henry Lyte (1793–1847) instead took Holy Orders and became curate of Taghmon, near Wexford, in 1815. Two years later he moved to Marazion, then on to curacies at Lymington, Hampshire; Charlton, Devonshire; and Dittisham. An appointment in 1823 as perpetual curate of Lower Brixham, Devonshire, served only to test to the limits his fragile health. His *Poems, Chiefly Religious* appeared in 1833; other publications included *Tales on the Lord's Prayer in Verse* (1826), *The Spirit of the Psalms* (1834), and an edition of *The Poems of Henry Vaughan* (1846).

No matter what else Lyte wrote—and he produced at least ninety hymns and psalm paraphrases that adapted easily to congregational worship—he will always be remembered as the author of one of the most popular of English hymns, "Abide with me." Most assuredly, that poem deserves the highest of praise, for it comes forth, despite all of the twentieth-century revisions and deletions, as a strong expression of personal grief and suffering that, in the end, will serve as an intense dedication to the glory of God. Although the hymn commonly celebrates an evening service, it may be equally valid as an ode in preparation for death, for in terms of the poet's own experience, he viewed the emergence of "Heav'n's morning" and the fading of "earth's vain shadows" on his deathbed. "In life, in death,

O Lord, abide with me"—certainly as simple and as direct a message as any worshiper would require. Unfortunately, the majority of hymnal editors tend to include only a portion of Lyte's original eight stanzas; most often omitted is the fifth section, which contains an intensely meaningful and highly accurate focal point for worshipers:

> Thou on my head in early youth did smile;
> And, though rebellious and perverse meanwhile,
> Thou hast not left me, oft as I left Thee,
> On to the close, O Lord, abide with me!

As with Henry Francis Lyte, the hymnodic reputation of John Henry Newman originates from a single effort—although as a poet and prose writer, the latter remains a major literary figure of the Victorian Age. Raised within the boundaries of the Evangelical faith, Newman (1801–1890) served as vicar of Saint Mary the Virgin University Church, Oxford, from 1828 to 1848. During that period and for two years afterward he wrestled with the principles of the Tractarians, which eventually led him toward the Roman Catholic Church. In 1845 he received Roman Communion, after which he spent his remaining years in seclusion at the Oratory of Saint Philip Neri, Edgbaston, Birmingham. Literary history remembers Newman for his "Tract XC" on the compatability of the Thirty-nine Articles with Catholic theology—a piece that brought the Tractarians under official Church of England ban. His *Lyra Apostolica* came in 1836 and the *Apologia pro Vita Sua* in 1864. In 1854 Newman received appointment as rector of the new Catholic University of Dublin; two years earlier he had delivered his lectures, *The Scope and Nature of University Education;* and *Lectures on Universities* appeared in 1859.

Newman's contribution to English hymnody cannot be considered large in terms of its quantity, but few hymnodists have surpassed him in poetic skill or religious dedication. For instance, in his "Praise to the Holiest in the height / And in the depth be praise," he negates the

objects of the world and concentrates upon the ultimate
that God can offer to any person.

> And that a higher gift can grace
> Should flesh and blood refine,
> God's presence and His very Self,
> And Essence all-divine.

In Newman's scheme of a God-ordered and God-
controlled world, all that appeared material was, in actuality, spiritual. However, his principal hymnodic effort came
in June 1833—a period during which he experienced both
physical and spiritual discomfort while traveling in Italy.
On a boat from Palermo to Marseilles, in the midst of a
week-long calm in the Straits of Bonifacio, he gave the
English-speaking world a hymn text of deep personal
emotion and extreme poetic sensitivity that continues to be
read and sung today.

> Lead, kindly Light, amid th' encircling gloom,
>   Lead Thou me on;
> The night is dark, and I am far from home,
>   Lead Thou me on.
> Keep Thou my feet; I do not ask to see
> The distant scene; one step enough for me.

Although Newman once proclaimed, "It is not the
hymn, but the tune ["Lux Benigna" (1865), by John
Bacchus Dykes (1823–1876)] that has gained the popularity," the sound and the sense of the language have always
been sufficient to create a sense of universality that really
obscures the poet's personal experience. Indeed, the
longevity of the piece may well be the result of the single
sentence resting securely but unobtrusively in the second
stanza: "I loved to choose and see my path; but now Lead
Thou me on." In other words, Newman gave to the English
worshipers of his own day a hymn that explained, specifically but succinctly, a primary relationship between human
beings and God—in his view the only relationship worthy

of consideration. His hymnodic gift continues to be received.

Table 20. The Major Hymns of Frederick William Faber

Opening Lines	Occasion	Written/ Published	Biblical Source
Sweet Saviour, bless us ere we go, Thy Word unto our minds instill	Evening	/1852	Psalms 27:1
O come and mourn with me awhile; O come ye to the Saviour's side	Passiontide: Good Friday	/1849	Mark 15:25
Jesu, gentle Saviour, Thou art in us now	Holy Communion	/1854	John 6:57
My God, how wonderful Thou art, Thy majesty how bright	General Hymn	/1849	Isaiah 57:15
Jesus is God: the solid earth, The ocean broad and bright	General Hymn	/1854	John 1:1, 3
Oh, it is hard to work for God, To rise and take His part	Church Work	/1862	Hosea 14:9
O come to the merciful Saviour Who calls you, O come to the Lord who forgives and forgets	Mission Service	/1854	Mark 10:49
My God! my God! and can it be That I should sin so lightly now	Mission Service	/1849	Psalms 51:4
Souls of man! why will ye scatter Like a crowd of fright'ned sheep?	Mission Service	/1854	John 12:47

Opening Lines	Occasion	Written/ Published	Biblical Source
Hark! hark, my soul! Angelic songs are swelling O'er earth's green fields and ocean's wave-beat shore:	Mission Service	/1854	Romans 13:12
Faith of our Fathers! living still In spite of dungeon, fire, and sword	National Hymn	/1849	

Frederick William Faber (1814–1863) and Newman stand side by side (or, more accurately, one year apart) as Anglican clerics who saw fit to turn to Roman Catholicism. However, the comparison ends rather abruptly at that point. Originally inclined toward the Calvinist wing of the Anglican Church, in 1838 Faber published *The Ancient Things of the Church of England,* in which he described the domination of the "Archbishop of Rome" as unscriptural and declared that the papists had added falsehoods to the sacraments. However, at Oxford he came under Newman's influence and began to shift directions. Taking Holy Orders in the Church of England, Faber served three years as rector of Elton, Huntingdonshire, before he turned from Protestantism and joined the Roman Catholic Church. In Birmingham he formed, with eight others, the Brothers of the Will of God—a community also known as the Wilfridians, because Faber had been rebaptized under the name of Wilfrid. In 1848 Faber and his followers joined with Newman at the Oratory of Saint Philip Neri; a year later he established a London branch of that order, presently known as the Brompton Oratory. Faber's hymns number approximately one hundred fifty, most of them intended to supply Roman Catholics with devotional readings.

Although Newman certainly ranks superior to Faber as a pure poet, Faber must be acknowledged as the more serious hymn writer. Nonetheless, the quantity of his hymns, as well as their serious intent, do not always carry the day in his favor. His hymnodic reputation comes to rest firmly upon the last poem in Table 20, "Faith of our Fathers! living still"—essentially a Roman Catholic hymn encouraging Britons to return to the one true religion. Notice the third stanza, especially.

> Faith of our Fathers! Mary's prayers
>   Shall win our country back to Thee!
> And through the truth that comes from God
>   England shall then indeed be free.

Leading Anglican hymnal editors would have nothing to do with the piece, as witnessed by its absence from *Hymns Ancient and Modern* (1861), the *Anglican Hymn Book* (1868), and *The Church Hymnary* (1870). The editors of other nineteenth-century Protestant collections in both England and North America, yielding to pressure from worshipers who demanded that the hymn be sung, included the piece—but with a number of serious revisions. Notice, again, the third stanza.

Original	*Popular Revision*
Faith of our Fathers! Mary's prayers	Faith of our fathers! faith and prayer
Shall win our country back to Thee!	Shall keep our country true to Thee;
And through the truth that comes from God	And through the truth that comes from God
England shall then indeed be free.	Our land shall then indeed be free.

For the editors of the Unitarian *Hymns for the Church of Christ* (1853), the opening lines of the stanza became "Faith of our Fathers! Good men's prayers, / Shall win our country all to Thee." Other examples can readily be cited to support what Louis Benson long ago identified as "the gentle art of hymn-tinkering" (*Hymnody of the Christian Church*, p. 215). Therefore, having been purged of its obvious and highly intentional doctrinal and national specificity, Faber's "Faith of our Fathers" continues to serve as one of the earliest representatives of hymnodic ecumenism.

Table 21. The Major Hymns of Cecil Frances Alexander

Opening Lines	Occasion	Written/ Published	Biblical Source
Forgive them, O my Father, They know not what they do	Passiontide	/1875	Luke 23:34
Jesus calls us; o'er the tumult Of our life's wild restless sea	St. Andrew's Day	1852/1852	John 1:40
The roseate hues of early dawn, The brightness of the day	General Hymn	/1852	2 Corinthians 4:18
Forsaken once, and thrice denied The risen Lord gave pardon free	General Hymn	/1875	John 21:16
Once in royal David's city Stood a lowly cattle shed	Children	/1848	Luke 2:27
There is a green hill far away, Outside a city wall	Children	/1848	Romans 5:8
Up in heaven, up in heaven, In the bright place far away	Children, Ascension	/1848	Matthew 25:31

Opening Lines	Occasion	Written/ Published	Biblical Source
We are but little children weak, And He is King above the sky	Children	/1850	Proverbs 20:11
Every morning the red sun Rises warm and bright	Children	/1848	Isaiah 33:17
Do no sinful action, Speak no angry word	Children	/1848	Isaiah 1:16–17
All things bright and beautiful, All creatures great and small	Children	/1848	Proverbs 16:4

Wife of the Reverend William Alexander, curate of Londonderry and later bishop of Derry and Raphoe (before rising to archbishop of Armagh and Primate of Ireland), Cecil Frances Alexander (1818–1895) published *Verses for Holy Seasons* (1846), *Hymns for Little Children* (1848), and *Hymns Descriptive and Devotional* (1858). Following her death, her husband collected the best of her poetry—most of it devotional pieces for children—and published them as *Poems by Cecil Frances Alexander.*

Of Alexander's nearly four hundred hymns, the vast majority attempt to meet the spiritual needs of children. In that context she can appear both similar to and different from her predecessors. At times she resembles Isaac Watts in her stern, almost Calvinistic, warnings against the evils of the present world.

> There's a wicked spirit
> Watching round you still,
> And he tries to tempt you
> To all harm and ill.

At other hymnodic moments, she takes her cue from Charles Wesley and assigns to little children responsibilities that may appear far beyond their spiritual capabilities.

> Oh, day by day each Christian child
> Has much to do, without, within;
> A death to die for Jesus' sake,
> A weary war to wage with sin.

But in the end, Cecil Frances Alexander sounds the trumpet of pure positivism. She stands against a background of a God-ordered nature, a strictly childlike nature of light and life.

> Each little flower that opens,
>   Each little bird that sings,
> He made their glowing colours,
>   He made their tiny wings.
> All things bright and beautiful,
>   All creatures great and small,
> All things wise and wonderful,
>   The Lord God made them all.

Reinforcing that childlike nature, Alexander relies upon images of color and shape and size. Thus,

> On the dark hill's western side
>   The last purple gleam has died,
> Twilight to one solemn hue
>   Changes all, both green and blue.
> In the fold and in the nest,
>   Birds and lambs are gone to rest,
> Labour's weary task is o'er.
>   Closely shut the cottage door.

One needs to keep in mind Alexander's distinct advantage over her eighteenth-century models. She evidences a concern for audience. She did not wish to preach to children; she wished instead to provide youngsters with poetry that, given the proper moment, they would willingly sing out and up to God.

To Sir Robert Grant belongs the credit for a truly universal hymn, a piece that transcends time as well as denominational philosophy and dictates. A lawyer, Grant served as king's serjeant in the court of the Duchy of Lancaster, and then entered parliament to represent (variously) the Elgin Burghs, Inverness Burghs, Norwich, and Finsbury. He became a privy councillor in 1831; rose to judge advocate general in 1833; and received appointment in 1834 as governor of Bombay.

In "O worship the King, / All-glorious above," one may observe a nearly perfect collective call to worship, a hymn meant to establish the theological sense and the emotional sound of congregational commitment to faith. Published in 1833, the year prior to Grant's appointment as Governor of Bombay, the hymn exists as a free version of Psalm 104, based on William Kethe's version in the 1561 *Anglo-Genevan Psalter*. Grant's strength as a hymnodist will be found not so much in his poetry as in his ability to reach inside the Old Testament psalms, grasp their active tone and diction, and recast their sentiments into his own sincere statement of praise. Grant thus emerges from the lines of his hymn as the parliamentarian and government official—the poet of intense action but few words, the herald of an All-glorious King who speaks amid the blare of the bugles and the beat of the drums.

> The earth with its store
> Of wonders untold,
> Almighty, Thy power
> Hath founded of old;
> Hath 'stablish'd it fast
> By a changeless decree,
> And round it hath cast,
> Like a mantle, the sea.

Amid all of that noise, however, Grant manages to reveal a gentle and sensitive side. An interesting aspect of his poetic and hymnodic personality permits him to view the beauty of God's work as it "sweetly distils / In the dew and the rain"; he thus asks his worshipers to "tell of His might" and to "sing of His grace," but he never loses sight of the "Ineffable Love" in which "Angels delight." In the end, Grant's purpose remains exceedingly clear, for he envisions all people as

> Frail children of dust,
> And feeble as frail,
> In Thee do we trust,
> Nor find Thee to fail.

His ornate style may seem anchored too heavily to the last vestiges of the Georgian Age, but few worshipers of the present day would argue with the overall assertiveness by which Grant transmits his fundamental theme of humanity's subordination to the glory and the power of Almighty God.

At this point in the discussion of hymnody in nineteenth-century Great Britain, a brief word needs to be inserted concerning the various references to one of the most significant volumes of hymnody published during this period—*Hymns Ancient and Modern.* In 1861 a committee representing more than two hundred Anglican clergy published a hymnal that remains one of the most comprehensive literary collections of words and music for congregational worship. After more than a century and a half of search, discovery, and experimentation; of paraphrase, translation, and original composition; of the very old and the very new, English Protestantism as well as Victorian conservatism in general, stood ready to accept and to bestride the middle ground. The Church of England looked forward, by mid-nineteenth century, to an unofficial hymnal that would include the old and the new, both in words and in music, ranging from old Latin hymns with their plainsong melodies to the then recent efforts of such contemporaries as John Keble, Henry Francis Lyte, John Mason Neale, Catherine Winkworth, and (despite his having left the Church) John Henry Newman. In addition, there existed a demand for the best of German hymnody and tunes that, for a generation and more, had proven congenial to English worshipers. The result came not from a single point of view, but by way of several opinions upon the vehicle of a determined effort—an effort worthy of examination because it reveals, almost step by step, the process by which a classic anthology of congregational song can be created.

The idea for a new Church hymnal came initially from the Reverend Francis H. Murray, rector of Chiselhurst and editor of *A Hymnal for the Use of the English Church* (1852), and Sir Henry Williams Baker (1821–1877), vicar of Monkland, Herefordshire. They shared their ideas with the Reverend G. Cosby White, vicar of Saint Barnabas, Pimlico, and compiler of *Hymns and Introits* (1852), a volume originally designed for the Collegiate Church at Cumbrae. The three clerics organized a meeting at Saint Barnabas in the fall of 1857, to which they invited several other interested colleagues who sensed the need for a new Church hymnal. In 1858 the editors of other popular hymn books expressed their readiness to cooperate with Murray's committee in the development of a single collection that would supersede their own extant volumes. Through an advertisement in the *Guardian* (27 October 1858), Murray and his committee secured the cooperation and assistance of no fewer than two hundred clergymen. At another meeting, in January 1859, the chair of the committee passed to Sir Henry Baker; on 18 November of that year, the group published a small preliminary text of 108 pages and 138 hymns—on the back page of which appeared a notice promising an enlarged version, by Advent 1860, of approximately 300 hymns and tunes.

On Sir Henry Baker's recommendation, the committee proceeded to appoint, as musical editor for the planned volume, Dr. William Henry Monk (1823–1889)—organist and director of the choir at King's College (London), a

prominent member of the Church Music Society, and a
laborer for the overall improvement of English congregational song. To Monk must be extended full credit for
suggesting a title for the volume: *Hymns Ancient and Modern
for Use in the Services of the Church.* As musical editor, he
completed most of the compiling and the arranging,
although the Reverend Frederick Arthur Gore Ouseley
(1825–1889), professor of music at the University of
Oxford, revised and approved the musical texts. The first
edition of the collection came forth in 1861, published in
London by Novello and Company; it contained 273 hymns
and accompanying tunes, with provisions for days of the
week, feasts, fasts, and services on the Book of Common
Prayer. Consideration had been extended in the direction
of special occasions and saints' days (including the Annun-
ciation and Purification of the Blessed Virgin Mary), as
well as 67 general hymns. Finally, the worshiper could find
132 versions of Latin hymns (most of them altered), 10
hymns from the German, and 119 hymns that had been
previously adapted for congregational worship.

Aside from the eighteenth-century hymnodic works of
Isaac Watts, Charles and John Wesley, and their major
Nonconformist contemporaries, the success of *Hymns Ancient and Modern* was without parallel. And as with Watts
and the Wesleys, the influence of the collection extended
beyond the spheres of hymnody and sacred music. The
work became an effective means by which members of
congregations assimilated the opinions, practices, and
overall atmosphere of the conservative elements of the
Church of England. As a hymnal, although technically an
unofficial publication of the Church of England, *Hymns
Ancient and Modern* established a literary tone—a literary
sentiment—for hymnody that came to characterize nineteenth-century Anglican congregational song. Be it known,
however, that its influence extended beyond the cathedrals
of London, Canterbury, Rochester, and York; the volume
affected other Protestant denominations, thus preparing

for it a lasting place in the history of hymnody within the English-speaking churches.

Because of its substance and its comprehensiveness, *Hymns Ancient and Modern* encountered is share of hostility, particularly within the first three months or so of its publication. Its critics viewed the volume as opposed to the even more traditional direction toward which its editors had turned it. The news-sheets of the period graphically record disturbances over attempts to introduce it into a number of churches. However, cold statistics underscore the degree to which the Anglican clergy united behind it: 350,000 volumes sold between 1861 and 1864; an appendix in 1868; a revised edition in 1875; an enlarged version in 1889; and a total revision in 1904. In 1895 a formal Church survey revealed that of 13,639 individual congregations, no fewer than 10,340 (75.8 percent) had embraced *Hymns Ancient and Modern,* as well as 28 cathedrals, practically the entire Scottish Episcopal Church, and the Royal Army and Royal Navy. By the end of 1912 the publishers claimed to have circulated more than sixty million copies, and revised editions have continued to be published since the end of World War I.

Setting aside for a moment the issues relative to editors, publishers, numbers and types of editions, and even sales figures, the key point at this juncture in the history and development of the English hymn focuses initially upon the book serving as the grand summation of Anglican hymnody from its beginning (around 1760) until 1861. The next item concerns the volume's influence on and dominance over those collections that followed it. *Hymns Ancient and Modern,* in its initial edition as well as by its very title, indicated that English hymnody would base its future upon *English* hymns, both of early and recent origin; upon translations from the Latin and the German; and upon a small number of hymnodic poems written especially for the 1861 collection. Further, Anglican hymnody, by way of *Hymns Ancient and Modern,* would take full advantage of the days of the week, festivals and fast days, services from the Book of Common Prayer, and significant occasions within the structure and the organization of the Church.

The publication of *Hymns Ancient and Modern* did not, however, bring to an end the composition of original Anglican hymns—or an end to hymns written by Anglicans. During the last half of the nineteenth century, the hymnodic efforts of a number of poets of the Church gained congregational acceptance, particularly because of their high literary quality. Limitations of space will not allow for discussion and analysis of each one of those hymnodists; however, six poets may serve to represent the so-called Literary Age of English hymnody—the approximate period between the publication of *Hymns Ancient and Modern* and the beginning of the twentieth century. Consider, then, the samplings from the hymnodic labors of Henry Alford, Sabine Baring-Gould, William Chatterton Dix, John Ellerton, Charlotte Elliott, and Samuel John Stone shown in Table 22.

Table 22. Later-Nineteenth-Century English Hymnodists

Opening Lines	Occasion	Written/ Published	Biblical Source
Alford:			
In token that thou shalt not fear Christ crucified to own	Baptism	1832/1832	2 Timothy 1:8
Ten thousand times ten thousand In sparkling raiment bright	General Hymn	/1867	Revelation 7:17
Come, ye thankful people, come, Raise the song of harvest-home	Thanksgiving, Harvest	/1847	Isaiah 9:3

Opening Lines	Occasion	Written/ Published	Biblical Source
Forward! be our watchword, Steps and voices join'd	Processional	1871/1875	Exodus 14:15
Baring-Gould:			
On the Resurrection morning Soul and body meet again	Easter	1864/1864	Psalms 17:16
Through the night of doubt and sorrow Onward goes the pilgrim band	General Hymn	/1867	Ephesians 4:5
Now the day is over, Night is drawing nigh	Children, Evening	/1867	Proverbs 3:24
Onward, Christian soldiers, Marching as to war	Children, Processional	1864/1864	Deuteronomy 31:7–8
Dix:			
As with gladness men of old Did the guiding star behold	Epiphany	1860/1861	Matthew 2:10
Alleluia! sing to Jesus! His the sceptre, His the throne	Holy Communion	1866/1867	Hebrews 7:17
Come unto Me, ye weary, And I will give you rest	General Hymn	1867/1867	John 6:37
To Thee, O Lord, our hearts we raise In hymns of adoration	Thanksgiving, Harvest	/1864	Psalms 65:12
Ellerton:			
Behold us, Lord, a little space From daily tasks set free	Midday	1870/1871	Revelation 11:15
The day Thou gavest, Lord, is ended, The darkness falls at Thy behest	Evening	1870/1870	Psalms 113:3

Opening Lines	Occasion	Written/ Published	Biblical Source
Our day of praise is done; The evening shadows fall	Evening	1871/1871	Revelation 7:11
Saviour, again to Thy dear Name we raise With one accord our parting hymn of praise	Evening, End of Divine Service	1866/1868	Psalms 29:10
This is the day of light: Let there be light to-day	Sunday	/1867	Revelation 1:10
Throned upon the awful tree, King of grief, I watch with Thee	Passiontide	1875/1875	Mark 15:34
Hail to the Lord Who comes, Comes to His temple gate!	Purification of the Virgin	1880/1881	Luke 2:22
O Son of God, our Captain of salvation, Thyself by suffering school'd to human grief	St. Barnabas the Apostle	1871/1871	Acts 4:36
Lift the strain of high thanksgiving! Tread with songs the hallow'd way	Restoration of a Church	1869/1871	Ezra 5:11
O Father, bless the children brought hither to Thy gate	Baptism	1886/1888	Matthew 28:19
O Father all-creating, Whose wisdom, love, and power	Holy Matrimony	1876/1880	Psalms 127:1
Now the labourer's task is o'er; Now the battle day is past	Burial	1871/1871	Wisdom of Solomon (Apocrypha) 3:1
Praise to our God, whose bounteous hand, Prepared of old our glorious land	Thanksgiving, National Blessings	1870/1871	Deuteronomy 8:10

Opening Lines	Occasion	Written/ Published	Biblical Source
Shine Thou upon me, Lord, True Light of men, to-day	Church Work	1889/1889	Numbers 22:35
Elliott:			
My God, my Father, while I stray, Far from my home, on life's rough way	General Hymn	/1834	Matthew 26:42
Christian! seek not yet repose, Hear they guardian Angel say	General Hymn	/1836	Matthew 26:41
Just as I am, without one plea But that Thy Blood was shed for me	Mission Service	1834/1835	John 6:37
Stone:			
The Church's one foundation Is Jesus Christ, her Lord	General Hymn	1866/1866	1 Corinthians 3:11
Round the Sacred City gather Egypt, Edom, Babylon	General Hymn	1874/1874	Psalms 46:5
Weary of earth and laden with my sin, I look at heav'n and long to enter in	General Hymn	1866/1866	Ephesians 1:7
Through midnight gloom from Macedon The cry of myriads as of one	Foreign Mission	1872/1875	Acts 16:9
Lord of the harvest! it is right and meet That we should lay our first-fruits at Thy feet	Thanksgiving for Missions	1872/1875	Psalms 72:19
Unchanging God, hear from eternal heaven: We plead Thy gifts of grace, for ever given	Missions	1885/1886	Romans 11:29

Opening Lines	Occasion	Written/ Published	Biblical Source
O Father, in Whose great design Our hearts are filled with love divine	Church Work: Temperance	/1889	Matthew 12:21
O Thou before Whose presence Naught evil may come in	Church Work: Temperance	/1889	Psalms 126:4
Our God of love who reigns above Comes down to us below	Children	/1899	Mark 10:14

Should one desire to consider the general contribution of the six hymnodists outlined in Table 22, the key point would be that each gave to English devotional poetry a hymn that will last as long as Christians gather for public worship. Henry Alford (1810–1871; Dean of Canterbury), in his thanksgiving hymn (especially popular in the United States), looked directly at the practical dimension of rural life, its activities, and its purposes.

> All is safely gather'd in,
> Ere the winter storms begin;
> God, our Maker, doth provide
> For our wants to be supplied.

As a churchman, Alfred never lost sight of the spiritual significance of the term *harvest,* an occasion upon which God "wilt come, / And will take Thy people home."

Similarly, Sabine Baring-Gould (1834–1924; rector of Lew Trenchard, Devonshire) considered the duality that manifests itself at some time during every human being's tenure upon earth. On the surface—or at least at an eager first reading—his "Onward, Christian soldiers," at one time one of the most popular of all English hymns, appears as a militant, emotional onslaught against anything and everything that might be termed anti-Christian. Notice the figures "forward into battle"; "like a mighty army"; "marching as to war"; and "though division harass."

However, a more careful reading produces the realization that Baring-Gould created a poem against a background of considerable movement and noise, reinforced by Arthur Seymour Sullivan's militant music, but with practically no violent action. Indeed, he wrote the piece for the children at Horbury Bridge—little children, who would march and sing as would most loyal children of the Victorian Age, children enthused with the spirit of God, Church, Nation. All Baring-Gould asked of those children was to "lift your voices, /Loud your anthems raise." War? Hardly—for see what emerges in the final stanza:

> Onward then, ye people,
> Join our happy throng,
> Blend with yours our voices
> In the triumph song;
> Glory, laud, and honour
> Unto Christ the King;
> This through countless ages
> Men and Angels sing.

Yet no matter how much noise they did create, Baring-Gould's juvenile parishioners at Horbury Bridge remained "All one body, we. / One in hope and doctrine, / One in charity." Those who currently denounce or reject outright this hymn of childlike exuberance would do well to read it thoroughly and to focus attention upon the sense of the poem rather than react to its sound.

If Baring-Gould's children had the opportunity for march and general jubilation, this scholar-poet of Devonshire also provided some hymnodic time for quiet reflection. Approximately three years after the publication of "Onward, Christian solders," he gave them a delicate and sensitive poem for divine worship. Those same youngsters (or their successors) at Horbury Bridge who followed "the Cross of Jesus /Going on before" would echo in the evening the tender sentiments from Proverbs: "yea, thou shalt lie down and thy sleep shall be sweet." Baring-Gould simply looked about him, first toward the heavens and then to his own earthly existence, embracing those obvious images of a

God-created universe: "the shadows of the evening," the peeping stars, the soon-to-be-sleeping "birds and beasts and flowers." The hymn straddles the thin line between a song of praise and a statement of prayer.

> Grant to little children
>   Visions bright of Thee;
> Guard the sailors tossing
>   On the deep blue sea.

Such sentiments, however, do not obscure the writer's traditional theological teaching. His little Christian soldiers constitute one body held firm by hope, doctrine, and charity. Those same little child-soldiers of Christ, after they awake "Pure, and fresh, and sinless / In Thy holy eyes," immediately and freely offer

> Glory to the Father,
>   Glory to the Son,
> And to Thee, Blest Spirit,
>   Whilst all ages run.

Of William Chatterton Dix (1837–1898; the manager of a marine insurance company in Glasgow), the best that can be said will always pertain to his abilities as a poet and translator, as well as his skill as a paraphraser of Scripture. Those references hold true particularly in terms of such pieces as the Epiphany hymn, "As with gladness men of old" and his general hymn, "Come unto me, ye weary." Given the proper musical accompaniment, his hymns usually motivate congregational singers toward serious and meaningful expression. Similarly, John Ellerton (1826–1893; rector of Barnes, Surrey, and finally of White Roding, Essex) could communicate hymnodically the sound and sense of the Scriptures, as witnessed by his effort on Barnabas, "O Son of God, our Captain of salvation." However, he could also transfer the occasion to specific concerns of the Church or to the needs of a particular congregation.

> And all true helpers, patient, kind, and skilful,
> Who shed Thy light across our darken'd earth,
> Counsel the doubting, and restrain the wilful,
> Soothe the sick bed, and share the children's mirth.

The lines may prove a bit too lengthy, too plodding, for some; yet few would disagree with Ellerton's attempts to direct the course of late-nineteenth-century hymnody toward actual late-nineteenth-century concerns. Those very concerns have transcended the specific age in which the poet and his contemporary congregational singers lived.

At the risk of stepping outside the chronological lines of nineteenth-century British hymnody, separate recognition should be extended to two hymns that encompass the full meaning of what is now embraced as congregational song. Both pieces represent the focus and intent of the congregational hymn: the individual spiritual needs of the worshiper and the collective doctrinal requirements of the congregation. On one level, the beautiful, sensitive, and emotional hymn by Charlotte Elliott (1789–1871), "Just as I am, without one plea," serves as the perfect symbol of the lifelong invalid who, after overcoming her sense of trouble, discomfort, and uselessness, suddenly achieves a state of complete peace and satisfaction.

> Just as I am, though toss'd about
> With many a conflict, many a doubt,
> Fightings and fears, within, without,
> O Lamb of God, I come.

The invalid suffering from pain and enduring the frustration resulting from that pain found a common hymnodic ground, more than thirty years later, with Samuel John Stone (1839–1900; rector of All-Hallows-on-the-Wall, London). In looking critically at the Church of England, Stone saw an institution "sore opprest, /By schisms rent asunder, / By heresies distrest." On that common ground, the two invalids—the human being and the religious institution—seek and eventually find salvation along similar paths.

'Mid toil, and tribulation,
  And tumult of her war,
She waits the consummation
  Of peace for ever more;
Till with the vision glorious
  Her longing eyes are blest,
And the great Church victorious
  Shall be the Church at rest.

If worshipers doubt the strength and influence of these two Anglican hymns, let them first review the contents pages of modern hymnals from England and North America, as shown in Table 23.

Table 23. "Just as I Am" and "The Church's One Foundation" in Modern Hymnals

Hymnal	"Just as I Am"	"The Church's One Foundation"
ENGLAND:		
Hymns Ancient and Modern (1922, 1950)	Yes	Yes
One Hundred Hymns for To-day (1969)	Yes	Yes
The Anglican Hymn Book (1965)	Yes	Yes
The Baptist Hymn Book (1962)	Yes	Yes
Praise for To-day (1974)	Yes	Yes
The BBC Hymn Book (1951)	Yes	Yes
Church Hymnary (1927, 1973)	Yes	Yes
Congregational Praise (1951)	Yes	Yes
New Church Praise (1975)	Yes	Yes
The English Hymnal	Yes	Yes
Methodist Hymn Book (1933)	Yes	Yes
Hymns and Songs (1969)	Yes	Yes
Praise the Lord (1972)	No	Yes
Worship Songs (1905)	Yes	Yes
UNITED STATES:		
Baptist Hymnal (1975)	Yes	Yes
The Brethren Hymnal (1951)	Yes	Yes
The Broadman Hymnal (1940)	Yes	Yes
Catholic Liturgy Book (1975)	Yes	Yes
Christian Hymnal (Mennonite, 1959)	Yes	Yes
Christian Worship (1949, 1970)	Yes	Yes
The Hymnal (Episcopal; 1940, 1943)	Yes	Yes
The Hymnal (Evangelical United Brethren, 1957)	Yes	Yes
The Hymnal (Army and Navy, 1942)	Yes	Yes
More Hymns and Spiritual Songs (1971)	Yes	Yes
Lutheran Book of Worship (1978)	Yes	Yes
Methodist Hymnal (1964, 1966)	Yes	Yes

Hymnal	"Just as I Am"	"The Church's One Foundation"
The Hymnal (Presbyterian, 1933)	No	Yes
The Worshipbook (Presbyterian, 1972)	No	Yes
Trinity Hymnal (1961)	Yes	Yes
Pilgrim Hymnal (1958)	Yes	Yes
Westminster Praise (1976)	Yes	Yes
Worship II (Roman Catholic, 1976)	No	Yes
CANADA:		
The Hymn Book (1971)	Yes	Yes
The Hymnary (1930)	Yes	Yes
The Book of Praise (1972)	Yes	Yes

Finally, only the most unemotional and insensitive of readers and singers would fail to grasp the reasons behind the popularity of "Just as I am, without one plea" among those who follow the efforts of the media-oriented Evangelical organizations that have established themselves in recent years, particularly in the United States. Despite the highly personalized circumstances in which Charlotte Elliott composed her poem, it has adapted easily to its dominant role as a hymn for missions, which include walking down the aisles of assorted stadia and assembly halls toward the altars of Evangelical conversion. The piece has served with equal adaptability as a celebration of personal or collective reaffirmation of faith.

> Just as I am, Thou wilt receive,
> Wilt welcome, pardon, cleanse, relieve:
> Because Thy promise I believe,
> O Lamb of God, I come.

A number of persons—inspired by Elliott's poem and the music ("Woodworth") of William Batchelder Bradbury (1816–1868; the American organist and music director), in addition to a wholesome dose of emotional pulpit oratory—have seen fit to leave their seats and proceed down the aisle to "Thou bidd'st me come to Thee, /O Lamb of God, I come." What better example to illustrate the long trail from the Evangelical revival of the nineteenth century to the televangelistic crusade of the twentieth.

Chapter Seven
ENGLAND IN THE TWENTIETH CENTURY

FEW WILL ARGUE THAT any discussion of a work of art from a chronological distance poses a minimum of problems once the critical criteria have been determined. To examine a body of music or literature composed during an earlier century means to observe ideas and groups, forms and modes, schools and philosophies—all of which have been firmly established in the minds of historians and commentators, all clearly outlined as to purpose, function, and method. However, once the examiner begins to consider a work within his or her own time frame—a work by an artist who may still be living and producing—the lines of form and purpose and the criteria of artist and audience may appear less clear than those from earlier moments in history. The theological, historical, musical, and literary labels of earlier centuries will usually suffice for categories into which artists of all forms and modes may conveniently and accurately be placed. The twentieth century, though, does not always offer those categories; or if the categories exist, they tend not to be apparent from such close proximity.

Nonetheless, despite the problems brought about by closeness, one cannot turn away from the present until it becomes a part of the past. In terms of my own particular area of study and interest, some attempt must be made to present an orderly discussion of twentieth-century British hymnody. At the risk of rigidity, let us look at the period in chronological stages, beginning with World War I. I will consider representative hymnodists and samples of their work rather than present an all-inclusive survey.

Table 24. British Hymnodists, 1915–1936

Date	Hymnodist	Opening Lines
1915	William Charter Piggott (1872–1943)	For those we love within the veil, Who once were comrades of our way
1916	Clifford Bax (1886–1962)	Turn back, O man, forswear thy foolish ways, Old now is earth, and more may count her days
1916	Howell Elvet Lewis (1860–1953)	Lord of light, whose name outshineth All the suns and stars of space
1916	Timothy Rees (1874–1939)	God of love and truth and beauty, Hallowed by Thy name
1916	Henry Arnold Thomas	Brother, who on thy heart didst bear The burden of our shame and sin
1918	Laurence Housman (1865–1959)	Father eternal, Ruler of creation, Spirit of life, which moved ere form was made
1919	Cyril Argentine Alington (1872–1955) and Ronald Knox	Awake, awake, put on thy strength, O Zion; God's purpose tarries, but his strength will stand fast
1921	Geoffrey Anketell Studdert-Kennedy	When through the whirl of wheels, and engines humming, Patiently powerful for sons of men
1925	Cyril Argentine Alington	Good Christian men, rejoice and sing
1925	George Wallace Briggs	Come, risen Lord, and deign to be our guest
1925	Percy Dearmer	Lo, in the wilderness, a voice, "Make straight the way," is crying
1925	William Charter Piggott	Heavenly Father, may Thy blessing
1925	Jan Struther	Lord of all hopefulness, Lord of all joy
1927	George Wallace Briggs	Son of the Lord most high, Who gave the worlds their birth
1930	Thomas Tiplady	Jesus, see Thy children Kneeling here tonight
1930	Thomas Tiplady	From Nazareth the Lord has come And walks in Galilee

Date	Hymnodist	Opening Lines
1930	Thomas Tiplady	O Ruler of the worlds of light That stand unveiled by silent light
1931	George Kennedy Allen Bell (1883–1958)	Christ is the King! O friends, rejoice; Brothers and sisters with one voice
1931	George Wallace Briggs (1875–1959)	Christ is the world's true light, Its Captain of salvation
1931	Percy Dearmer (1867–1936)	As the disciples, when Thy Son had left them, Met in a love-feast, joyfully conversing
1931	Percy Dearmer	Sing praise to God, who spoke through man In differing times and manners
1931	Jan Struther (1901–1953)	God, whose eternal mind Rules the round world over
1936	Jan Struther	When Mary brought her treasure

At first glance at Table 24 there emerges the notion that the initial six items—from Piggott to Housman—ought to be governed nicely by their historical context. If not reactions to the Great War, those hymns can easily be seen as reverberations from the scenes of its tragedies. Bax, for instance, points to a world caught up in strife, a world in which human beings, as children of the earth, find themselves "crowned with flame, / Still wilt not hear thine inner God proclaim— / 'Turn back, O man, forswear thy foolish ways.' " In the pieces by Lewis and by Rees, one may observe examples of prayer hymns. The former relies heavily upon such traditions as "Father, as in highest heaven / So on earth Thy will be done," and he comprehends, in the heaviness of the historical moment,

> the toil of lowly workers
> In some far outlying field;
> By the courage where the radiance
> Of the Cross is still revealed.

Rees, on the other hand, engages in a form of collective self-chastisement. Praying on behalf of "the conscience of the nation," he asks God to "remove our guilty blindness," a reference to people's willingness to maim and to kill one another without really knowing why. Nonetheless, the hymns of Piggott, Bax, Lewis, and Rees contain sufficient general sentiment to allow adaptation to contexts far outside their immediate historical boundaries.

The hymns of Henry Arnold Thomas and Laurence Housman cited in Table 24 may not enjoy such easy chronological transfer. "Brother, who on thy heart didst bear" clearly awaits the moment of world peace, the moment when "the burden of our shame and sin" can be lifted—or at least lightened. The piece responds well to a call for Christian service, but Thomas obviously considers the major event of the times as responsible for "sick and lame and maimed and blind." In the end, practically hand in hand with Rees, Thomas asks that "ours may be the holy task / To help and bless, to heal and save." Housman, however, does not attempt to smooth his own grief and despair over the issue of world war, and he leaves little doubt concerning his strong sense of pacifism: "By wars and tumults love is mocked, derided." Thus he builds his poem amid piles of harsh language and equally harsh imagery—amid envy, blindness, wrath, fear, jealousy, and lust. The world has gone mad, and in the final stanza, Housman poses the major question, "How shall we love Thee, holy, hidden Being, / If we love not the world which thou hast made?" No hymn tune written could dull the sharpness of that direct inquiry; no organ or choir could deter its passage from the printed page into the collective conscience of even the most insensitive congregation.

Those hymns composed "between the wars" serve well as models of the artificial calm that hung over the Western world during the 1920s and 1930s. The worshipers of those times, concerned with social and economic problems, witnessed extreme variations in original hymn compositions, which reflected both glances back into the past and gazes into the future. For example, in their piece on prophecy—"Awake, awake! put on Thy strength, O Zion"—Knox and Alington revealed once more the degree to which a hymn text could anchor itself in Scripture: its four six-line stanzas paraphrase passages from Isaiah, Habakkuk, Genesis, Revelation, Psalms, John, Luke, and Matthew—all of which combine to underscore the idea that "God's purpose tarries, but His will stands fast." In similar fashion, but without the quantity of obvious biblical paraphrase, Struther's wedding hymn, "God, whose eternal mind," addresses a God whose image has, traditionally, come forth with the utmost of clarity.

> God, who art Three in One,
>   All things comprehending,
> Wise Father, valiant Son
>   In the Spirit blending.

From the perspective of content, the hymn contains little that could possibly reveal its age, and should the proponents of the traditional concepts about marriage prevail, its sentiment and language will endure for at least another fifty years.

The congregational hymns of Percy Dearmer's have long been respected for holding to the middle ground between turn-of-the-century traditionalism and full-blown twentieth-century modernism. In a hymn entitled "Make Straight the Way" ("Lo, in the wilderness a voice"), he calls upon a God "Unchanged" and "unchanging" to stem "the creeds of hate, contempt, and fear / That crash and overturn us." In other words, he raises the major Christian moral and ethical concerns of post-World War I Britons, particularly those caught up in the rush toward the better life of the twentieth century (or at least a hope for such an existence). However, there seems nothing especially current about Dearmer's phrases or his figures. The Anglican divine may best be described as a skilled poet who knew clearly and on a distinctly religious level the relationship between the artist and his product.

> For all the poets, who have wrought
> Through music, words, and vision
> To tell the beauty of God's thought
> By art's sublime precision,
> Who bring our highest dreams to shape
> And help the soul in her escape,
> To God be thanks and glory.

Dearmer knew the craft of verse, and he seemed willing to test contemporary poetic form against the criteria of its adaptability to congregational song.

> As the disciples, when Thy Son had left them,
> Met in a love-feast, joyfully conversing,
> All the stored memory of the Lord's Supper
> fondly rehearsing.

There may indeed be moments when worshipers find Dearmer's lines difficult to sing; nonetheless, there are also congregational singers who prefer his regular measures to the more unconventional forms that blossomed during the 1970s and 1980s.

The shift from the neotraditional hymns of Percy Dearmer to those pieces bulging with the imagery of twentieth-century life and worship may be observed in a hymn by Geoffrey A. Studdert-Kennedy, with its stack of modern utensils: wheels, engines, furnaces, miners' picks, and workers' jackets. His industrial Christian fellowship hymn would hardly be termed erudite. To the contrary, the piece echoes "the boundless energy" of God. However, the hymnodist's deity represents a total updating of the conventional biblical vision of God. Studdert-Kennedy asks the worshiper to extol the virtues of an omnipotent laborer, to conjure forth the vision of

> God in a workman's jacket as before,
> Living again in the eternal gospel-story,
> Sweeping the shavings from His workshop floor.

Similarly, George Wallace Briggs, canon of Worcester and adviser to education authorities, strove hard to update the context of his hymns. In "Son of the Lord most high," he presents the congregational singer with a "humbly bred" image of Christ, a Son of God who labors "by His brethren's side" to fulfill His ministry of healing. Briggs describes Christ as a "lowly majesty, / Lofty in lowliness," working physically as well as spiritually to glorify the common lot. Nevertheless, the hymnodist achieves the same finality as his more traditionally minded predecessors, although the parting image stresses the individuality and uniqueness of Christ.

> Toiling by night and day,
> Himself oft burdened sore,
> Where hearts in bondage lay,
> Himself their burden bore.

Both Briggs and Studdert-Kennedy appeal directly to the industrial element within postwar England and Western society in general; both echoed the spirit of a new revival, a sociotheological awakening in which the energy of a new era complemented the renewal of religious commitment.

If the British hymnodists of the 1920s and 1930s believed in a renewal of faith, they also sensed the pulsation of a new positivism. They spoke out for a new world rising out of the tragedy and the despair of the recent war. In their hymnody, Christ not only heralds the arrival of that new moment, He takes His place at its head. "New life, new hope awakes," proclaimed George Briggs.

> The world has waited long,
> Has travailed long in pain;
> To heal its ancient wrong
> Come, Prince of Peace, and reign.

Brigg's concept of Christ cuts the darkness and the pessimism of the world and emerges as a bright beacon of hope, the world's "Captain of salvation." Thomas Tiplady, on the other hand, seems a bit softer, slightly more tender and even pastoral, not at all caught up on the industrial motif. His Christ walks in "beauty, grace and power," like "the dawn in summer time / Awakes the voice of praise." The poet expresses sentiments not far removed from those of Byron's maiden, "whose love is innocent." Despite the one or two tinges of romanticism, the Christ in Tiplady's hymn still comes to lead a new world, to sever "the bonds of sin and fear" that—in the familiar theme from Saint John's Gospel "the truth shall make us free." G.K.A. Bell sounds much the same theme and the same tone, summarizing effectively the pronouncements of his contemporaries: "New lamps be lit, new tasks begun, / And the whole Church at last be one." The entire final stanza of Bell's "Christ is King! O friends, rejoice" emphasizes an ecumenical spirit that parallels the "new life, new hope" of Briggs and the "sweet celestial grace" envisioned by Thomas Tiplady.

The next period to be considered extends from the end of World War II to 1960 (see Table 25).

Table 25. British Hymnodists, 1945–1960

Date	Hymnodist	Opening Lines
1945	George Bradford Caird	Not far beyond the sea, nor high Above the heavens, but very high
1949	Thomas Charles Hunter-Clare	God of the pastures, hear our prayer, Lord of the growing seed
1950	Cyril Argentine Alington	Ye that know the Lord is gracious, Ye for whom a corner-stone
1950	Cyril Argentine Alington	Lord of beauty, Thine the splendour
1950	Cyril Argentine Alington	O loving Father, to Thy care

Date	Hymnodist	Opening Lines
1950	Cyril Argentine Alington	O Father, by whose sovereign sway
1950	Albert Frederick Bayly	O Lord of every shining constellation That wheels in splendour through the midnight sky
1950	Albert Frederick Bayly	What doth the Lord require For praise and offering?
1950	Thomas Charles Hunter-Clare	Lord, Thy Word hath taught That our deeds are naught
1951	Leslie Thomas John Arlott	We watched the winter turn its back, Its grip is loosened now
1951	Leslie Thomas John Arlott	God, whose form is all creation, Take the gratitude we give
1951	Leslie Thomas John Arlott	By the rutted roads we follow
1951	Albert Frederick Bayly	Thy love, O God, has all mankind created
1951	George Bradford Caird	Almighty Father, Who for us Thy Son didst give That men and nations in His precious death might live
1951	Henry Child Carter	Give me, O Christ, the strength that is in Thee, That I may stand in every evil hour
1951	Andrew Young	Lord, by whose breath all souls and seeds are living With life that is and life that is to be
1954	George Wallace Briggs	God, who hast given us power to sound Depths hitherto unknown
1957	George Wallace Briggs	Jesus, whose all-redeeming love No penitent did scorn
1958	Albert Frederick Bayly	A glorious company we sing

As mentioned at the outset of this discussion, the closer one focuses upon the "hymnodic present," the greater the difficulty in determining the neat niches for the grouping of hymnodists and their hymns. However, even though the "pockets" may become smaller, they do indeed exist, and the student of hymnody may even discover three or four surprises. For example, three poems from the listing in Table 25 demonstrate once again the importance of Scripture in hymnodic composition. George Caird's "Not far beyond the sea, nor high" seeks to guide human beings out of the darkness of yet another world war and onto a plain of "truth and light." The hymnodist chooses a path of four stanzas lined with seven distinct paraphrases of Scripture, and his purpose resounds clearly from within the second section (with its three New Testament paraphrases):

> The babe in Christ Thy Scriptures feed
> With milk sufficient for His need,
>   The nurture of the Lord.
> Beneath life's burden and its heat
> The full-grown man finds stronger meat
>   In Thy unfailing Word.

Caird traverses similar ground in his stewardship hymn, "Almighty Father, who for us Thy Son didst give," with seven of the sixteen lines originating directly from the Gospels and the Pauline Epistles. In addressing those who "know the Lord is gracious," Alington smoothly slides scriptural references beneath his already traditional pronouncements.

> Ye, a royal generation,
>   Tell the tidings of your birth,
> Tidings of a new creation
>   To an old and weary earth.

Nonetheless, the effect of a "new creation" upon an "old and weary earth" catapults Alington's apparent traditionalism into the midst of a recognizable mid-twentieth-century setting.

Four other pieces from the list in Table 25 can carry the label of prayer hymns, although form rather than content governs the classification. According to Louis Benson (*Hymnody*, pp. 162–163), "The Hymn of Prayer is rather one in the form of prayer, with its petitions versified. Its contents cover life. No one can limit them except by abridging our desires. All we can demand is that the subject-matter be submitted to the same tests that determine edification in the hymns of experience." Therefore, in calling upon God to send His spirit down among the peoples of the world, T. C. Hunter-Clare asks worshipers to pray for "love that never faileth, / Love that o'er all foes prevaileth." Hunter-Clare takes his cue from 1 Corinthians, while Henry Carter relies upon Ephesians 6:10–15 to offer a prayer for Christian strength, specifically for "the armour that can guard, / Over my breast Thy blood-bought righteousness. George Briggs (see Table 24) offered two prayer hymns for worshipers of the 1950s and beyond. His piece, "Science," sounds a strong note of caution—"That as to knowledge we attain / We may in wisdom grow"; from another view, his hymn for sinners, directed to the "Physician of the soul," advises worshipers (sinners and faithful alike) to seek "the pitying love of God."

Consider, also, another group of hymns from this fifteen-year period following World War II, a group of congregational songs that constitute a miscellany of tone and subject matter. For instance, Hunter-Clare's hymn on the theme of labor begins with an address to "God of the pastures," moves on to "God of the rivers" and of "the swelling sea," proceeds through the "dark and sombre mine" and the city's "throbbing heart," and comes to rest upon an appeal to "authority and right," a plea to "God of the nations." Bayly tends to stockpile the modern images of God, to classify them in terms of "the secrets of Thy work on high"; "the atom's hidden forces" and an "awakening life in cell and tissue" both "help us trace, from birth to

final issue / The sure unfolding of Thine ageless plan."
Still, Bayly does not lose sight of the conscience of man, of
the knowledge that God remains responsible for whatever
successes human beings may achieve. "How shall my soul
fulfill," the poet asks, "God's law so hard and high?" The
answer comes in the final refrain of the hymn.

> Let Christ endue Thy will
> With grace to fortify
>   Then justly;
>   In mercy
> Thou'lt humbly walk with God.

Finally, L.T.J. Arlott offers two country hymns (pastoral rather than political) of an obviously practical nature.
Despite the ancient themes, he provides his worshipers
with some freshly hewn imagery: the "ambushed frost that
kills by night" complements "the storm with bludgeoned
hand"; to counter those, Arlott asks for "soft rain" and
"gold and red" sun to "Give us our daily bread." God's
heaven and God's earth emerge as an agricultural creation
governed by an interesting concept of "our calendar of
care" that, in the end, plots "the crops of Your creation."
Andrew Young's hymn of thanksgiving focuses, in similar
fashion, upon the visual products of God's craft. The
worshiper praises the virtues of a "summer's golden sea"
that has yielded the harvest. Only superficially does that
product represent human effort, for it actually exists as the
result of "Thee, who art our living Bread."

The 1960s was a period that appears to have been
most productive for British hymnody—once again, variety
of theme and form emerged as the order of the day. The
decade saw not only the publication of individual hymn
texts in periodical literature, but also witnessed the publication of a number of hymn collections representing theologically independent individuals as well as traditionally
organized religious institutions. The former began to
compete seriously with the latter in the pews of fairly well

established congregations. However, as tempting as it may be to examine complete volumes, we must remain fixed to our purpose and focus almost entirely upon the hymn texts themselves, of which the following (Table 26) may serve to represent the sixth decade of the twentieth century in Great Britain.

Table 26. British Hymnodists, the 1960s

Date	Hymnodist	Opening Lines
1961	Timothy Dudley-Smith	Tell out, my soul, the greatness of the Lord! Unnumbered blessings, give my spirit voice
1962	Sydney Carter	Catch the bird of heaven, Lock him in a cage of gold
1962	Sydney Carter	Every star shall sing a carol. Every creature, high or low
1962	Sydney Carter	It was on a Friday morning that they took me from the cell, And I saw they had a carpenter to crucify as well
1964	Ian Fraser	Christ burning Past all suns
1964	John Brownlow Geyer	Our risen Lord we will adore Who broke the gates of hell
1964	George Osborn Gregory	Go ye, said Jesus, and preach the Word
1964	David Stanton Goodall	When the pious prayers we make Are a wall of pride
1964	Richard G. Jones	God of concrete, God of steel, God of piston, and of wheel
1964	Brian Arthur Wren	God, your glory we have seen in your Son
1964	Brian Arthur Wren	Lord Christ, the Father's mighty Son, Whose work upon the Cross was done
1967	Albert Frederick Bayly	Lord of all goods, our gifts we bring to Thee
1967	Albert Frederick Bayly	O God, Thy life-creating love
1967	Ian Ferguson	"Am I my brother's keeper?" The muttered cry was drowned

Date	Hymnodist	Opening Lines
1967	Frederick Hermann Kaan	If you have ears, then listen To what the Spirit says
1967	Frederick Hermann Kaan	We meet you, O Christ, In many a guise
1967	Frederick Hermann Kaan	Lord, as we rise to leave this shell of worship Called to the risk of unprotected living
1967	Frederick Hermann Kaan	As we break the bread And take the life of wine
1967	Erik Routley	All who love and serve your city, All who bear its daily stress
1968	Frederick Hermann Kaan	For the healing of the nations Lord, we pray with one accord
1968	Frederick Hermann Kaan	Now let us from this table rise Renewed in body, mind and soul
1969	Emily Chisholm	Peter feared the Cross for himself and his Master; Peter tempted Jesus to turn and go back
1969	Ian Fraser	Lord, bring this day to pass When forest, rock and hill
1969	John Brownlow Geyer	We know that Christ is raised and dies no more: Embraced by futile death He broke its hold
1969	Rosamund E. Herklots	"Forgive our sins as we forgive," You taught us, Lord, to pray
1969	Michael Hewlett	When God almighty came to be one of us, Masking the glory of His golden train
1969	Donald W. Hughes	Creator of the earth and skies, To whom the words of life belong
1969	Frederick Pratt-Green	Christ is the world's Light, He and none other; Born in the darkness, He became our Brother
1969	Frederick Pratt-Green	When Jesus walked by Galilee And cried to Andrew, "Follow me!"
1969	James Quinn	Angel voices, richly blending
1969	James Quinn	Father, most loving, listen to Thy children

Date	Hymnodist	Opening Lines
1969	James Quinn	Forth in the peace of Christ we go: Christ to the world with joy we bring
1969	James Quinn	God is love, and where true love is, God Himself is there; Here in Christ we gather, love of Christ our calling
1969	James Quinn	Now at last He takes His throne
1969	Malcolm Stewart	In a garden one night on a bed of bracken and grief Two men slept while another man cried in grief
1969	Malcolm Stewart	You are blessed who are poor in desires, Never seeking the riches of earth, which the fires

    The decade of the 1960s marks a period of political, social, and theological extremes in Britain—all brought about by problems arising from war and technology, from complex domestic and international tensions. Although the hymnody certainly reflects those tensions and problems, there were moments of hymnodic respite—a middle ground, so to speak—wherein the worshiper could grasp a more serene and traditional view of the mid-twentieth century. Frederick Pratt-Green writes of the uniqueness of Christ, but in the context of scriptural imagery his Christ remains "the world's Peace, He and none other; / No man can serve Him and despise His brother." Pratt-Green's hymn in honor of Saint Andrew ("When Jesus walked by Galilee") comes through as a conventional paraphrase, but the twentieth-century congregational singer may relate, with a sense of hope and commitment, to the refrain from each of the five four-line stanzas, "Would I were such a saint!" James Quinn also strides the middle road of British hymnody, although at times his litany echoes the frankness and the directness of the late 1960s:

God is love, and where true love is, God Himself is there;
Here in Christ we gather, love of Christ our calling.
Christ our love, is with us, gladness be His greeting.

Still, Quinn holds to conventional imagery and, as in "Forth in the peace of Christ we go," he conveys the idea of a truly personal commitment—a far cry from the denominational utterances of his nineteenth-century predecessors. "We are the Church," he maintains; governed by the bidding of Christ, nations will seek and ultimately find "True peace, true love, to all mankind."

Slightly to one side of such traditional moderates as Pratt-Green and Quinn there exist a number of British hymnodists who record the sights and sounds of the 1960s. They seek to transmit what they see and what they hear by way of the worship service. Thus, Richard Jones finds a ready repository for his images of power, speed, truth, and love.

> Lord of cable, Lord of rail,
> Lord of motorway and mail;
> Lord of rocket, Lord of flight,
> Lord of soaring satellite.

Erik Routley's meter may be more convenient for singers than that of Jones; yet, the former's concerns seem no less current, as he reminds worshipers of the "daily stress" of the city, the cries for "peace and justice" during a time of "wasted work and wasted play." Then one needs to consider Fred Kaan, who moves around a number of hymnodic categories with considerable facility. His hymn for Human Rights Day touches the heart of a sensitive but very real theme from the 1960s:

> All that kills abundant living,
> Let it from the earth be banned;
> Pride of status, race or schooling,
> Dogmas keeping man from man.

Kaan's quest for justice in a nation known historically for its status and tradition carries through even to the post-Communion ceremony as he asks the "father God" to "help us to accept with joy / The challenge of tomorrow's day." Such transition marks Kaan's own hymnodic route, since he began his career as a hymnodist by concentrating upon the post-Communion and baptism, then eventually shifted his focus to the complexities arising from urbanization, industrialization, human rights, war, and peace.

Prayer hymns continued to be written in noticeable quantity during the period from 1960 to 1969. They appear especially pertinent and applicable when placed beside the drama and the trauma of the times. Although David Goodall offers a commentary about pious prayers rather than an actual prayer, he does force his worshipers to examine the motives behind the expression of their faith. He cautions against prayers becoming a "wall of pride" surrounding "our lust and greed," thereby causing people to lose sight of the most important of all images: "then see Him conquering come to die / For the world He loves." Brian Wren, who may become the central figure upon which late-twentieth-century British and American hymnody will focus, offers a clear prayer for Christian unity, one that asks to "make all our scattered churches one, / That the world may believe." Three of his four five-line stanzas end on the hope "that the world may believe," which constitutes the pattern by which the peoples of the world may eventually reconcile their major political, theological, and social differences. In asking for forgiveness from sin and pardon for an "unforgiving heart / That broods on wrongs, and will not let old bitterness depart," Rosamund Herklots directs congregational singers to another mode of reconciliation—one between God and humanity, after which perhaps "our lives will spread Your peace."

The Scripture-based hymns of the 1960s would fit into a number of the categories already discussed. Dudley-

Smith's "Magnificat" (Luke 1:46–54) has the effect of a contemporary litany, as the poet begins each of his four stanzas with "Tell out, my soul"; then in the final four lines of the hymn, he creates a chant effect through reliance upon some strategic repetition.

> Tell out, my soul, the glories of His Word!
> Firm is His purpose, and His mercy sure.
> Tell out, my soul, the greatness of the Lord
> To children's children and for evermore!

Geyer's hymn, "Our risen Lord we will adore," with its six paraphrases of and references to Scripture, appears fairly conventional in form and language, while he anchors his baptism-resurrection hymn almost totally to Romans 6:9 ("knowing that Christ being raised from the dead dieth no more; death hath no more dominion over him") and the idea that "A new Creation comes to light and grows." If Ferguson begins his piece with the question of Genesis 4:9—"Am I my brother's keeper?"—he ends the poem by transposing the point of inquiry into a clear statement: "I *am* my brother's keeper." He thus creates a highly rhythmic and obviously contemporary closing stanza.

> As long as people hunger,
>   As long as people thirst,
> And ignorance and illness
>   And warfare do their worst,
> As long as there's injustice
>   In any of God's lands,
> I am my brother's keeper;
>   I dare not wash my hands.

Although Donald Hughes's hymn on penitence— "Creator of the earth and skies"—owes considerable debt to John and Philippians, its conventional language, imagery, and theme serve as stark contrast to one of the most interesting hymns written during the 1960s: Emily Chisholm's "Peter feared the Cross for himself and his Master."

Her seven stanzas of six lines each presents an *abcdeb* rhyme scheme (which means that she really writes free verse), while each one seems, visually, to represent what Peter feared.

> Peter feared the Cross for himself and his Master;
> Peter tempted Jesus to turn and go back.
>   O Lord, have mercy,
>   Lighten our darkness.
>   We've all been tempters,
>   Our light is black.

Shapes and pictures and images exist principally in the mind's eye, which means that everyone does not see the same things. At any rate, the advantage of Chisholm's hymn is its congregational flexibility. One can place it within the traditional context of singing by worshipers during service, or employ it for responsive singing—by choir and congregation, by soloist and congregation, or by solo reader and singing congregation—to inject variety into the service.

The folk hymn of the 1960s presents the imaginative congregation with a wide range of options. The language and the meter of the folk hymn differ drastically from earlier, more traditional forms—so much so that few (if any) of the immediately recognized hymn tunes of the past can adapt to them. The advantage, of course, is that the music cannot conveniently obscure the sense of the poem; in fact, the accompaniment of folk hymns by a single, soft instrument—or even no accompaniment at all—forces the worshiper to pronounce and to concentrate upon one idea at a time.

In the refrain from Sydney Carter's "Catch the bird of heaven," one understands how, by itself, the rhythm of the folk hymn can serve as sufficient musical accompaniment.

> Ah! the bird of heaven!
>   Follow where the bird has gone;
> Ah! the bird of heaven!
>   Keep on traveling on.

When he chooses, Carter can be both folksy and traditional, as in the lines "God above, man below, / Holy is the name I know." However, he can also bring a frown of concern to the thoughtful worshiper's brow.

> Now Barabbas was a killer, and they let Barabbas go,
> But You are being crucified for nothing here below.
> Your God is up in heaven, and He doesn't do a thing:
> With a million angels watching, who never turn a wing.
> "It's God they ought to crucify instead of you and me."
> I said to the Carpenter a-hanging on the tree.

The entire text of "It was on Friday morning" needs to be discussed, analyzed, and explicated before a congregation can express its purpose, its tone, and its language within the context of a particular worship service or church-related event. The advantage of the folk hymn lies in that very point: the form allows (it may force) congregations to view and then express the hymn as a true representative of creative art, as a folk poem set to music. It emerges from the pages of the hymnal as something more than merely a song.

Ian Fraser sees Christ in a variety of sharp images and literary forms that affect the sensitive natures of those who follow Him: "Christ burning / Past all suns," "Christ, holding / Atoms in one / Loom of light and power," "Christ, festive / In gay bird." The poetry of the folk hymn can charge worshipers with emotion, fill them with pure joy, and cause them to participate fully and sincerely in the spirit of the piece.

> Old men and maidens, young men and children
>   Black ones and coloured ones and white ones, too,
> God on His birthday, and to eternity,
>   God took upon Himself the need of you.

Michael Hewlett does not create simply a themeless sense of joy and excitement; in his folk-poetic environment, "love needs a universe of folk to love," which in turn parallels the final line of his hymn, "God took upon Himself the need of you."

An examination of Fred Kaan's folk hymns reveals immediately why his work remains extremely popular among congregational singers of all ages and of all persuasions. His work conveys an overall informality of language and rhythm—joyful but not exuberant, serious but not erudite, lucid but not overly folksy.

> If you have buds for tasting
> The apple of God's eye,
> Then go, enjoy creation
> And people on the way.

Kaan traverses the various avenues of life, from the palace to the shack, proclaiming what he terms "the rising love of Christ!" There may be moments for him when he wishes to "lift from our life the blanket of convention," but his multiple images of God and Christ serve well to unify the various, extreme, and unexpected patterns of human existence. On the surface, Kaan's hymns appear calmer than those of David Goodall, who reflects the true spirit of late-twentieth-century individualism. One is not surprised when asked to cry out,

> I want to go out,
> I want to go home.
> I want to be single,
> I want to belong.
> I want to grow up.
> I want to stay young.

For the traditionalist, the hymn takes on an aspect of human capriciousness, but it represents the individual who, with utmost sincerity, wants to know the way, the truth, and the direction of life. Goodall touches on a serious problem related directly to the folk hymn: worshipers may certainly come to an understanding of the poetic texts, either independently or in group discussion; whether they can actually bring themselves to sing the piece during a worship service, to treat it as a pertinent aspect of the order of worship, is another matter. For a number of individuals, the distance between Samuel Stone's "Church's one foundation" and David Goodall's "I want to go out, / I want to go home" may be too far and too difficult too travel.

Turning to the period from 1970 on, the principal problem may well center upon determining what to include and what to omit. British hymnody of this era has not suffered from any lack of creative activity. Once again, however, one can only seek examples as representative as possible. Contemporary hymnals continue to be storehouses of plenty, and congregations searching for new hymns (or for the newest hymns) need not look far or long. Table 27 considers the hymnodic contributions of several poets, a number of whom have managed to make the transition from previous decades.

Table 27. British Hymnodists, 1970–1986

Date	Hymnodist	Opening Lines
1970	Albert Frederick Bayly	From age to age God summons men To take the pilgrim way
1970	James Quinn	Easter glory fills the sky
1971	Albert Frederick Bayly	Joy wings to God our song, For all life holds
1971	Albert Frederick Bayly	Good news for this new age Our song of Christmas brings
1971	Brian Foley	See, Christ was wounded for our sake And bruised and beaten for our sin
1971	Brian Foley	Lord, as I wake I turn to you, Yourself the first thought of my day
1971	Frederick Hermann Kaan	Sing we of the modern city
1971	Frederick Pratt-Green	Love is the greatest of the three, And Faith one step behind
1971	Frederick Pratt-Green	When, in man's music, God is glorified, And adoration leaves no room for pride

Date	Hymnodist	Opening Lines
1971	Brian Arthur Wren	I come with joy to meet my Lord, Forgiven, loved and free
1972	Luke Connaughton	Bread from the earth, wine from the soil, Adam made of clay: Bring to the Lord—sing to the Lord!—gifts of red and gold
1972	Frederick Hermann Kaan	While still the earth is full of people, And earth to man her increase gives
1972	Frederick Hermann Kaan	Faith, while trees are still in blossom Plans the picking of the fruit
1972	Frederick Hermann Kaan	Modern man has the city for his home, Where his life is walled in by want and dread
1973	Archibald Macbride Hunter	Though in God's form He was, Christ Jesus would not snatch
1973	Ian Robertson Pitt-Watson	God's perfect law revives the soul
1973	Ian Robertson Pitt-Watson	O God, be gracious to me in Thy love
1973	Ian Robertson Pitt-Watson	Thou art before me, Lord, Thou art behind, And Thou above me has spread out Thy hand
1973	Frederick Pratt-Green	Rejoice in God's saints This day of all days
1974	Timothy Dudley-Smith	Not to us be glory given But to Him who reigns above
1975	John K. Gregory	Good is our God who made this place Whereon our race in plenty liveth
1975	Carol Micklem	We praise you, Lord, for all that's true and pure— Clean lives, clear water, and an honest mind
1975	Carol Micklem	Give to me, Lord, a thankful heart And a discerning mind
1975	Brian Arthur Wren	Lord Jesus, if I love and serve my neighbour Out of my knowledge, leisure, power, or wealth
1975	Brian Arthur Wren	Thank you, Lord, for water, soil, and air— Large gifts supporting everything that lives

Date	Hymnodist	Opening Lines
1976	Erik Routley	In praise of God meet duty and delight, Angels and creatures, men and spirits bless'd
1977	Frederick Pratt-Green	It is God who holds the nations in the hollow of His hand; It is God whose light is shining in the darkness of the land
1980	Timothy Dudley-Smith	Lord, as the day begins Lift up our hearts in praise
1981	Timothy Dudley-Smith	Father on high, to whom we pray
1981	Timothy Dudley-Smith	Jesus, my breath, my light, my Lord
1981	Timothy Dudley-Smith	Remember Lord, the world You made
1982	Frederick Pratt-Green	Let us all, in hymns of praise, Bear witness with one voice
1982	Frederick Pratt-Green	Prepare us, Lord, in quietness of mind To meet You where our jaded spirits find
1983	Rae E. Phillips Whitney	In the beginning, Before pain and sinning
1984	Frederick Pratt-Green	Jesus, I know you came To seek and find me
1984	Christopher Idle	As the light upon the river At the rising of the sun
1985	Timothy Dudley-Smith	Behold a broken world, we pray, where want and war increase
1985	Rae E. Phillips Whitney	Lead me from death to life, From falsehood into truth
1985	Brian Arthur Wren	We want to care for blind or evil enemies, giving blessings, meaning what we say
1986	Brian Arthur Wren	Welcome the wild one, the desert declaimer, urgently, awesomely, crying his news

Throughout this discussion of late-twentieth-century British hymnody, I have focused primarily upon distinct social and theological themes. At this point there appears a definite advantage to concentrating upon individual hymnodists, particularly since certain themes tend to carry over from poet to poet, from hymn to hymn, from decade to decade. Fred Kaan, for example, always perfectly at home in the city, continues to rely upon the language and the imagery of the busy, crowded urban moment. His "Sing we of the modern city" incorporates such contemporary signs of activity as graphs, masses, numbers, and statistics into his declaration that Christ has proven "By his timeless presence" that "People matter, people count!" Even when translating the words and the ideas of another poet—as in João Dias de Araujo's "Modern man has the city for his home"—Kaan seems to have no trouble transcribing "the dark of our noisy city life" and the "skyscrapers blotting out the sun." Through all of those massive images conjured by the technicians, the poet's Christ still manages to be "the light to shine," that which effectively conceals 'the high-rising blocks of steel and stone." Of all contemporary British hymnodists, Kaan spends the most time photo-graphing and recording the sights and sounds of the present.

Two praise hymns by Timothy Dudley-Smith assume fairly conventional features and appear anchored to traditional form and traditional language. His "Not to us be glory given" paraphrases Psalm 115, while his morning hymn ("Lord, as the day begins") recognizes that "Christ be in words and skill, / Serving each other's needs." Wren's Communion hymn, "I come with joy to meet my Lord," raises again the issue of Christian unity and the idea that the love of Christ "makes us one, / And strangers now are friends." However, the hymnodist demonstrates that he remains a true child of the present; in his ecology hymn, "Thank you, Lord, for water, soil, and air," Wren seeks, on one hand, forgiveness for man's "reckless plundering and waste," and on the other, asks for divine guidance in reestablishing "A hope for us and ages yet unborn." There exists in certain of Wren's hymns a rare quality of urgency tempered by respect and reserve, and those traits make his hymns acceptable to a wide range of congregational singers—especially to those who cannot adapt (easily or readily or willingly) to the folk-hymn movement.

One example of how certain British hymnodists attempt to reach the largest possible audience may be seen in Fred Pratt-Green's "Rejoice in God's saints," a piece written to celebrate, at Norwich, the six hundredth anniversary of the *Revelations of Divine Love*. Pratt-Green wrote two versions; the first looks directly upon the occasion.

> Rejoice in their courage,
> Their spiritual skill:
> In Julian of Norwich
> Rejoice all who will!

The second transcends the occasion—for those without knowledge of or interest in Lady Juliana of Norwich (1343–1443) and her *Sixteen Revelations of Divine Love*—to that which promotes the celebration of any saint. Thus, the hymnodist altered this stanza to read,

> Their joy in exploring
> Far reaches of prayer,
> Their depth of adoring,
> Lord, help us to share.

Even his piece on the occasion of Queen Elizabeth II's Silver Jubilee, "It is God who holds the nations in the hollow of His hand," contains strong declarations that apply to the entire human race, not merely to the inhabitants of Great Britain and the Commonwealth: "May all races live together, share its riches, be at peace." Such sentiments appear more at home at the headquarters of the United Nations than at Buckingham, Windsor, or Edinburgh. The fact that a Presbyterian church in La Porte, Indiana, and a Zion Lutheran congregation in Wooster, Ohio, can commission hymns from a Methodist minister (himself a former Congregationalist) from Norwich, England, tells us all something about the catholicity of the English hymn during the latter decades of the twentieth century.

So does Albert Bayly. His hymn, "From age to age God summons men"—written in England for the three hundred fiftieth anniversary of the Pilgrims' departure for America—translates history for the present generation on both sides of the Atlantic Ocean. The hymnodist writes of "A great new world," of "God's new world," governed by a vision of and a call to a God "whose help our fathers knew." In his Christmas hymn, which he entitles "Good News for This New Age," Bayly appears more lighthearted, more effervescent—perhaps caught up in the sheer joy of the occasion.

> Good news for this new age,
> Our song of Christmas brings;
> Around this troubled world
> God's word of healing rings.
> Sing joy, sing peace, sing freedom, life,
> For Christ is born to end man's strife.

Bayly manages to hold on to his vision of God. Practically every line of almost every one of his hymns forces the focus of singers upward; the lines cry out for people to probe, to reflect upon "the secrets of Thy work on high." For that purpose, he never seems to lose sight of the relationship between an ageless God and twentieth-century people, the latter confronted with coming to grips with what Bayly so aptly terms "Thine ageless plan."

Samples from the works of the remaining hymnodists who claim attention in this discussion would comprise a representative miscellany of late-twentieth-century British congregational song. The reader can easily contrast the long, loud, tambourine-like lines of Luke Connoughton ("Bring to the Lord—sing to the Lord!—gifts of red and gold") to the familiar and regular appearance of one of Brian Foley's stanzas.

> Lord, as I wake and turn to You,
>   Yourself the first thought of my day:
> My King, my God, whose help is sure,
>   Yourself the help for which I pray.

John Gregory, in his offertory hymn, takes his metrical cue from Robert Bridges' 1899 *Yattendon Hymnal.*

> Good is our God who made this place
> Whereon our race in plenty liveth.
> Great is the praise to Him we owe,
> That we may show 'tis He that giveth.

A. M. Hunter demonstrates that a hymn may be built upon free verse and a three-line stanza.

> Though in God's form He was,
> Christ Jesus would not snatch
> At parity with God.

Caryl Micklem provides singers with four lines of free verse, but manages to end the third and fourth lines of each of four stanzas (in "We praise you Lord!") with "hearts" and "things."

British hymnodists continue to praise God through a variety of rhyme schemes, poetic forms, and images. As poets, they differ from their "secularist" brothers and sisters in terms of audience and purpose—in terms of how and when others will pronounce their poems as congregational songs. Pitt-Watson, for example, in his paraphrase of Psalm 139 (from the *New English Bible*), understands that unique relationship between poet-hymnodist and congregation, and he relates with equal certainty the problems facing the hymnodist writing for Britons of the late twentieth century.

> Search me, O God, search me and know my heart,
>   Try me, O God, my mind and spirit try;
> Keep me from any path that gives Thee pain,
>   And lead me in the everlasting way.

Pitt-Watson skillfully holds on to the repetitive motif that has characterized psalmodic translation and paraphrase since the early seventeenth century. Only his sounds have changed. Rae Whitney confronts similar problems on a less personal but still highly eucmenical plain, and in her hymn for the Sixth Assembly of the World Council of Churches, "In the beginning, before pain and sinning," she declares how "God's Spirit moves us / To tell how God loves us." And finally, the noted hymnodist-hymnologist-composer Erik Routley, six years before his death, wrote a hymn with but a single world title, "Praise," that now seems to identify the scope and the purpose of the British hymnodists of the later twentieth century.

> In praise the artist and the craftsman meet,
> Inspired, obedient, patient, practical;
> In praise join instrument and voice and mind
> To make one music for the Lord of all.

If that stanza does not satisfactorily identify the purpose of contemporary British hymnody, then perhaps one might consider another statement by Routley, this one in prose. "The hymnody of tomorrow," he maintained, constitutes "the developing counterpoint of good conversation. It is a conversation which will continue for a long time yet."

The question of how much longer cannot be answered readily. This discussion of twentieth-century British hymnody, with its references to individuals and examples of hymnodic titles and passages, has attempted to provide some general indication of recent trends, of future directions. Beyond that, the readers will have to end for themselves, examining carefully the pages of hymnals and collections of hymnodic poetry. In addition, large libraries will house information on the Hymn Society of Great Britain and Ireland (founded 1936; 7 Little Cloister, Westminster Abbey, London SW1P 3PL) and the Society for Promoting Christian Knowledge (or SPCK, founded 1698; Holy Trinity Church, Marylebone Road, London

NW1 4DU)—two of several organizations existing as sources for recent hymn texts. As Erik Routley suggested, hymnody continues as an art form that will never cease to be, a form whose creative machinery will never cease to function. Therefore, individual worshipers and congregations must themselves never cease in their search for texts and tunes to fit both their individual and collective needs.

Chapter Eight
AMERICA, AMERICA,
GOD SHED HIS GRACE ON THEE!

To FULLY APPRECIATE THE opening chapters in the history of American hymnody, one needs to recall, if only momentarily, the transition from psalmody to hymnody that occurred in England during the seventeenth and eighteenth centuries. The individual interested in American hymnody needs, first, to visualize certain hymnodic parallels between Great Britain and the American colonies; then proceed to the study of American psalmody; and then observe, during the seventeenth century and the first half of the eighteenth century, the colonial American psalter and its influence over the hymn collections published in the United States—principally in Philadelphia, Boston, and New York—between 1795 and 1835. Since the issue of psalmody in Britain and America appears in Chapter 4, "Psalter and Psalm Paraphrase" (see particularly Tables 8 and 16), the discussion in this chapter will focus upon the initial stages of American hymnody.

The dent in the armor of American psalmody came about when Mennonites and Moravians emigrated to the New World and brought with them their songs, songbooks, and hymn collections, which consisted of German texts that eventually gained wider acceptance with the appearance of English-language editions published in America. Then in the middle and late eighteenth century, prompted by the general lack of spirit of psalmody, and encouraged by the Evangelical zeal of George Whitefield, American imprints of Isaac Watts and John and Charles Wesley attempted to provide Americans with alternatives to chanting psalm paraphrases. The opening chapter in the hymnody of the United States of America would soon become a written reality.

The immediate consideration for the study of a truly American hymnody, or hymnody by those labeled truly American, concentrates specifically upon two figures: Samuel Davies (1723–1761) and Timothy Dwight (1752–1817). Davies, president of New Jersey Presbyterian College at Princeton (having succeeded Jonathan Edwards), followed closely the sound and the sense of Isaac Watts. His principal poetic piece, "Great God of wonders! all Thy ways / Are watchless, godlike, and divine," appears as an exercise in the rhetoric of hymnody. At the outset, he extols the glories of God's creative acts and the divine forgiveness of human sins—the latter being described as "Thy grand prerogative." Each of the five stanzas terminates with a dual question, "Who is a pardoning God like Thee? / Or who has grace so rich and free?" Davies undoubtedly has confidence in what he terms "The godlike miracle of love," but he seems terribly overwhelmed by the incomparable power of God's influence over the entire world.

Dwight, a member of the American literati, served as president of Yale College and editor (for the General Association of Connecticut) of an edition of Isaac Watts's *Psalms of David* (1800)—in which he included a number of his own paraphrases of psalms. Assuming an attitude somewhat different from that of Davies, Dwight approached the glory of God with utmost confidence, completely assured by the common image of "Jesus, Thou Friend divine, / Our Saviour and our King." His paraphrase of Psalm 137—with asides to Deuteronomy and Isaiah—remains a clear picture of the relationship between God and the very institution that has been established as a symbol of divine will and divine power on earth.

> I love Thy kingdom, Lord,
> The house of Thine abode,

> The Church our blest Redeemer saved
> With His own precious blood.

Dwight's hymn underscores the entire issue of human faith, of the human commitment to "The highest glories earth can yield, / And brighter bliss of heaven." A careful reading of Dwight's hymns and paraphrases from Scripture reveals a distinct relationship between those odes and the longer poetic pieces—for instance, *The Conquest of Canaan* (1785), *Greenfield Hill* (1794), and *The Triumph of Infidelity* (1788). As poet or as hymnodist, Dwight defended Calvinist orthodoxy while keeping both eyes open for the images associated with Connecticut and the overall rural American scene.

Once congregational song in the United States emerged from the protective influence of British psalmody and British Nonconformist hymnody, it assumed, during the first half of the nineteenth century, its own sound and sense as fashioned by its own hymnodists. Then one can embark on a substantive discussion of American hymnody, which, insofar as it pertains to the early part of the nineteenth century, has an extremely rich poetic heritage—not all of it originally intended for congregational worship. Consider, for example, the summary seen in Table 28.

Table 28. American Hymnody, 1817–1840

Date	Hymnodist	Opening Lines
1817	Henry Ware, Jr.	Lift your glad voice in triumph on high, For Jesus has risen, and man cannot die
1824	George Washington Doane	Thou art the Way; to Thee alone From sin and death we flee
1824	John Pierpont	O Thou to whom in ancient time The lyre of Hebrew bards was strung
1827	Sarah Elizabeth Miles	Thou Who didst stoop below To drain the cup of woe

Date	Hymnodist	Opening Lines
1831	Ray Palmer	My faith looks up to Thee, Thou Lamb of Calvary
1832	Samuel Francis Smith	My country, 'tis of thee, Sweet land of liberty
1832	Thomas Hastings	Gently, Lord! Oh, gently lead us Through this lonely vale of tears
1832	Thomas Hastings	How calm and beautiful the morn
1832	Thomas Hastings	Return, O wand'rer, to thy rest
1832	Thomas Hastings	Hail to the brightness of Zion's glad morning
1833	Ralph Waldo Emerson	We love the venerable house Our fathers built to God
1833	Charles William Everest	"Take up thy Cross," the Savior said, "If thou wouldst my disciple be"
1834	Edmund Hamilton Sears	Calm on the list'ning star of night Come heaven's melodious strains
1837	John Greenleaf Whittier	Lord, for the things we see We trust the things to be
1840	William Cullen Bryant	Look from Thy sphere of endless day, O God of pity and of might

There is a tendency among present-day American worshipers to dismiss as totally inadequate both the theological sense and the poetic sounds of the pieces that early-nineteenth-century American hymnodists produced. Such dismissal and negative criticism, most of it highly generalized, have little justification. Nineteenth-century America quickly proved to the world that it existed as an entity separate from Great Britain. Politically, sociologically, and theologically, the United States had become separate from the culture that had given it birth. Indeed, the hymnody of the new republic sought to echo the optimism of its own people as they moved out of New England and the Middle Atlantic territories and cast their hearts westward. George Washington Doane (1799–1859), a member of the New England intellectual establishment, caught the spirit of that optimism. Ordained in the Episcopal Church, professor of belles lettres at Trinity College, Hartford, rector of Trinity Church, Boston, and bishop of New Jersey, he edited the first American imprint of John Keble's *Christian Year* (1834) and published his own collection, *Songs by the Way* (1824). One of the principal poems in the latter volume proclaims the very moment for the young nation's opportunity.

> Thou art the Way, the Truth, the Life;
> Grant us that way to know,
> That truth to keep, that life to win,
> Whose joys eternal flow.

Doane's "way" serves as a spiritual indicator rather than as a geographical sign, but the poet's concern for the protection of his nation's collective soul seems quite capable of penetrating heavy layers of contexts and occasions. All of early-nineteenth-century American hymnody cannot relate directly (or even peripherally) to westward expansion, but one would be less than prudent to ignore the influence of the times upon so widespread an activity as congregational worship.

Doane's hymns, although they certainly do reflect their creator's sensitivity to poetic language and meter, nonetheless appear stiff and conventional when placed beside the literati of American hymnodists—Bryant, Emerson, and Whittier. One may reasonably argue the unfairness of such a comparison, since Doane represents the term *hymnodist* in its purest and most legitimate sense, while Bryant, Emerson, and Whittier came to hymnody indirectly, through verse that others later adapted to congregational song. And only Emerson received ordination and held (if only for less than a year) a pastorate; Bryant was engaged in journalism and the law, while Whittier remained the self-educated controversialist and man of letters. In the end, however, comparisons tend to be on the basis of what actually exists rather than on what was intended to be. In the end, one must proceed directly to the texts.

Although critical commentators and historians of American literature have been quick to react to Bryant's Puritan heritage and Calvinist orthodoxy, they tend to minimize his debt to William Wordsworth and S. T. Coleridge, as well as his enthusiasm for the romantic ideal of nature. Together, the Calvinism and the romanticism produced hymns to which congregational singers (particularly those in New England) could become sincerely and easily committed. His "Look from Thy sphere of endless day" dwells upon a "land of light" that, although seemingly protected by a "God of pity and of might," nonetheless contains an abundance of persons who wander about in a state of theological confusion and "Hear not the message sent by Thee." For Bryant, a world without God was a stagnant pool, a waste, "a dreary scene, / That makes us sadden as we gaze." As with his secular poetry in general, the passages adapted as congregational hymns express indecision. One cannot escape the poet's pronouncements of an intellect possessed of varying thoughts about the relationships among nature, God, and human beings. Bryant represents the hymnody of the yearning heart and of the inquiring mind.

Emerson, always alert to the historical significance of any occasion, wrote "We love the venerable house" for the ordination of Chandler Robbins, who succeeded him in 1833 as minister of the Second Unitarian Church in Boston. As such, the piece would appear to have little or no value beyond the event that its poet celebrates. But Emerson skillfully concealed the occasion beneath a host of images reinforcing the "faith, and peace, and mighty love, / That from the Godhead flows." Robbins's ordination provided Emerson the opportunity to underscore the function of the Church and to explore, for those who had not yet undertaken the search, the relative positions of those who "live with God" and the Church that has functioned as a blessing to them.

John Greenleaf Whittier shall be discussed further in the context of the later part of the century. From 1817 to 1840, his "Lord, for the things we see" stands out as a strong, individualized commentary upon the social, moral, and ethical ills of the still-new world. Those poetic comments arise at least partly from the poet's equally strong Quaker background and beliefs as well as from his antislavery sentiments. Whittier could indeed rise to rhythmical and emotional heights when he proclaimed,

> The love of God and neighbour,
> An equal band at labour,
> The richer life where beauty
> Walks hand in hand with duty.

Although these lines might appear to have come from Isaac Watts's hymns for children, Whittier manages to rise above a superficial sense of morality. His principal concern is "what mankind shall be," a concern that he shared, most obviously, with Bryant and Emerson. Unfortunately the three of them came to hymnody only slightly and indirectly, which means that congregational singers have not received the maximum benefits from their theological and poetic qualities. Equally unfortunate, not all congregational singers can appreciate the transition from poet to hymnodist and from poem to hymn—as well as the opposite flow of that literary transformation.

However, the remaining hymnodists selected as representatives of the early nineteenth century need not be slighted or relegated to the back of the book. The younger Henry Ware, another of the ministers of the Second Unitarian Church, Boston, left his pastorate to join the faculty of Harvard Divinity School. His contribution to the celebration of Easter comes on a truly dramatic note; the poet also provided doses of refreshing energy to the hymnody of his own times. Taking a cue from Charles Wesley, Ware literally commanded worshipers to "Lift your glad voices in triumph on high, / For Jesus has risen, and man cannot die." From there, he proceeds to describe the terrors that surrounded Christ in the grave during His "short . . . dominion" there; then Christ "burst from the fetters of darkness," an image "resplendent in glory to live and to save."

While John Pierpont (1785–1866) may not seem poetically so exuberant as Ware, he did rely on metrical symmetry that allows congregations to sing his lines with relative ease. Another of the Massachusetts Unitarians, Pierpont served the Hollis Street Church, Boston; the Unitarian Church, Troy, New York; and the First Unitarian Church, Medford, Massachusetts. In addition, he found time for active (sometimes overly so) involvement in issues relating to antislavery and temperance, sentiments that indirectly find their way into his verse. At any rate, Pierpont seemed to be accompanying himself on some imaginary linguistic instrument, as he concluded,

> O Thou, to Whom in ancient time
> The lyre of prophet bards was strung,
> To Thee at last, in every clime
> Shall temples rise, and praise be sung.

"O Thou, to Whom in ancient time" constitutes a hymn on hymn singing, although Pierpont took aim at all forms of expressions of worship. He characterized with utmost sensitivity congregational song and public prayer as "the incense of the heart," an image that establishes a multidimensional tone for the entire poem.

Sarah Miles (1807–1877), wife of the headmaster of the Boston High School, published a number of her hymnodic pieces in *The Christian Examiner*. Those verses demonstrate how the American hymnodist reacted to the Christ/human being relationship. As did Ware and Pierpont, she wove a number of images that, after more than a

century and a half, continue to attract the worshiper. Her
Christ wears "the form of frail mortality"; His earthly
journey may be appreciated by seeing "The holy head by
earth's fierce storm . . . bowed"; the love of God may be
imagined to "Beam, like a bow of promise, through the
cloud." Nonetheless, Miles tended to fall back upon the
security offered by traditional and often trite imagery: "the
crown of victory," "the narrow way," and "the light of love
our guiding star shall be."

No less a traditionalist, Charles William Everest, a
Connecticut Episcopalian, published a collection entitled
Visions of Death and Other Poems (1833), a key to both the tone
and the substance of his hymnodic contributions. He found
an appropriate theme in Mark 8:34—"If any man would
come after me, let him deny himself and take up his cross
and follow me"—which he then applied to the first line of
each stanza in "Take up thy Cross." The initial stanza
paraphrases the New Testament verse, while the remaining
four expand upon what the hymnodist perceived as a clear
vision, by the committed Christian, of death. Everest seemed
to have mastered Thomas Gray's "Elegy," the popularity of
which remained high in America throughout the first half of
the nineteenth century. Thus, one notices

> Take up thy Cross, then, in His strength
> And calmly sin's wild deluge brave;
> 'Twill guide thee to a better home,
> And point to glory o'er the grave.

The influence (or coincidence, perhaps) may well serve as
the strongest poetic virtue of Everest's hymn, although the
standard references and allusions have done well to keep it
alive for those of the present century who like their
hymnody anchored deeply and firmly to Scripture.
Whether the inclusion of the piece in the first edition of
Hymns Ancient and Modern reflects Everest's denominational persuasion or his poetic regularity or both remains a
matter of speculation.

Despite the literary reputations of Emerson, Whittier, and Bryant, the single hymn from early-neneteenth-century America that stands apart—and that does so as a congregational hymn—begins with those lines that we continue to sing more than a century and a half after its composition and publication, "My faith looks up to Thee, / Thou Lamb of Calvary." Ray Palmer's poem exists as a testimony to personal religious commitment that manifests the quality that we know and recognize as faith.

> May Thy rich grace impart
> Strength to my fainting heart,
> My zeal inspire;
> As Thou hast died for me,
> O may Thy love to me
> Pure, warm and changeless be,
> A living fire.

Palmer, a graduate of Phillips Andover Academy and Yale College, became minister of the Central Congregational Church, Bath, Maine. From there he moved on to the First Congregational Church of Albany, New York, and finally received appointment as secretary of the American Congregational Union. As a hymnodist, he did not attempt to obscure the emotional impact of serious religious commitment—although one would hardly describe him as Evangelical. His poetry represents the soul struggling in a dark labyrinth of grief, groping for light that leads, eventually, out of that darkness—out of "life's transient dream"—and into the embrace of Christ's love, the "pure, warm and changeless . . . living fire." In the end, that dark soul, wallowing in "sorrow's tears," is borne by Christ "safe above, / A ransomed soul." The passage upward, at least in terms of the singer-worshiper's personal faith, becomes fairly easy when accompanied by Lowell Mason's now-popular hymn tune, "Olivet." In fact, the poetry and the music of the piece have been united since its original publication in *Spiritual Songs for Social Worship* in 1832.

The strong ties between hymnody and religious poetry continued in mid-nineteenth-century America, as lines and stanzas of poems were converted to congregational hymns. Unlike those written earlier in the century, the hymns dating from the middle decades have generally stood the test of time, and thus they continue to be found in American hymnals and to be sung by American congregations. Table 29 considers a number of examples.

Table 29. American Hymnody at Mid-Nineteenth Century

Date	Hymnodist	Opening Lines
1840	Arthur Cleveland Coxe	How beauteous were the marks divine That in Thy meekness used to shine
1841	Lydia Huntley Sigourney	Not for the summer hour alone, When skies resplendent shine
1844	Arthur Cleveland Coxe	Who is this, with garments gory, Triumphing from Bozrah's way
1844	James Russell Lowell	Once to every man and nation Comes the moment to decide
1848	Oliver Wendell Holmes	Lord of all being, throned afar, Thy glory flames from sun to star
1849	Edmund Hamilton Sears	It came upon the midnight clear, That glorious song of old
1851	Arthur Cleveland Coxe	Saviour, sprinkle many nations; Fruitful let Thy sorrows be
1856	John Greenleaf Whittier	Lord and Master of us all, Whate'er our name or sign
1857	John Henry Hopkins, Jr.	We three kings of Orient are, Bearing gifts, we traverse afar
1858	George Duffield, Jr.	Blessed Saviour! Thee I love, All my other joys above
1858	George Duffield, Jr.	Stand up!—stand up for Jesus! Ye soldiers of the Cross
1858	Ray Palmer	Jesu! Thou joy of loving hearts! Thou fount of life, Thou light of man!

Date	Hymnodist	Opening Lines
1858	Ray Palmer	Jesus, these eyes have never seen That radiant form of Thine
1858	Ray Palmer	Lord, my weak thought in vain would climb To search the starry vault profound
1858	Ray Palmer	O bread to pilgrims given, O food that angels eat
1859	Oliver Wendell Holmes	O love divine, that stooped to share Our sharpest pang, our bitterest tears
1860	Samuel Johnson	City of God, how broad and far Outspread Thy walls sublime
1861	Oliver Wendell Holmes	O Lord of hosts! Almighty King! Behold the sacrifice we bring
1862	Julia Ward Howe	Mine eyes have seen the glory of the coming of the Lord; He is trampling out the vintage where the grapes of wrath are stored
1864	Samuel Johnson	Life of ages, richly poured, Love of God unspent and free
1864	Samuel Longfellow	Holy Spirit, Truth divine, Dawn upon this soul of mine
1864	Samuel Longfellow	I look to Thee in every need, And never look in vain
1865	James Russell Lowell	"What means this glory round our feet?" The Magi mused, "More bright than morn?"
1866	John Greenleaf Whittier	Immortal love, for ever full, For ever flowing free
1867	John Greenleaf Whittier	All as God wills, Who wisely heeds To give or to withhold
1867	John Greenleaf Whittier	O Love! O Life! our faith and sight Thy presence maketh one
1867	John Greenleaf Whittier	Who fathoms the eternal thought? Who talks of scheme and plan?

The first figure to claim our attention, Lydia Sigourney (1791–1865)—still another in the long line of Connecticut hymnodists—first published her wedding hymn, "Not for the summer hour alone," in England, which permits some justification for her identification as a truly transitional figure of congregational song. In reality, though, Sigourney practiced a rather high level of poetic art; in fact, nine or ten of her hymns may stand scrutiny as moral poems that found their way from the anthology to the hymnal. She paraphrased closely and carefully the traditional and the biblical vows of matrimony, and not until the final stanza of her wedding hymn does one observe the transfer from moral poem to congregational song.

> But for a being without end
>   This vow of love we take:
> Grant us, O Lord, one home at last,
>   For Thy great mercy's sake!

The hymn begins with the traditional journey from the "summer hour" of youth and pleasure, moves forward through the "stern and wint'ry days" of late maturity, and comes to rest, before the final stanza, on the well-worn but still pleasant image of "the transient flowers of grass" that eventually "blossom, droop, and die." Sigourney seems to have lost favor among congregational singers in the United States, most probably because she represented a type of quiet, sentimental, and even nostalgic attitude toward hymnody that appears, at least for the moment, out of tune with the abrasive reverberations of late-twentieth-century offerings.

Not so with at least one of George Duffield's efforts— his major effort, perhaps—a hymn that promises to endure as long as Christians sing and find enough room for spiritual exercise between the pews. Duffield's noteworthy contribution to both hymnody and popular culture came from the pre-Civil War abolitionist movement, was occasioned by the death of a close friend and colleague, matured within the milieu of the Young Men's Christian Association and the Baptist Sunday school, and eventually anchored itself to the high waves of religious enthusiasm and Gospel militance that always demand expression. As the Sunday school children of Baring-Gould's provincial parish marched exuberantly upon the high roads of their English countryside, so do Duffield's singers of all ages still stand in their worship services and club meetings throughout the United States—no less militant and certainly no less exuberant in proclaiming,

> This day the noise of battle,
>   The next the victor's song:
> To him that overcometh,
>   A crown of life shall be;
> He with the King of Glory
>   Shall reign eternally!

In his own way, Duffield (1818–1888)—a graduate of Yale and Union Seminary, as well as an ordained Presbyterian minister—perceived the true spirit of popular religion, and his contribution to American hymnody ought not to begin and end abruptly with the blaring notes of "Stand up!—stand up for Jesus!" He could—as in "Blessed Saviour! Thee I love"—quietly advance the interests of personal prayer, of individual religious commitment. And he did so without really losing his sense of corporate expression and poetic regularity: "Ever shall my glory be, / Only, only, only Thee!"

Two close contemporaries with classic literary names, Samuel Johnson (1812–1882) and Samuel Longfellow (1819–1892), not only provided Americans with consistently high poetic quality, but allowed them to observe for the first time some evidence of a truly American hymnodic spirit. Johnson and Longfellow collaborated on two collections—*A Book of Hymns* (1846) and *Hymns of the Spirit* (1864). Johnson left the Unitarian ministry in 1853 to form the independent Free Church at Lynn, Massachusetts, and to write his most interesting treatise, *The Worship of Jesus, Past and Present* (1868). Perhaps more conventional than his colleague, Longfellow served Unitarian congregations at Fall River, Massachusetts; Brooklyn, New York; and Germantown, Pennsylvania; he then retired to write the biography of his older brother, Henry Wadsworth Longfellow.

In his "Life of ages, richly poured," Johnson wrote of "the thinker's creed, / Pulsing in the hero's blood," of the "holy book and pilgrim way . . . / Widening freedom's sacred sway." He concluded his series of spiritual and political images with the most obvious of American sanctuaries, "the people's liberty." Further, his "City of God, how broad and far," contains an abundant supply of "chartered freemen . . . / Of every age and clime" under the direction of a single Church, a single God, and a strong army of the faithful. The worshiper can even imagine, in "Thine empire grown / Of freedom, love, and truth," an idealized form of mid-nineteenth-century American republic, the essence of what has come to be known as "one nation under God." Longfellow appears slightly more personal than his fellow divinity school student, particularly in "I look to Thee in every need," but his narrator-worshiper-singer reflects the spiritual height of a particularly American perspective on human activity.

> Discouraged in the work of life,
>   Disheartened by its load,
> Shamed by its failures and fears,
>   I sink beside the road;
> But let me only think of Thee,
> And then new heart springs up in me.

Even in his most popular hymn, "Holy Spirit, Truth divine," Longfellow sensed the energy generating from the rite of confirmation. The spirit and the love glow, kindle, "Bravely bear, and nobly strive." Above all, the poet conveyed, in his six stanzas, the image of a multifaceted omnipotence—the Holy Spirit representing truth, love, power, right, peace, and joy. Such sentiments, although

certainly not limited to nineteenth-century American hymnody, heralded a fresh, poetic approach to a conventional
form.

The venerable Ray Palmer reappears at midcentury,
first with two Latin translations. His "Jesu! Thou joy of
loving hearts!"—from "Jesu, dulcedo cordium," attributed
to Bernard of Clairvaux (see Chapter 2)—constitutes one
of the highest poetic achievements in all of American
hymnody, principally because of the skill with which the
translator-poet displays to advantage the congregational
"we." Recognizing their frailty, the worshipers, as a single
entity, "turn unfilled to Thee again" for salvation.

> We taste Thee, O Thou living Bread,
> And long to feast upon Thee still;
> We drink of Thee, the fountain-head,
> And thirst our souls from Thee to fill.

Palmer continued the imagery of spiritual nourishment in
another translation from the Latin, this one beginning "O
Bread to pilgrims given." Perhaps the most interesting
aspect of this hymn concerns the alteration of the second
stanza in the 1974 British collection, *Hymns for Celebration:*

Palmer, 1858	*Hymns for Celebration, 1974*

O Water, life-bestowing
    From out the Saviour's
    heart,
A fountain purely flowing
    A fount of love Thou art!
	O Fountain, purely flowing
	    Forth from that sacred
	    heart,
	Our Saviour's grace bestowing,
	    True wine of life Thou art.

O let us, freely tasting,
    Our burning thirst assuage!
Thy sweetness, never wasting,
    Avails from age to age.
	O let us, freely tasting
	    Our spirit's thirst assuage;
	Thy goodness, never wasting,
	    Avails from age to age.

Exactly what has been gained from such alteration remains
a subject for discussion. A number of hymnal editors and
ministers of music have spent, and will continue to spend,
considerable time and labor changing older hymn texts to

fit what they believe to be the needs of current congregational singers. That effort, after all, may well be an
intellectual escape from or compromise for the encourage-
ment and promotion of new, original hymnodic texts.
Similarly, one may find some editors (although admittedly
in the minority) who refuse to tamper with original
texts—with the creativity of others; thus, certain congregations (again in the minority) continue to sing hymns as their
writers intended them to be sung.

Two of Ray Palmer's original hymn compositions,
both based upon New Testament passages, appeared
initially in the 1858 *Sabbath Hymn Book: For the Service of
Song in the House of the Lord,* (edited by Edwards Amasa
Park [1808–1900], Austin Phelps [1820–1890], and Lowell
Mason [1792–1872]). In "Jesus, these eyes have never
seen," from 1 Peter 1:8 ("Whom having not seen, ye love;
in whom, though now ye see him not, yet believing, ye
rejoice with joy unspeakable and full of glory"), he
considers the various images of Christ as they enter the
mind's eye of the faithful. He then summarizes the
experience as "some bright dream that comes unsought,
/ When slumbers o'er me roll." The piece begins with the
notion of a "veil of sense" that "hangs dark between / Thy
blessed face and mine." Palmer concludes on the note of
human death, at which time "the rending veil shall Thee
reveal / All glories as Thou art."

Romans 11:31 serves as Palmer's next thesis: "Even so
have these also now not believed, that through your mercy
they also may obtain mercy." Thus in his hymn, "Lord, my
weak thought in vain would climb," he appears to shift the
emphasis from the visual comprehension of Christ to the
intellectual understanding of the Son of God. The human
mind seeks to soar heavenward "to find creation's utmost
bound," but the narrator of the poem discovers that to be
a vain exercise based only upon the frailty of "dim reason."
The serious student of poetry thinks immediately of
Alexander Pope's dictate at the outset of the second epistle

of *The Essay on Man:* "Know then thyself, presume not God to scan; / The proper study of Mankind is Man." Palmer phrases the idea in terms clearly applicable to an assembly of public worshipers.

> Be this my joy, that evermore
>   Thou rulest all things at Thy will;
> Thy sovereign wisdom I adore,
>   And calmly, sweetly, trust Thee still.

The two pieces from the *Sabbath Hymn Book* may be identified, with all confidence, as Ray Palmer's own version of an essay written to and about (in a generic sense) "Man."

Arthur Cleveland Coxe served a number of churches before he received appointment as bishop of western New York in 1865: Saint John's Church, Hartford, Connecticut; Grace Church, Baltimore; and Calvary Church, New York. He most certainly represents a hymnodist of poetic ability and stature equal to that of Ray Palmer, emphasizing (in at least three of his hymns written at midcentury) the breadth of Christ's strength and influence. Christ moves through Bishop Coxe's hymns, from stanza to stanza, "ransoming, with priceless payment, / And delivering with power." The hymnodist introduces the image of the Son of God as "unwearied comer / From His journey's sultry length," and in so doing paints (in "Who is this, with garments gory") a figure of sublime strength and action, a figure striding gloriously, a conqueror in the midst of raging heathens. Even in a relatively sedate piece, "How beauteous were the marks divine," he writes of "Thy lonely pathways trod . . . / So patient through a world of woe." One difference emerges when, in the final stanza, the narrator (as singer and worshiper) leaps up and commences a journey of his own.

> Oh, in Thy light be mine to go,
>   Illuming all my way of woe!
> And give me ever on the road
>   To trace Thy footsteps, Son of God!

In the relatively lively "Saviour, sprinkle many nations," an obvious mission hymn, the image shifts slightly to the extended power and influence over the lands of the world. The stretched hands and strained sights of the world's people wait, according to Coxe, impatient for "Love's pure flame, and wisdom's light."

The discussion now turns to three hymnodists who each produced a single congregational song that overwhelmed everything else he or she wrote. The common denominator among the three is that each produced a substantial quantity of verse, the vast majority of which has faded peacefully into literary oblivion. John Hopkins, rector of Christ Church, Williamsport, Pennsylvania, published *Carols, Hymns, and Songs* (1862) and *Poems by the Wayside* (1883). Edmund Hamilton Sears, (1810–1876) held several pastorates in Massachusetts, claimed descent from the 1620 Pilgrims, edited *The Monthly Religious Magazine*, and published a number of volumes with fascinating titles: *Regeneration* (1854), *Pictures of the Olden Time* (1857), *Athanasia; or, Foregleams of Immortality* (1872), *The Fourth Gospel, the Heart of Christ*, and *Sermons and Songs of the Christian Life* (both 1875). Julia Ward Howe (1819–1910) who managed to extend her life one decade into the twentieth century, embraced such causes as social reform, women's suffrage, and international peace, and produced three volumes of verse: *Passion Flowers* (1854), *Words for the Hour* (1856), and *Later Lyrics* (1866).

As Christmas hymns, both Edmund Sears's "It came upon the midnight clear" and John Hopkins's "We three kings of Orient are" have suffered from having been anchored so steadfastly to their late-winter occasions. Worshipers have come to know the pieces so well— especially their opening stanzas and accompanying tunes— that they do not always fully appreciate their value as hymnodic praise. For example, the simple but effective exchange in Hopkins's hymn, wherein "Heav'n sings Alleluia: / Alleluia the earth replies" underscores the entire thesis of the Three Kings' being guided to "Thy perfect light," a state of being governed by a "king for ever, / Ceasing never over us all to reign." And, of course, as with so many of the exceedingly popular hymnodic pieces, the familiarity of the accompanying music dulls the singers' minds to the point where they fail to pause at the proper places, thus failing to comprehend the meanings of phrases and sentences within the text.

Similarly, once past the initial eight lines of Sears's hymn—once past the hypnotic fog of rote, rhyme, and melody—the attentive worshipers come upon (if they choose to awake) a number of interesting pastoral images introduced by the unfurling of peaceful, angelic wings, "through the closing sky they come." Sears writes for the entire world; he sees that audience as a weary world, suffering beneath "Two thousand years of wrong." He imagines before him a painful and a tragic world, waiting for the coming of love and of peace, a world eagerly expecting the fulfillment of a prophecy and the time when it can "give back the song / Which now the angels sing." It seems a shame to hide such sentiments in a materialistic holiday closet, to let them out for one brief week of the year, and then shut them back inside again—forgetting (or perhaps never even comprehending) their plain and direct lessons.

But if Edmund Sears and John Hopkins receive only yearly airings, think of how few and how irregular the occasions upon which congregations may sing, collectively and during worship, Julia Ward Howe's militant but also extremely sensitive hymn, "Mine eyes have seen the glory of the coming of the Lord." Her poem stands as a fine example of what may happen to a hymn if, by chance of title or historical occasion, it becomes too closely associated with political, social, or regional events. No one will really argue that the piece does not deserve to be placed upon the same historical perch as the American Civil War, resting alongside the loyal and antislavery elements who wore the blue uniforms of the United States of America. Nonetheless, its lines and its tone also belong to Scripture.

Howe	*Scripture*
He is trampling out the vintage where the grapes of wrath are stored	Isaiah 63:3—I have trodden the wine press alone, and from the peoples no one was with me
Let the hero born of woman crush the serpent with his heel	Genesis 3:15—I will put enmity between you and the woman, and between your seed and her seed; he shall bruise your head, and you shall bruise his heel.
He is coming like the glory of the morning on the wave	Hosea 6:3—His going forth is sure as the dawn; He will come to us as the showers, as the spring rains that water the earth.

The lines of the hymn further express an extremely personal commitment, a statement of personal faith, both singular and collective. Howe emphasizes "*Mine* eyes," "*I* have seen," "*I* have read," "*my* soul," "*my* feet," "*my* grace": in all, the hymn contains eight references in the first person (singular and plural). Further, she underscores "the glory in His bosom that transfigures *you* and *me*" and the recognition that "as He died to make men holy, let *us* die to make men free." The "Battle Hymn of the Republic" remains with us as still another example of imbalance in hymnody between language and music, of what happens to a poem when one aspect of the complete congregational song (language and music) obscures the other.

Three prominent members of the American poetic fraternity contributed to the hymnody of mid-nineteenth-century America. In fact one, John Greenleaf Whittier, we have observed in our discussion of the first half of the century. Again, his "hymns" constitute passages from larger poetic works, although this does not diminish the quality of those pieces as congregational songs. Collectively, the strength of the selections lies in the freshness of the poet's imagery, particularly in his facility for providing substantive figures to theological abstractions. Death is thus a "covered way / Which opens into light"; some comfort comes from the "solemn shadow of the Cross / . . . better than the sun"; a sense of security comes from observing "where His islands lift / Their fronded palms in air." Whittier also attunes one's senses to the rhythmic beat of love and of faith as they relate to a higher order of nature.

> Blow, winds of God, awake and blow
>   The mists of earth away;
> Shine out, O Light divine, and show
>   How wide and far we stray.

In the end, he achieved a reasonable balance between the artist's conception of Christ as eternal Lord and Master and the worshiper's translation of that concept through Scripture and traditional theological commentary. His "Immortal love, for ever full" indicates various debts to Romans, Mark, and Acts; "Our Lord and Master of us all" echoes fragments from 1 John, while "O Love! O Life! our faith and sight" and "Who fathoms the eternal thought" bow ever so slightly in the direction of, respectively, John 14:6 and Isaiah 42:3.

The observation that the elder Oliver Wendell Holmes (1809–1894) displayed his best poetic talents when he wrote serious religious verse seems too lengthy an issue to pursue here. There exists little doubt, however, that the poet, novelist, essayist, and physician recognized the essential ingredients of the congregational hymn, and he approached it with spirit and force, even gusto. He wrote, in "Lord of all being, throned afar," of the glory of God as it "flames from sun to star" and functions as the "Centre and soul of every sphere." Even in the midst of sorrowful

or tragic surroundings, Holmes created a sense of action—
a form of Augustan tension—brought about by the distance between pleasure and grief.

> O Love divine that stooped to share
>   Our sharpest pang, our bitterest tear!
> On Thee we cast each earth-born care;
>   We smile at pain while Thou art near.

But what Holmes really thrived on for hymnodic context
focuses upon a stirring occasion where he could ask
worshipers to "lift the starry flag on high / That fills with
light our stormy sky." Indeed, one would expect no less
from the author of "The Chambered Nautilus" and "Old
Ironsides" than such lines as

> From treason's rent, from murder's stain,
> Guard Thou its folds till peace shall reign,
> Till fort and field, till shore and sea,
> Join our loud anthem, praise to Thee!

A bit singsong perhaps? But those who wish to sing the
hymns of Oliver Wendell Holmes must be prepared to
accept the spirited reverberations of an equally spirited
aristocrat, an intellectual patrician who loved his nation no
less than he loved his God.

Another member of the New England intellectual
elite, James Russell Lowell, contributed somewhat indirectly to the development of American hymnody. His long
poem, "The Present Crisis," yielded, more than fifty years
after its publication, the hymn, "Once to every man and
nation." In that passage Lowell focused upon "Some great
cause, God's new Messiah," in terms of the religious and
moral dilemmas that confront every person who seeks to
determine the truth and who strives to distinguish, within
the framework of an extremely orthodox but complex
world, right from wrong. Lowell sought to ease those
dilemmas by creating a network of graphic roads upon
which human beings might, with confidence, traverse.

> By the light of burning martyrs,
> Jesus' bleeding feet I track,
> Toiling up new Calvaries ever
> With the Cross that turns not back.

The poetry of such passages clamors for recitation, although those who have attempted to sing it may express their reservations about it as a hymn for collective public worship. Not so, however, with Lowell's piece for Epiphany, "What means this glory round our feet?" That ballad-carol avoids the poetic clamor and clash of the preceding piece, relying instead upon the traditional images of the season. Nonetheless, Lowell did recognize the frustrations surrounding his own sensitive times:

> 'Tis eighteen hundred years and more
> Since those sweet oracles were dumb;
> We wait for Him, like them of yore;
> Alas! He seems too slow to come.

There is little doubt of Lowell's superiority as a poet over the likes of Oliver Wendell Holmes. The former succeeded in his efforts to explicate the simple, direct faith—the faith epitomized by those "kindly clasping hand in hand, / . . . 'Peace on earth, good will to men.' " In the end Lowell should be thanked for producing, however unintentionally, hymns that have caused worshipers to think as they utter his words and phrases. Such artistic and intellectual quality has indeed been rare in the history of American congregational song.

The post-Civil War period in the United States witnessed not only the unification and expansion of the nation, but also the development of American hymnody in new directions and into new dimensions. The latter portion of the nineteenth century gave rise to what has become known as the *gospel* song or the *Sunday school* song. No matter what label one chooses, the form possesses the same qualities: exhilarating combinations of simple repetition, clear and exact language, the syntax of conversation, and images that even the smallest schoolchild can comprehend, recite, and eventually memorize. The period also produced its share of reasonably mature hymnodic poetry, and that aspect, carried over from the earlier literary periods, ought not to be forgotten. Table 30 examines the diversity of the form.

Table 30. Late-Nineteenth-Century American Hymnody

Date	Hymnodist	Opening Lines
1865	Robert Lowry	Shall we gather at the river, Where bright angel feet have trod
1869	William Cullen Bryant	O North, with all thy vales of green, O South with all thy palms!
1870	Philip Paul Bliss	"Whosoever heareth," shout, shout the sound! Spread the blessed tidings all the world around
1870	Frances Jane Crosby Van Alstyne (Fanny Crosby)	Rescue the perishing, care for the dying, Snatch them in pity from sin and the grave
1871	Philip Paul Bliss	"Almost persuaded," now to believe; "Almost persuaded," Christ to receive
1872	John Greenleaf Whittier	All things are Thine; no gift have we, Lord of all gifts, to offer Thee
1872	John Greenleaf Whittier	Dear Lord and Father of mankind, Forgive our foolish ways!
1873	Frances Jane Crosby Van Alstyne (Fanny Crosby)	Blessed assurance, Jesus is mine! Oh what a foretaste of glory divine!
1874	Philip Paul Bliss	Sing them over again to me, Wonderful words of Life
1874	Phillips Brooks	O little town of Bethlehem, How still we see thee lie
1876	Daniel Crane Roberts	God of our Fathers, whose almighty Hand, Leads forth in beauty all the starry band
1877	Mary Artemisia Lathbury	Break Thou the bread of life, Dear Lord, to me

Date	Hymnodist	Opening Lines
1879	Washington Gladden	O Master let me walk with Thee In lowly paths of service free
1882	John Greenleaf Whittier	When on my day of life the night is falling, And in the winds, from unsunned spaces blown
1884	Denis Wortman	God of the prophets! Bless the prophets' sons
1887	Mary Baker Eddy	O'er waiting harpstrings of the mind There sweeps a strain
1887	Mary Baker Eddy	Shepherd, show me how to go O'er the hillside steep
1887	Ernest Warburton Shurtleff	Lead on, O King eternal, The day of march has come
1893	Katharine Lee Bates	O beautiful for spacious skies, For amber waves of grain
1896	Mary Baker Eddy	Brood o'er us with Thy shelt'ring wing, 'Neath which our spirits blend
1896	Mary Baker Eddy	O gentle presence, peace and joy and power; O Life divine, that owes each waiting hour
1896	Mary Baker Eddy	Saw ye my Saviour? Heard ye the glad sound
1899	Edgar Lewis Jones	Would ye be free from the burden of sin? There's power in the Blood, power in the Blood

Representatives of the American literati may be said to head the list of late-nineteenth-century American hymnodists, not necessarily because they wrote hymns of the highest literary level, but because their lines echo the very sounds that have reverberated through the entire century. The immediately recognizable poets of the nineteenth century were the most consistent element of American hymnody, and for that quality they must receive their due.

William Cullen Bryant's attempts to create a unified nation through hymnody—or at least to suggest the advantages of unity—stand as a most ambitious project. From the outset, he looked forward to the day "When He shall reign from pole to pole, / The Lord of every human soul." Bryant directed his worshipers' attentions to the possibility of a time when the mercy, truth, and righteousness of God would come down to obliterate the superficial boundaries of state and nation. Whittier, on the other hand, reinforced the power of prayer and the trauma of human frailty, both popular hymnodic themes of the period. On one level he exposed an exceedingly practical side, as in his hymn for church building and consecration, "All things are Thine; no gift have we." In that poem, he balanced the "mortal motive, scheme, and plan" with the glory of God, as seen in "Thy children's good, / Thy joy, Thy tender Fatherhood." Nevertheless, Whittier was obviously a sensitive poet, an artistic individual confronting a serious moral, spiritual moment. He reflected, in "When on my day of life the night is falling," upon the last possible mortal instance, the time when the individual finds himself "by hands familiar beckoned / Unto my fitting place." But Whittier remained the child of God and of nature, a reconciliation that had served him intellectually throughout his long life. Taking a cue from Revelation 22:1—"And he showed me a pure river of water of life, clear as crystal, proceeding out of the throne of God and of the Lamb"—he wrote of "heaven's green expansions, / The river of Thy peace." For him, that river served as a trial leading, "at last, beneath Thy trees of healing" to "The life for which I long."

In his most popular, and perhaps his best, hymn, beginning with a direct address, "Dear Lord and Father of mankind," Whittier proposed to speak on behalf of all faithful people. He strove for increased commitment—for "purer lives" and for "deeper reverence." The principal element in his hymn, however, was its tone and its mood of ultimate serenity—a quality that characterizes a considerable portion of Whittier's religious verse. He described "The gracious calling of the Lord" that compels human souls, "without a word," to "Rise up and follow Thee." The hills above Galilee remain "calm"—"The silence of eternity / Interpreted by love"—the perfect backdrop for Christians' orderly lives that "confess / The beauty of Thy peace." To summarize the ultimate qualities of God's potency, the poet tuned his lyre upon the notes of heavenly coolness and omnipotent balm, a "still, small voice of calm" to balance the strain and the stress of a tense world. The effectiveness of that hymn lies in its generalizations, which continue to create a sense of absolute timelessness—a mood that transcends the generations.

Whittier's "Dear Lord and Father of mankind" serves as a transition from the hymns of the American literati of the late nineteenth century to those generally popular congregational pieces which achieve poetical and musical merit. For instance, Katharine Lee Bates (1859–1929), professor of English at Wellesley College, gave to her nation "O beautiful for spacious skies," a poem that continues on a note of exhilarating pride, but does so without any need for congregational movement—either literal or figurative. She required her singers neither to march nor to rise from their seats; they need only "Confirm thy soul in self control, / Thy liberty in law!" Indeed, the "stern, impassioned stress" of Bates's pilgrims sufficiently secures both the "success" and the "nobleness" of this truly national hymn. There periodically arises public clamor to take the piece out of the sanctuary and place it in whatever context may be required for status as a national anthem. A poem similar in intent is the centennial hymn of Daniel Crane Roberts, who served in the Union Army prior to his ordination and subsequent appointments as rector of Saint Thomas Church in Brandon, Vermont, and Saint Paul's Church in Concord, New Hampshire. Roberts established clearly and early the relationship between God as ruler-guardian and mortals as followers. The predominantly American flavor of the hymn sets it apart from British prototypes, particularly when the congregation recognizes "Thy love divine hath led us in the past: / In this free land by Thee our lot is cast." Roberts extended throughout his poem the idea of an active God: "Thy strong arm" as a means of defense, "Thy bounteous goodness" as a means to achieve peace. Thus, the final stanza becomes the signal announcing a new day for a new, energetic and dynamic world.

> Refresh Thy people on their toilsome way,
> Lead us from night to never ending day;
> Fill all our lives with love and grace divine,
> And glory, laud and praise be ever Thine.

Worshipers can easily argue for the inclusion of two additional hymns in the same category as those by Bates and Roberts. Ernest Warburton Shurtleff (1862–1917) held pastorates in Ventura, California, Plymouth, Massachusetts, and Minneapolis, Minnesota, before organizing the American Church in Frankfurt, Germany, and working with students in Paris, France. Denis Wortman (1835–1922), before assuming the presidency of the General Synod of the Reformed Church, held pastorates in Brooklyn, Philadelphia, and Schenectady. Shurtleff's "Lead on, O King eternal" may appear a bit too militant for certain tastes, while Wortman's "God of the prophets" seems too firmly anchored to the rite of ordination. Those familiar with Shurtleff's effort recall "the day of march," the "fields of conquest," "Thy tents," the "swords loud clashing," the "roll of stirring drums," and—perhaps most emphatic of all—"The crown [that] awaits the conquest." Such phrasing ought not to surprise or to offend anyone, for the hymnodist himself identified the purpose of his piece at the end of the initial stanza: "And now, O King eternal, / We lift our battle song."

Wortman's intent bears similar marks of linguistic clarity and specificity within an extremely broad context.

Thus, in the third stanza of "God of the prophets," he pleads,

> Anoint them priests! Strong intercessors they
> For pardon, and for charity and peace!
> Ah, if with them the world might pass, astray,
> Into the dear Christ's life of sacrifice!

The hymnodist's exuberance appears dedicated to the renewal, the revitalization, of a "weary world," a place wherein the collective human need remains synonymous with the collective human right. At the very outset of Wortman's poem, his clerics become missionaries— apostles and heralds who "Forth may . . . go to tell all realms Thy grace."

The final hymns in this popular group appear originally to have been rooted to their roles as occasional pieces. Nevertheless, the occasions themselves have become sufficiently widespread as to arouse the interests and the emotions of worshipers in a variety of circumstances. For instance, the communion hymn of Mary Artemisia Lathbury (1841–1918), "Break Thou the bread of life," allows the congregation to reflect upon the theme and the content of the ritual. It also permits the group to examine the essential issues underlying one of the most sacred acts in the worship service. If nothing else, the singers of Lathbury's hymn ought to at least pause in the middle of the piece to reflect upon the statement, "Beyond the sacred page, / I seek Thee, Lord." The opportunity surely exists to ponder the concept of truth as it functions upon an individual in terms of "my peace, / My All in All." Lathbury appears to have been one of those hymnodists associated with the Chautauqua (New York) Assembly; although she also wrote and edited materials for the Methodist Sunday School Union, her hymns can hardly be termed denominational.

Gladden's well-known "O Master, let me walk with

Thee" and Brooks's equally popular "O little town of Bethlehem" seem not to promote such multidimensional discussion as Lathbury's communion hymn. Gladden simply placed the worshiper-singer in the position of asking personally for directions on the roads of discipleship, brotherhood, and service. The singer seeks advice, help, teaching, guidance, and hope—all of which will create a corporate peace "that only Thou canst give." Brooks, Episcopal bishop of Massachusetts, appears to have viewed Christmas as the one solution to "The hopes and fears of all the years," but he really aimed for transcendence beyond the season, to a time—an age, if you will—where "God imparts to human hearts / The blessings of His heaven." Christmas, for Brooks, was the grandest intervention underscoring the purpose of the entire year, "Where charity stands watching / And faith holds wide the door."

One segment of late-nineteenth-century American hymnody best characterizes both the nation and the times: the gospel songs of the Evangelical church and of the Evangelical Sunday school. These pieces arose out of the need for free, collective, and highly emotive expression, a form of expression that owed little to denominational tradition and even less to liturgical convention. The American gospel hymn paid only passing attention to poetry—to imagery, meter, and even poetic rhythm. Instead the form gathered strength from its music and from such actions as singer-worshipers applied with spirit and spontaneity. The hymns of the American gospel church and the American Sunday school tend to be so numerous that all or even a significant portion of them cannot reasonably be surveyed or discussed within the confines of a discussion of the history of American hymnody. All one can do is provide a platform upon which to parade a number of representative minstrels of the gospel form and permit them to demonstrate their wares.

Initially, P. P. Bliss (1838–1876) went from his native

Pennsylvania to Chicago in 1864 to conduct musical institutes and to compose Sunday school melodies for Dr. George F. Root. Ten years later he joined the evangelist D. W. Whittle (who held the rank of major) as music director—in much the same way as Ira David Sankey assisted Dwight Lyman Moody. When Moody and Sankey returned from their first evangelical campaign to Great Britain, they decided to join forces with Bliss to combine their *Sacred Songs and Solos* with his *Gospel Songs.* The result appeared as *Gospel Hymns and Sacred Songs.*

Bliss's name comes quickly to mind whenever the subject of gospel hymnody arises. He exhibited the ease with which anyone with a sense of musical rhythm and religious exuberance could produce a gospel song. Bliss seemed to have mastered the craft of sheer repetition; his " 'Whosoever heareth,' shout, shout the sound" constitutes the essence of unadulterated thumping redundance. For instance, the word "whosoever" appears no less than seventeen times in the course of three eight-line stanzas. Notice the final section:

> "Whosoever will," the promise is secure;
> "Whosoever will," for ever must endure;
> "Whosoever will!" 'tis life for evermore:
>   "Whosoever will may come."
> "Whosoever will, whosoever will,"
> Send the proclamation over vale and hill;
> 'Tis a loving Father calls the wand'rer home:
>   "Whosoever will may come."

In Bliss's caesural lines he employs internal pauses to enrich, through obvious association, the regularity of his thought. Each line thus tends to stress a single, complete thought, but Bliss also divides it—nicely and evenly—in the center:

> Whosoever will / / the problem is secure;
> Whosoever will / / for ever must endure.

Through such internal division, Bliss simplified even the simple. He reduced the effect of language while increasing the importance of rhythm, motion, emotion, and (most important), sound.

Bliss wrote his own music as well, which expedited the process of complete gospel hymn composition. Therefore, in his "Sing them over again to me," he managed to inject his thesis, "Wonderful words of life," into each line. In the event the singer happened to forget that thesis, Bliss provided a refrain that, to no one's surprise, reads, "Beautiful words, wonderful words, / Wonderful words of Life." His "Almost persuaded, now to believe" reveals an extremely interesting introductory choral effect whereby the central idea of the entire hymn ("Almost persuaded") surrounds the main idea of each stanza.

(1)   "Almost persuaded," now to believe;
      "Almost persuaded," Christ to receive. . . .

(2)   "Almost persuaded," come, come to-day;
      "Almost presuaded," turn not away. . . .

(3)   "Almost persuaded," harvest is past!
      "Almost persuaded," doom comes at last!

Having effectively "hammered home" his point—the vast chasm between *almost* and the actual commitment to Christ—Bliss could then move, with ease and confidence, to the ultimate result of the issue.

"Almost" cannot avail;
"Almost" is but to fail!
Sad, sad, but bitter wail,
   "Almost," but lost.

We may directly observe, then, the formula for both moral communication and hymnodic success within the gospel song form. Bliss represents the triumph of method over language, of the simplest rhetorical technique over poetic image, of sound over sense.

Another obvious technique employed by gospel hymnodists of the past consisted of simple question and answer—the strongest exponent of that method having been E. L. Jones. In his especially popular turn-of-the-century contribution to American gospel song, Jones loosed upon his singers a series of superficial inquiries—almost a catechism in rhyme—all of which produce the same hymnodic response: "There's power in the Blood." Since the initial publication of that piece in a collection entitled *Songs of Praise and Victory,* however, few have paid serious attention to those interrogative statements. Thus, the real merit of Jones's gospel hymn focuses upon the emotive refrain that sweeps away practically every other sentiment from the campground.

> There is power, power, wonder-working power
> In the blood, in the blood of the Lamb;
> There is power, power, wonder-working power
> In the precious blood of the Lamb.

One does not require too many fingers and toes to determine that the words "power" and "blood" comprise fully thirty percent of all words within the stanza.

Certainly Robert Lowry (1826–1899) brought quality credentials to the field of gospel hymnody: a baccalaureate from and a professorship of rhetoric at Bucknell University, and a pastorate at the Hanson Place Baptist Church in Brooklyn, New York. He also served as an editor with the New York city music firm of Biglow and Main, superintending such gospel collections as *Happy Voices, Chapel Melodies, Bright Jewels, Pure Gold, Royal Diadem, Tidal Wave, Fountain of Song,* and *Welcome Tidings.* His most noticeable contribution begins with a question.

> Shall we gather at the river,
> Where bright angel feet have trod;
> With its crystal tide for ever,
> Flowing by the throne of God?

However, his effort differs substantially from that of E. L.
Jones, principally because Lowry strove steadily (if not
always directly) toward some attempts at poetry. He asked
worshipers to consider such images as "bright angel feet,"
the river's "crystal tide," "the bosom of the river," and "the
melody of peace." All of this appears forced and even trite,
but it does not really matter. As had Jones, Lowry
composed a refrain that not only answered his introductory query, but managed to neutralize the thinness of his
imagery as well.

> Yes, we'll gather at the river,
> The beautiful, the beautiful river,
> Gather with the saints at the river
> That flows by the throne of God.

By his own account, Lowry composed both words and
music of the hymn at a single sitting, during a summer's
day and in the midst of an influenza epidemic. Thus, the
piece is the result of a highly traumatic experience, but one
must not lose sight of Bliss, Jones, and Lowry (as well as
legions of their likeminded contemporaries), for whom the
music of the hymn meant considerably more than its
language and its thought. Late-nineteenth-century American gospel hymns reflect the priorities of those who
produced them.

No matter what the conclusion about its quality or
effects, no discussion of the gospel element in American
hymnody can terminate before due consideration of the
grande dame of the movement, Frances Jane Crosby Van
Alstyne. Blind from infancy, she began to write verse at the
age of eight—and seemingly never stopped. She wrote
hundreds of hymns and songs under scores of different
names and different initials. She wrote for countless
occasions and countless congregations; at one period she
labored for the firm of Biglow and Main, supposedly
under contract to furnish three gospel songs per week.
Indeed, she may well have surpassed Charles Wesley in

terms of quantity—and let the comparison end abruptly on that point. No matter how many occasions Fanny Crosby set in hymnodic stone, however, she managed to universalize each one to the extent that the specifics of the moment meant little.

Most certainly, Fanny Crosby capitalized upon the technical simplicity of the gospel form: rhythm, repetition, refrain, and above all, the most elementary levels of language again parade before and echo from the singers and worshipers. With equal certainty, however, she surpassed her contemporaries by showing extreme sensitivity to language by balancing carefully the meaning with the rhythm—a balance generally ignored by the majority of her colleagues. Thus, her songs resound with intense energy, with the crisp commands of an Evangelical drill-master who orders one to "Rescue the perishing," "care for the dying," "snatch them in pity." She tells one directly and frankly to weep, to lift, to praise. Fanny Crosby's hymns go forward in sheer determination, upon the dictum that "duty demands it." She asks few questions, but provides a lengthy series of answers, the essence of which grasps firmly to the concept of "strength for thy labor the Lord will provide." Even in her most popular piece, "Blessed assurance, Jesus is mine!" the singer-worshiper's path to salvation, to the "foretaste of glory divine," has been expedited somewhat by a rousing refrain of spiritual declaration and personal testimony.

> This is my story, this is my song,
> Praising my Savior, all the day long;
> This is my story, this is my song,
> Praising my Savior all the day long.

The blessed assurance leads to two aspects of a "perfect submission": one synonymous with "perfect delight," the other with blessed "rest." The strength of Fanny Crosby, as seen particularly in "Blessed assurance," comes because she knew how to achieve a balance between stanza and refrain. She did not overindulge the one at the expense of the other, and thus she came close to writing what may be termed, with accuracy, a gospel poem.

This survey of hymnody in the United States during the nineteenth century could easily come to a close upon the rousing notes of the gospel hymns popular during the last half of the period. However, as a final consideration, I now turn to a personality known more for her work as a denominational founder and administrator than as a writer of hymns for congregational worship. The hymns of Mary Baker Glover Eddy (1821–1910), produced as early as 1887, deserve analysis because they are examples of poetic sensitivity that few persons have bothered to understand and even fewer to sample. She appears to have tuned her hymnodic muse closely to higher Nature; her images reflect both spiritual and intellectual commitment, as in "Brood o'er us with Thy shelt'ring wing" she beckoned one to consider "Love whose finger traced aloud / A bow of promise on the cloud." Similarly, Christ, as a shepherd figure (in "Shepherd, show me how to go") will tear away the facade of stubbornness, callousness, and self-righteousness, thus allowing Him, in the end, to "Break earth's stupid rest" and quietly inspire to His presence a band of committed followers.

The reader of Eddy's hymnodic efforts will discover a tone of controlled but natural serenity that permits worshipers to think as they sing. In that context, her hymns present a refreshing contrast to the choral bombasts of her more evangelically inclined brothers and sisters in sacred song. However, when she did drift toward the popular at the altar of gospel hymnody, she lost considerable stature as a writer of hymnodic verse.

> Saw ye my Saviour?
> Heard ye the glad sound?
> Felt ye the power of the Word?
> 'Twas the Truth that made us free,

> And was found by you and me,
> In the life and the love of our Lord.

The piece stands as a tribute to hymnodic redundance; its four six-line stanzas contain nothing not already seen or heard. Further, its identification as a Communion hymn proves particularly offensive in light of the seriousness of that liturgical occasion and the availability of a vast number of stock images and references of greater respectability—any of which would do justice to that particular moment in the worship service.

Fortunately, Mary Baker Eddy did not linger long under the influence of the gospel song. Her real strength lies in the hymn as poetic prayer and divine ode. Her verse rises to excellence in such pieces as "O gentle presence, peace and joy and power" and "O'er waiting harpstrings of the mind," wherein her language demonstrates its sufficiency both to feed and to reflect upon her imagination. She continued to emphasize Love—to provide that state of being and feeling with substance and with action; then (as in "O gentle presence, peace joy and power") she managed to relate Love to divine "peace and joy and power." The protection of God becomes, for Eddy, "a sweet secret of the narrow way," and she in turn reduces the entire cycle of human existence to a moment "When heaven's aftersmile earth's tear-drops gain." Continuing the theme of refuge and protection in "O'er waiting harpstrings of the mind," Eddy envisions "earth's troubled, angry sea" as the road upon which "I see Christ walk, / And come to me." The real poetry of the piece comes at the outset.

> O'er waiting harpstrings of the mind
>   There sweeps a strain,
> Low, sad and sweet, whose measures bind
>   The power of pain.

Once again the writer's attentiveness to language underscores her ability to construct images that intentionally intimidate worshipers to think and to see. Remove such hymns from their hymnal (textual) surroundings, print them without musical notations for public recitation and for public prayer, and even the most insensitive of worshipers will come to appreciate the importance of poetic art and poetic craft to the overall purpose of congregational song.

Chapter Nine
LET US *ALL* BE FREE!

A NUMBER OF HYMNOLOGISTS and critical commentators on popular culture would quickly and loudly maintain that the black spiritual hymn (or black gospel song) requires little attention to text, since the form itself depends principally upon the various melodies associated with it. In other words, the same effect may be achieved through humming the tune as may be obtained from singing its words. Such commentary may well be accurate, but any hymnodic composition—no matter what its purpose or the cultural or ethnic background of its development—continues to exist as a combination of linguistic and musical expression. The one cannot exist without the other. True, the so-called Negro spiritual, as it has come to be recognized, grew out of a noninstitutional, nondenominational atmosphere, one derived from captivity, trial, deprivation, harassment, suffering, and even tragedy; it arose from an environment spawned by a fusion of personal and collective expression, by a need to weep and to pray, to sing and to dance, to praise and to curse. Nevertheless, in spite of its outward signs of spontaneity, as well as the apparent lack of literary convention and form, the black spiritual hymn can be classified as verse, as rhythmic expression directed upward to, for, and in the name of an omnipotent being. At the same time, however, it cannot rank with or be compared with the form and the level of hymnodic poetry of those pieces which have long been associated with traditional denominational establishments and institutions.

Before discussing a selection of black spiritual hymns, it is worthwhile to examine a list of the most recognized for

easy and ready reference. They have been set forth below
in alphabetical order and identified, as is the usual practice
with hymnody, by opening lines:

> Deep river, my home is over Jordan;
> Deep river, Lord

> Go down, Moses,
> 'Way down to Egypt land

> Go tell it on the mountain,
> Over the hills and everywhere

> God called Ezekiel by His word,
> "Go down and prophesy!"

> He's got the whole world in His hands,
> He's got the big round world in His hands

> It's me, it's me, it's me, O Lord,
> Standing in the need of pray'r

> Joshua fit de battle of Jericho, Jericho, Jericho

> Kum bayah, my Lord, Kum bayah!

> Let us break bread together on our knees

> Lit'le David, play on yo' harp, Hallelu, hallelu

> Rock o' my soul, in de bosom of Abraham

> Sometimes I feel like a motherless chil'

> Steal away, steal away,
> Steal away to Jesus

> Swing low, sweet chariot,
> Coming for to carry me home

> We are climbing Jacob's ladder

> Were you there when they crucified my Lord?

> When de saints come marchin' in

The simplicity of the black spiritual does not always
lend itself to simple classification and/or analysis of any of
its representatives. One needs to identify key words and
terms within the text—to discover a thesis, as it were.

Such an exercise does not always yield the clearest of results, but it does allow for orderly discussion of a not-too-orderly form. For example, one might begin with those spirituals wherein a singer-narrator focuses on nature as the means by which to project an idea or to communicate an emotional state. The refrain, "Go tell it on the mountain, / Over the hills and ev'rywhere," serves as a platform from which to announce the notions of the three principal stanzas: (1) the Lord's reforming the sinner, (2) the Lord's teaching the sinner to pray, and (3) the sinner's ultimate transformation to the point at which he or she can declare, "I am a Christian, / I am the least of all." Similarly, the Jordan River, the "deep river," is the last barrier into "that promised land, where all is peace," where if one manages to "cross over into campground," the wearisome journey of life on earth will finally achieve a happy end, a home.

The ultimate hymn within the realm-of-nature category appears to be "He's got the whole world in His hands." In that piece, the singer-narrator manages to covey a sense of anticlimactic order; in the five four-line stanzas, the narrator refers to (stanza 1) the whole big round world; (stanza 2) wind, ran, sun, moon; (stanza 3) tiny little itsy bitsy baby; (stanza 4) you and me brother and sister; and (stanza 5) everybody. The unity of the piece comes from the thesis line that concludes each stanza: "He's got the whole world in His hands." That refrain conveys an image that continues to hold firm and fresh, despite its age and the various religious and secular objects to which it has been applied—even soap and automobile insurance.

The tone and the tempo of the musical settings of black spiritual hymns have long borne the mantles of heaviness and pervading depression. Certainly those elements do exist within the form but these same pieces yield just as much spirited action, physical as well as textual.

Notice, for instance, the emotional energy and the potential for physical expression bursting from this linguistically elementary hymn:

> When de saints come marchin' in,
> When de saints come marchin' in,
> Lord, I want to be in dat number
> When de saints come marchin' in. .

By introducing and concluding each stanza, those four lines essentially oversee the entire spiritual. In fact, depending upon the whim of the singers, the lines can be inserted wherever and whenever convenient. The oral tradition by which the black spirituals have come to the present allows a congregation to do as it pleases. Certainly a text exists for each one of those spirituals, but apparently anyone is free to add, delete, or alter as the occasion demands or the spirit moves.

The titled refrain of "When de saints come marchin' in" does not provide the only opportunity for action and activity, however. Each stanza functions as a self-contained spiritual, with its own echo and refrain.

> I have a lovin' brother.
> He is gone on before.
> An' I promised I would meet him
> When they crown Him Lord of all
> When the crown Him Lord of all,
> When they crown him Lord of all,
> Lord, I want to be in dat number
> When dey crown Him Lord of all.

The weakness of the piece, as well as the rhetorical frailty of its structure, lies in its vulnerability to musical and gymnastic gimmicks. With all of the marching, clapping, chanting, and repeating, the singers hardly have time to digest what little meaning they might derive from its lines and stanzas. It can and has all too easily become a showpiece rather than a legitimate spiritual for congregational worship.

Not all of the action in the black spiritual comes in the form of an outward display of exuberance. As the name of the form clearly implies, the movement may indeed be purely spiritual. The "sweet chariot" "swings" low and "comes" to "carry"; the line "Coming for to carry me home" concludes each stanza of the song which has come to be known as "Swing low, sweet chariot." That refrain underlines the spiritual transition from earth to heaven, from life to death, from death to renewed life. Another piece generates activity through "climbing Jacob's ladder" an act leading to and demonstrating the love of and service to God and Christ. That action automatically intensifies by the simple identification in each stanza of the various "We," "Brother," and "you" as "Soldiers of the Cross." Further spiritual action takes place in "Steal away, steal away," wherein the thunder and the sounds of the trumpet announce God's call to the "poor sinner," one who "stands a-trembling." A Judgment Day theme appears to have taken hold of the singer-narrator, for the lines graphically depict the "bending" trees, the "bursting" tombstones, and the "lightning" calls of God.

Finally, one may wish to consider that "Rock o' my soul" may fit into the action/activity category, although this spiritual does contain a certain degree of ambiguity. One version reads, "Rock *o'* my soul in the bosom of Abraham," which identifies the God of Abraham as the rock (or shelter) *of* or *for* the soul. Another text (again a transcript from the oral tradition) declares, "Rock-*er* ma soul in de bosom ob Abraham," which can easily allude to the action of cradling the soul within the refuge of God. Both versions yield essentially the same meaning; the "Rock o' " versus "Rock-er" debate thus exists within the framework of a linguistic exercise—perhaps one of the most interesting facets of the black spiritual hymn.

An obvious heading under which to place specific spirituals is prayer—whether that prayer be personal or collective, direct or peripheral. At one end of that group appear hymns in which the singer-worshiper announces emphatically his or her need for prayer. The opening chant of "It's me, it's me, it's me, O Lord" gives way easily to a series of staccato confessions:

> Not my brother, not my sister, but it's me, O Lord,
>   Standing in the need of pray'r;
> Not my brother, not my sister, but it's me, Or Lord,
>   Standing in the need of prayer.

Few singers, readers, or general observers can fail to realize the sense of urgency running through the hymn, just as others will readily perceive, the pure melancholy of the "motherless chil', / Far, far away from home," who has no other recourse but to get "down on my knees an' pray, / Get down on my knees an' pray." Balancing the need for prayer is the next step in the process: the actual praying. The singer-narrator of that type of spiritual conveys the idea, for example, of breaking "bread together on our knees," of turning "my face to the rising sun," of asking "O Lord, have mercy on me." From another point of view, the title and the opening stanza of "Kum bayah, my Lord" serve as the prayer itself, while subsequent lines describe an unidentified "someone" as crying, singing, and praying.

Although practically all black spiritual hymns have taken their cues from Scripture, some appear to emphasize specific biblical themes, events, or personages. David, the boy harpist of Israel, comes immediately to mind as a favorite among the singer-narrators of black spiritual hymnody. In him one perceives rhythmically the "Li'tle . . . shepherd boy" who killed the monster Goliath "an' shouted fo' joy." Joshua, too, appears in the "Lit'le David" piece as "de son of Nun; / He never would quit till his work was done." Joshua has been featured as leader, in his own spiritual—a ballad, of sorts, that describes the hero's military exploits leading to that morning at Jericho when "de walls come tumblin' down." Jehova's directives to Moses and Ezekiel, respectively, have produced two of the most popular among the spirituals, both containing themes sufficiently universal to the present historical moment. Despite the resemblance between "Dry Bones" and an elementary school anatomy lesson, the lively rhythm and light language of that song are merely facades. Between the lines lurks the dual specter of sterility and death that characterized the Babylonian exile wherein the prophet Ezekiel labored to carry out the commands of Jehovah.

Similarly, "Go down, Moses," perhaps one of the lengthiest of black spiritual hymns, focuses upon the tragedy of enslavement and the harsh journey out of the spiritual wilderness. It begins with the simple, sad plea for deliverance: "Go down, Moses, way down in Egypt land, /Tell ole Pharaoh, let my people go." It ends with a note of hope, a ray of pure idealism and strong faith: "O let all from bondage flee . . . / And let us all in Christ be free." Last, the question relative to the crucifixion—"Were you there when they crucified my Lord"—refers to remembrance and significance rather than to actual presence. The trauma of that experience—more accurately, the recollection of the account of that experience—produces a deep emotional response, relating the singer's narrative to the one based upon Old Testament experiences: "Oh! Sometimes it causes me to tremble, tremble, tremble." As with the vast number of black spiritual hymns, the universality of its theme—the search for freedom, for an end to pain and suffering—carries the day for the form and secures its niche in the history of hymnody in the United States. That very theme, because it continues to hold center stage in contemporary history, effectively negates the major problem of superficiality arising from the poetry and the language of black spiritual hymnody.

Chapter Ten
AMERICA IN THE TWENTIETH CENTURY

THE IMMEDIATE REACTION TO a preliminary consideration of twentieth-century American hymnody may well resemble a quick step backward—half in awe, half in trepidation— after having just seen a large container filled with literally thousands of puzzle pieces that must, at some point, be fitted together to form a single and unified entity. Where does one begin? With what does one begin? How does one locate the pieces? How does one fit everything together? How long before one finishes the project? Does one ever actually finish? In other words, by virtue of its sheer bulk, twentieth-century American hymnody, much like its counterpart in Great Britain, presents problems of selectivity, arrangement, classification, and analysis—not to mention likes, dislikes, and prejudices among congregational singers. In the end, however, there must be an end. Decisions will be determined and answers will be formulated. If the method for selection appears somewhat arbitrary, so be it. In the end, the pieces selected for preview and discussion will serve at least as accurate and ample representatives of the giant jigsaw puzzle that constitutes congregational song in the United States from 1900 to the present—or at least as close to the present as we can get.

Table 31 focuses upon hymnody produced from 1901 to 1919—from the turn of the century until shortly after the Great War.

Table 31. American Hymnody, 1901–1919

Date	Hymnodist	Opening Lines
1901	Maltbie Davenport Babcock	This is my Father's world, And to my listening ears
1901	Alice Elvira Freeman	How sweet and silent is the place, Alone, my God, with Thee!
1902	Julia Bulkley Cady Cory	We praise Thee, O God, our Redeemer, Creator, In grateful devotion our tribute we bring
1903	Richard Watson Gilder	To Thee, Eternal Soul, be praise, Who, from of old to our own days
1903	William DeWitt Hyde	Creation's Lord, we give Thee thanks That this Thy world is incomplete
1903	Frank Mason North	Where cross the crowded ways of life, Where sound the cries of race and clan
1907	Shepherd Knapp	Lord God of hosts, whose purpose never swerving, Leads toward the day of Jesus Christ, Thy Son
1907	Henry Van Dyke	Joyful, joyful we adore Thee, God of glory, Lord of love
1907	Howard Arnold Walter	I would be true, for there are those who trust me; I would be pure, for there are those who care
1908	Robert Davis	I thank Thee, Lord, for strength of arm To win my bread
1908	Shepherd Knapp	Not only where God's free winds blow, Or in the silent wood
1909	Ozora Stearns Davis	At length where dawns the glorious day, By prophets long
1909	Ozora Stearns Davis	We bear the strain of earthly care But bear it not alone
1909	Carl Doving, (trans.)	Built on the rock the Church doth stand, Even when steeples are falling
1909	William Pierson Merrill	Not alone for mighty empire, Stretching fair o'er land and sea

Date	Hymnodist	Opening Lines
1909	William Merrell Vories	Let there be light, Lord God of Hosts! Let there be wisdom on the earth
1910	Louis Fitzgerald Benson	O splendor of God's glory bright, From light eternal bringing light
1910	Louis Fitzgerald Benson	The light of God is falling Upon life's common way
1910	Walter Russell Bowie	O holy city, seen of John, Where Christ the Lamb doth reign
1910	Henry Webb Farrington	I know not how that Bethlehem's babe Could in the Godhead be
1911	John Coleman Adams	We praise Thee, O God, for harvests earned, The fruits of labor garnered in
1911	William Pierson Merrill	Rise up, O men of God! Have done with lesser things
1911	Frances Whit-marsh Wile	All beautiful the march of days, As seasons come and go
1912	Jay Thomas Stocking	A Master-Workman of the race, Thou man of Galilee
1912	Henry Van Dyke	O Lord our God, Thy mighty hand, Hath made our country free
1913	George Bennard	On a hill far away stood an old rugged cross, The emblem of suff'ring and shame
1913	John Edgar Park	O Jesus, Thou wast tempted, Alone in deserts wild
1913	John Edgar Park	We would see Jesus, lo! His star is shining Above the stable while the angels sing
1914	Walter Russell Bowie	God of the nations, who from dawn of days, Hast let Thy people in their widening ways
1915	George Angier Gordon	O will of God beneath our life, The sea beneath the wave
1916	John Wright Buckham	O God, above the drifting years, The shrines our Fathers founded stand
1916	Milton Smith Littlefield	O Son of man, Thou madest known, Through quiet work in shop and home

Date	Hymnodist	Opening Lines
1917	Frank Mason North	O Master of the waking world, Who hast the nations in Thy heart
1917	Frank Mason North	The world's astir! The clouds of storm Have melted light
1917	Frank Mason North	Thou Lord of light, across the years Thy shining path of love we see
1919	Calvin Weiss Laufer	We thank Thee, Lord, Thy paths of service lead To blazoned heights and down the slopes of need
1919	Frank Mason North	Touch Thou, O Lord, our waiting hearts with light, Kindle with holy flame our sacrifice

Fitting it is, indeed, that one of the most popular hymns of twentieth-century America—published very early in the century—suggests the arrival of a new time for a relatively old world. Maltbie Davenport Babcock (1858-1901) barely made his mortal way into the twentieth century, after having served churches in Lockport, New York, Baltimore, and New York City (Brick Presbyterian Church). Babcock's singer-narrator describes an exhilarating moment when the human heart and mind, standing squarely and securely amid the phenomena of a God-created world, harmonize to "The music of the spheres." The hymnodist projected for all people the image of "my Father's world," a place, a time, a state of mind where, "In the rustling grass I hear Him pass, / He speaks to me everywhere."

Recognizing that within that same world live people with limited visions of God's works and God's grand scheme, William Merrill' (1867–1954)—one of several of the Presbyterian ministers at Brick Presbyterian Church, New York—challenged the twentieth century to "Rise up" and "Have done with lesser things." His hymn of brotherhood still manages to prod the offspring of modernity to devote their collective "heart and soul and mind and

strength" to the service of God and to a Church that will
hopefully contribute to the defeat of what he poetically
termed "this night of wrong." The Reverend Ozora Davis
(1866–1931), a Congregationalist minister and a president
of Chicago Theological Seminary (1909–1920), wrote
concerning brotherhood, a condition wherein Christ
accompanies the faithful, shares their common hopes, and
helps to lighten their burden of the "strain of earthly care."
Shepherd Knapp (b. 1873), a Congregationalist minister
and another hymnodist associated with the Brick Presbyterian Church, expressed the far-ranging sentiments of his
fellow composers of congregational hymnody, directing
his hymns toward an essentially pre-World War I urban
environment.

> Not only where God's free winds blow
>   Or in the silent wood,
> But where the city's restless flow
> Is never still, His love we know,
>   And finds His presence good.

Hymnologically as well as politically and economically,
the first two decades of the twentieth century witnessed a
flexing of the nation's spiritual and physical muscles. The
hymns of the period, although not bombastic in tone or
content, nonetheless reflected the pride of American
worshipers in their nation. Milton Littlefield (1864–1934),
a product of Johns Hopkins University and Union Theological Seminary, was but one example of a hymnodist who
turned his attention to the activities of shop and home. He
emphasized with acute accuracy "The sacredness of common things, / The chance of life that each day brings,"
which constituted a purpose proclaimed by God and
embraced by those whom He had placed upon earth. Part
of that "sacredness of common things" concerned the
fundamental American quality of freedom, an issue that
reverberated throughout the administrations of McKinley,
Roosevelt, and Taft. According to Henry Van Dyke

(1852–1933), a God-created freedom gave rise to a "broad and happy land." A graduate of Princeton University and Princeton Theological Seminary, yet another of the Brick Presbyterian Church pastors, and a professor of English literature at Princeton, Van Dyke served as U.S. minister to the Netherlands and Luxembourg, as a U.S. navy chaplain during World War I, and as chairman of the Committee of Revision of the Presbyterian *Book of Common Worship.* In one of his more noted hymns, he extended, albeit indirectly, the image of the holy and golden city of Jerusalem to the vastness of the United States, which he envisioned

> In union's golden chain;
> Her thousand cities fill with peace.
> Her million fields with grain.

For any hymnodist, of course, only one leader can point the way to the ideal site of peace and plenty. Walter Russell Bowie (1882–1969), a member of the committee that prepared the American Revised Standard Version of the Bible and professor of practical theology at Union Theological Seminary (New York), served Emmanuel Church (Greenwood, Virginia), Saint Paul's (Richmond), and Grace Church (New York). In his mind, the strength of early-twentieth-century America manifested itself in the contributions of those who, directed by the light of God, eagerly swarmed to the shores of the United States to establish anew their lives and their hopes within "the borders of our promised land." Merrill's thanksgiving hymn, "Not alone for mighty empire," places new hopes and new strengths in proper perspective. Even with the magnitude of the bounteous harvests and earthly glories and conquests, there arises the need for serious national prayer—for an expression that seems somewhat futuristic for the year 1909.

> God of justice, save the people
> From the clash of race and creed,

> From the strife of class and faction,
>   Make our nation free indeed;
> Keep her faith in simple manhood
>   Strong as when her life began,
> Till it find its full fruition
>   In the brotherhood of man!

If nothing else, Merrill's hymn heralded the role of American congregational song in the battles for social justice and human equality that, later in the century, would range long and rage hard—and would eventually give birth to new hymns.

Although the ideals of America blazed brightly and strongly within the lines of its hymns, early-twentieth-century hymnodists did not lose sight of the institutions that initiated and sponsored the various ministries of God's people. Thus, Carl Doving's translation of Nicolai F. S. Grundtvig's poem—which has come to be known as "Built on the rock the Church doth stand"—underscores the symbolic rather than the organizational nature of the Church. For Doving as translator, the Church looms large as a "house of living stones, / Builded for His habitation," a symbolic structure that all worshipers must come to imagine as "High above the earth . . . / All earthly temples excelling." On a similar level stands George Bennard's "Old Rugged Cross," a true child of the nineteenth-century gospel song tradition in which the structure atop Doving's solid rock yields for the moment to an "emblem of suff'ring and shame," but nonetheless a sign that the narrator-singer will cherish and cling to. What brings unity to two pieces apparently so different in form and purpose (not to mention audience) rests on the notion of human beings realizing, through faith and through the Church, an eventual rendezvous with God. Doving's God, in the end, "would deign with us to dwell, / With all His grace and favor"; Bennard's faithful narrator, on the other hand, awaits the "call some day to my home far away, / Where

His glory for ever I'll share." Both narrators, of course, seek their places as heirs to God's kingdom.

A number of hymns written during the initial decades of the twentieth century contain similar themes or, at least, seem to be governed by particular key terms. For instance, the trilogy of "light," "purity," and "beauty" resides most conspicuously within "Splendor of God's glory bright," a translation from Ambrose of Milan by Louis Fitzgerald Benson (1855–1930)—the noted hymnologist and hymnodist who edited hymnals for the Presbyterian Church, lectured on liturgics at Auburn Theological Seminary, taught hymnology at Princeton Theological Seminary, and authored the significant *English Hymn: Its Development and Use in Public Worship* (1915). Henry Wilder Foote (*Three Centuries*, p. 325) has termed *The English Hymn* a volume without "rival as a mine of accurate information about the development and use of English and American hymns and hymnbooks."

At any rate, Benson began his translation from Ambrose with the idea of "light eternal bringing light," a description of heavenly radiance, and he proceeded through a half-dozen similar images: "Sun of heav'n's love"; "lasting radiance from above"; "Dawn's glory gilds the earth"; "Light of light, light's living spring"; "all days illumining"; "Holy Spirit's ray"; and "faith her eager fires renew."

William Vories's light comes forth in no less abundance or intensity. This hymnodist (b. 1880) served as an independent missionary in Japan and founded the Omi Mission in the Japanese province of the same name; no doubt his Eastern associations influenced the imagery of his hymnodic texts. In his "Let there be light," the phrase, "peace of vision clear" serves as the spiritual beacon that magnifies the love of God and the useful labor of humankind, while at the same time it neutralizes human fear. In fact, the final stanza of that hymn could easily have

been composed yesterday instead of three quarters of a
century earlier.

> Let woe and waste of warfare cease,
>   That useful labor yet may build
>   Its home with love and laughter filled;
> God, give Thy wayward children peace.

The light from above most easily transfers to a strong
sense of purity—a vision, if you will—filtered through the
idealism of youth. Thus Howard Walter writes of truth and
trust, of purity and strength. He directs the attentions of
congregational singers to the manifestation of one who
"would be friend to all, the foe, the friendless," who always
"would look up, and laugh, and love, and lift." As with
Vories's "Let there be light," Walter's "I would be true"
manages to defy the span of years between the date of its
composition and the present age.

Light unearths purity of and in the world, and the
combination of light and purity creates for singer-
worshipers a sense of the beautiful, of the earthly sublime.
Frances Wile (1875–1939) composed a hymn to mark the
seasons, thus conveying the idea of the progression of
nature's moments. Her "All beautiful the march of days"
notes clearly the passage of time in relation to the
transcience of her own years. But, at the same time, one
needs to take note of God's splendors, of nature's being
and of nature's actions.

> O'er white expanses sparkling pure
> The radiant morns unfold;
> The solemn splendors of the night
> Burn brighter through the cold.

Beauty exists also in the sheer emotion of adoration, in
the harmonious expression of faith and commitment.
Little wonder, then, that Henry Van Dyke's tribute to
"joyful" praise of God leans heavily upon the beauty of a

God-created nature, upon the hearts of the faithful that "unfold like flowers before Thee, / Opening to the sun above." Few hymnodic expressions have surpassed, in terms of pure exuberance, the positiveness of Van Dyke's "Joyful, joyful we adore Thee"; it serves as a testimony and a tribute to clear, pure, and beautiful life, to the utter ecstasy that lifts hearts and minds heavenward in the direction of the "Joyful music" that ultimately leads "Sunward / In the triumph song of life." No less a genius than Beethoven allows us to sing this hymn, but the "Well-spring of the joy of living" originates from the wellspring of creative power and vivid imagination generated by a truly thankful American hymnodist.

Surely one of the most prominent hymnodists of the twentieth century expended considerable talent and time in developing the images of light, purity, and beauty. In a composition entitled "The Shadowed Lands," beginning "Touch Thou, O Lord, our waiting hearts with light," Frank Mason North (1850–1935)—secretary of the New York City Missionary Society and also secretary of the Methodist Board of Foreign Missions, president of the Federal Council of the Churches of Christ in America, and one of the founders of the Methodist Federation for Social Services—asked for inspiration, commitment, and a sense of holy service. He sought expression through the "holy flame" that would "Unveil Thy glorious purpose to our sight" and "Give clearer vision to our lifted eyes." North carried the light of the dedicated missionary and the professional Church administrator in an effort to "save the suff'ring peoples." Nonetheless, he tuned himself most finely to what he termed the "throb of surging life." If nothing else, he emerged as a hymnodist of action, a poet most determined to hymnodize the traumas of the twentieth-century world. In terms of images of light, purity, and beauty, North seemed to have marshaled their symbolic and linguistic equivalents and directed them toward the vibrant actions and reactions of American youth.

> The world's astir! The clouds of storm
> Have melted into light,
> Whose streams aglow from fountains warm
> Have driven back the night.
> Now brightens dawn toward golden day;
> The earth is full of song;
> Far stretch the shining paths away;
> Spring forward! Hearts, be strong!

Young America, for North, could be found in its people—
the old as well as the young—and in the urban centers of
the United States: "the crowded ways of life, / Where
sound the cries of race and clan." But he also perceived the
dangers and the ills within the city, a "noise of selfish strife"
that gave way eventually to "haunts of wickedness and
need." From the unattractive side of America's relatively
recently developed industrial strength, from its toil and
sorrow and pain and ugliness, would come one day a new
light and a new beauty. North, ever the missionary,
imagined a transformation—a conversion, perhaps—in
the form of the ultimate symbol of light, beauty, and
purity: "glorious from Thy heaven above, / Shall come
the city of our God." Thus, the New Jerusalem had been
transplanted from its Middle Eastern origins to a nation of
new people and of new hopes.

The years 1920 through 1940—between the wars, as
historians have tended to label them—proved a period of
hymnodic stability in America, a time when the traditional
establishment of the Church appeared content to develop
hymnodic themes similar with those which had emerged at
the turn of the century. Such apparent stability, however,
in no way brought about a decline in the quality of hymns;
there was not even a sign of staleness or stagnation.
Indeed, such poets of the Church as Benson and North
continued to seek the means by which to raise the overall
poetic level of congregational song in the United States,
while the likes of Henry Hallam Tweedy, Walter Russell
Bowie, Harry Emerson Fosdick, and Calvin Weiss Laufer

set standards for hymnodic expression that remain to this day. Table 32 considers some examples from these poets of the Church, as well as others from among their equally talented contemporaries.

Table 32. American Hymnody, 1923–1940

Date	Hymnodist	Opening Lines
1923	Louis Fitzgerald Benson	O Love that lights the eastern sky And shrouds the evening rest
1924	Louis Fitzgerald Benson	For the bread, which Thou hast broken; For the wine which Thou hast poured
1925	Louis Fitzgerald Benson	O sing a song of Bethlehem, Of shepherds watching there
1925	Edward Grubb	Our God, to whom we turn When weary with illusion
1925	D. P. McGeachy	God of the marching centuries, Lord of the passing years
1925	Frank Mason North	With Thee, our Master and our Lord, We greet this wondrous day
1925	Henry Hallam Tweedy	O gracious Father of mankind, Our spirits' unseen Friend
1926	Louis Fitzgerald Benson	I name Thy hallowed Name, I bring Thee a new day
1926	Earl Bowman Marlatt	"Are ye able," said the Master, "To be crucified with me?"
1927	Stuart Wesley Keene Hine	O Lord my God! when I in awesome wonder Consider all the works Thy hands have made
1927	Milton Smith Littlefield	Come, O Lord, like morning sunlight, Making all life new and free
1927	Frank Mason North	O wondrous Child! the lowing kine Have never gazed on face like Thine
1928	Walter Russell Bowie	Lord Christ, when first Thou cam'st to men, Upon a Cross they bound to Thee
1928	Henry Webb Farrington	O God Creator, in whose hand, The rolling planets lie

Date	Hymnodist	Opening Lines
1928	Earl Bowman Marlatt	Spirit of Life, in this new dawn, Give us the faith that follows on
1928	Nancy Byrd Turner	O Son of man, who walked each day A humble road serene and strong
1928	Henry Hallam Tweedy	Eternal God whose power upholds Both flower and flaming star
1930	Harry Emerson Fosdick	God of grace and God of glory, On Thy people pour Thy power
1931	Thomas Curtis Clark	While restless crowds are thronging Along the city ways
1931	James Gordon Gilkey	Outside the Holy City, Unnumbered footsteps throng
1931	Calvin Weiss Laufer	Thee, Holy Father, we adore; We sing Thy praises o'er and o'er
1931	Howard Chandler Robbins	And have the bright immensities Received our risen Lord
1931	Wilbur Fisk Tillett	O Son of God incarnate, O Son of man divine!
1932	Henry Hallam Tweedy	O Holy Spirit, making whole Thy sons in body, mind and soul
		O Spirit of the living God, Thou Light of fire divine
1935	Samuel Ralph Harlow	O young and fearless Prophet of ancient Galilee
1935	Nancy Byrd Turner	Men go out from the places where they dwelled, They know not why, nor whither, over-borne
1937	Howard Chandler Robbins	Put forth, O Lord, Thy spirit's might And bid Thy Church increase
1938	Katherine K. Davis (John Cowley, pseud.)	Let all things now living a song of thanksgiving To God the Creator triumphantly raise

Date	Hymnodist	Opening Lines
1939	Howard Chandler Robbins	Sunset to sunrise changes now, For God doth make His world anew
1939	Henry Hallam Tweedy	Lord of starry vasts unknown, Make my heart Thy spirit's throne
1939	Henry Hallam Tweedy	True lovers of mankind, The Lord of life adore!
1940	Francis Bland Tucker	All praise to Thee, for Thou, O King divine Didst yield the glory that of right was thine
1940	Francis Bland Tucker	Alone Thou goest forth, O Lord, In sacrifice to die
1940	Francis Bland Tucker	Father, we thank Thee, who hast planted Thy holy Name within our hearts
1940	Francis Bland Tucker	The great Creator of the worlds, The sovereign Lord of heaven

The hymns of Frank Mason North continued in evidence during the third decade of the twentieth century, and the two pieces selected for discussion here represent the diversity of both his skill and his professional interests. The one entitled "O Wondrous Child," a Christmas hymn, captures the tenderness of the Nativity scene as the poet praised the peace and the serenity of the moment, the joy that promotes both strength and love. But North also demonstrated an awareness of truth, of reality, of the real purpose that places the apparent joy of the occasion in proper context and in proper prospective.

> The mysteries of Thy life begin
> Here in this stable of an inn;
> The paths Thy tender feet must tread
> Reach out from this, Thy humble bed;
> Thy outstretched hand, so soft, so wee,
> Must know Thy cross's agony.

North remained the idealist, the missionary who, in company "With Thee, our Master and our Lord," would "greet this wondrous day." His creative eye focused upon the distant horizons, where "Afar the troubled lands await / The rescue from distress." And as a missionary, North basked in the glory of God's service; the Cross became the vessel upon which to launch forth the glory of God throughout the world. The essence of his hymnody may be observed in the final lines of his missionary commission hymn, a song dedicated to "Thy conquering love in every land, / Thy triumph, Christ, our King!"

Although Louis F. Benson, during the period of the 1920s and 1930s, held fairly firm to the "light" motif that characterized his early hymnodic efforts, he demonstrated a willingness to vary the focus of his principal images. The discussion may easily begin with his hymn on life everlasting—"O Love that lights the eastern sky"—and its depiction of the various relationships between light and life: "Life's new dawn," the light that "breaks through / To melt the mist away," and the love that "lights the evening star." In a different vein, Benson became a paraphraser of the Hebrew psalms and demonstrated to congregational singers that he could create a fresh poem without obscuring the language or the sentiment of the original. Notice the opening phrase of each of the five stanzas of his 1926 piece, "I name Thy hallowed Name, / I bring Thee a new day": (stanza 1) "I name Thy hallowed Name"; (stanza 2) "Thy kingdom come to me"; (stanza 3) "Thy will be done by me"; (stanza 4) "Give me my bread today"; and (stanza 5) "If any tempt me, lead." Rather than simply mimic the Hebrew poets (or the English translators thereof), Benson allowed the psalmodist to set the tone, in each stanza, for his own extremely personal prayer for intercession. One ought not to ignore Benson's moving Communion hymn ("For the bread which Thou hast broken") or his Christmas piece ("O sing a song of Bethlehem"). In the former poem, the hymnodist again relied upon love and peace as thematic notes upon which to sound the "call to heaven above us," while in the latter work he simply took advantage of the singsong effect of the season.

> O sing a song of Bethlehem,
> Of shepherds watching there,
> And of the news that came to them
> From angels in the air.

From Bethlehem, Benson guided his worshipers through Nazareth, Galilee, and Calvary (twice within each stanza). Certainly the ground appears all too familiar, yet few congregational singers have been bothered by the hymnodist's sincere attempts to develop a modern direction for an essentially ancient form.

The attraction to Henry Hallam Tweedy's hymns by a large number of American (as well as British) worshipers may be the result of the middle ground upon which that poet placed his offerings before the congregation. Educated for the Congregationalist ministry, Tweedy (1868–1953) served the Plymouth Congregational Church, Utica, New York; South Congregational Church, Bridgeport, Connecticut; and Yale Divinity School as a professor of practical theology. Tweedy as poet rarely aimed too high or too low. His language reflects his own piety and religious commitment, while his images prove neither esoteric nor oversimplistic. One may state with confidence that he sought and generally achieved a transition from the traditions of the nineteenth century to the new and fresh ideas of his own time.

In "O gracious Father of mankind," Tweedy produced the image of God the Father within the nice, easy context of "High heaven's Lord, our hearts' dear Guest." Most assuredly, the end of the final stanza of that piece summarizes well both the poet's purpose and his method.

> No more we seek Thee from afar,
> Nor ask Thee for a sign,
> Content to pray in life and love
> And toil, till all are Thine.

Tweedy's reliance upon the most common elements of nature to provide his verse with substance and dimension can be seen clearly in "O Spirit of the living God," wherein the dominant image comes immediately in terms of "Thou Light and Fire divine." From there, the "wind" becomes the instrument by which God transmits wisdom and clears away the "mists of error, clouds of doubt"; "fire" inspires "our lips / With flaming love and zeal." Those easily recognizable images complement Tweedy's secondary thesis—the universality of truth communicated in "the language all men understand / When love speaks loud and clear."

In terms of an obviously identifiable twentieth-century point of view, Henry Hallam Tweedy's best effort appears to have been his forty-line dedication to love, truth, and beauty—"Eternal God, whose power upholds." Again, the language and the imagery remain on a middle ground similar to those hymns discussed previously. However, the poet appeared to have achieved especially accurate and comprehensive figures. God's power "upholds / Both flower and flaming star"; science seeks God's truth; God's "heralds of good news" gain inspiration from righteousness and grace and thus "live Thy life divine." Tweedy's sensitivity comes forth in perhaps the most artistic section of the hymn, when he calls out,

> O God of beauty, oft revealed
> In dreams of human art,
> In speech that flows to melody,
> In holiness of heart.

Rather than merely extol the virtues of heaven-sent beauty, Tweedy hurled his image forward and outward on a divine mission; his errant beauty "teaches us to ban all ugliness / That blinds our eyes to Thee," creating ultimately an atmosphere of "loveliness / Of lives made fair and free."

Three hymns by Howard Chandler Robbins reflect the degree to which a hymnodist of the 1930s could take advantage of the emerging interest in space, flight, and the physical sciences without necessarily scrapping traditional images. The opening stanza of his Ascension hymn may not be the easiest lines for congregational singers to express, but the language and the relationship among the images prove interesting reading.

> And have the bright immensities
>   Received our risen Lord,
> Where light years frame the Pleiades
>   And point Orion's sword?
> Do flaming suns His footsteps trace
>   Through corridors sublime,
> The Lord of interstellar space
>   And conqueror of time?

Such a passage would indeed cause problems for worshipers and singers were it not for the fact that Robbins posed therein two questions that obviously require answers. His view of Christ among the stars, the constellations, and the planets—his image of Christ striding the endless regions of space and time—would appear to weaken the relationship between the faithful and the Being to which they direct their faith.

However, Robbins answered the questions in the second stanza of his hymn. Heaven remains an idea rather than a geophysical entity; as such, it is as "An altar candle sheds its light / As surely as a star." The very act and place of worship bridge the distance between earth and heaven.

> And where His loving people meet
>   To share the gift divine,
> There stands He with unhurrying feet;
>   There heavenly splendors shine.

The beauty of "And have the bright immensities" originates from the relationship between its imagery and its structure; together, the two force the congregational singer to think as well as to utter.

In two other hymns—"Put forth, O Lord, Thy spirit's might" and "Sunset to sunrise changes now"—Robbins continued to roam the vastness of space and time, although he abandoned his practice of posing direct questions to singers. The first piece constitutes a plea for unity and peace as a means of expunging hatred and fear. Robbins asks us to remember and to apply the lessons from Christ learned by the apostles: "Their steadfast faith our unity, / Their peace our heritage." In "Sunset to sunrise changes now," Robbins worked well with the concept of light, particularly as a contrast from the sunlight to "a more heavenly lamp" that "shines . . . / . . . from the Cross, on Calvary's height." Such a beacon, of course, serves as a sign that "The Lord of life hath victory"—still one more spark of hope that forms a new image for the modern world.

Francis Bland Tucker (1895–1984), an Episcopal priest and a member of the committee that compiled the 1940 Episcopal *Hymnal,* served as rector of Christ Church, Savannah, Georgia—the same pulpit that John Wesley had occupied more than two centuries before. A poet of decided merit, Tucker effectively captured the substance and the expression of his equally artistic and imaginative sources: Peter Abelard, Philippians, the second-century *Epistle to Diognetus,* and the *Didache* of the same general period. Notice what transpires in one context when the poet appears beside one of those sources:

Paul (Philippians 2:5–9)	Tucker ("All praise to Thee," lines 5–12)
Christ Jesus . . . did not count equality with God a thing to be grasped, but emptied Himself, taking the form of a servant, being born in the likeness of men, and being found in human form He humbled	Thou cam'st to us in lowliness of thought; By Thee the outcast and the poor were sought, And by Thy death was God's salvation wrought, Alleluia!

Himself and became obedient unto death, even death on a cross.	Let this mind be in us which was in Thee, Who wast a servant that we might be free Humbling Thyself to death on Calvary, Alleluia!

Tucker's art as a poet carried over to his skill as a paraphraser of Scripture. He possessed sufficient control to construct his own lines as echoes of the originals. He certainly did not obscure the words of Paul (or the translators of Paul) or even change the thematic intent of the passage from the New Testament epistle. By itself, however, the piece serves as a fine example of a twentieth-century praise hymn, one that fully and reasonably utilizes congregational expression and exhilaration. And so at the conclusion of the poem, the singers of Tucker's "All praise to Thee" rise to "confess with one accord / In heaven and earth that Jesus Christ is Lord." The movement from Christ's "humbling" on Calvary and the bowed knees of the faithful to the endnote of adoration on the part of the singing congregation underscores the strain of humility that dominates the hymns of Francis Bland Tucker.

For those who, in the relative silence that separated the two world wars, preferred Evangelical exuberance in hymnody to poetic diction and figures, the hymns of Earl Marlatt beckoned. Marlatt (1892–1976), served as professor of philosophy and religious literature and dean of the School of Religion at Boston University (1925–1946), before moving on to the faculty at Perkins School of Theology, Southern Methodist University. He armed his hymns with all of the accoutrements of the old time religion. His "Are ye able," with its emphasis upon discipleship, provides an interesting variation upon what may be termed a question-and-answer form of hymnody. Each of the four stanzas opens with a question from "the Master," followed by responses from a variety of sources:

"sturdy dreamers" and "heroic spirits." However, the ultimate answer lies within the refrain, in the congregational response that serves also as the congregational commitment and answer to the grand Call:

> "Lord, we are able." Our spirits are Thine.
> Remold them, make us, like Thee divine.
> Thy guiding radiance above us shall be
> A beacon to God, to love and loyalty.

One may observe that Marlatt did not always pay strict attention to rhythm, and on more than one occasion he absolutely forced the issue. Nonetheless, he had learned from his nineteenth-century predecessors. He relied heavily upon repetition, as in his piece on the Holy Spirit ("Spirit of life in this new dawn"), where the initial word in each of the five stanzas is the same—(1) "Spirit of Life," (2) "Spirit Creative," (3) "Spirit Redeeming," (4) "Spirit Consoling," and (5) "Spirit of love." Other than his experiments with the style and the structure of hymnodic verse, Marlatt offered little in the way of fresh language or imaginative imagery.

If Evangelical hymnody demonstrated any degree of maturity during the period from 1920 to 1940, it would have to be observed in a piece by S.W.K. Hine, a translation of a poem by Carl Boberg that most congregational singers have come to know by its popular title, "How Great Thou Art." On one level, Hine's effort relies heavily upon the simple utterances of nature—the brightness of stars, the rolling of thunder, the singing of birds, the sounds of brooks and breezes. Those natural manifestations in turn provide the prelude to the single, most significant act of God and witnessed by the inhabitants of the earth.

> When Christ shall come with shouts of acclamation
> And take me home, what joy shall fill my heart?

> Then I shall bow in humble adoration
> And then proclaim, my God how great Thou art!

Harry Emerson Fosdick's testimony to congregational exuberance, "God of grace and God of glory," serves also as a perfect example of controlled expression. Ordained to the Baptist ministry in 1903, Fosdick (1878–1976) lectured in homiletics and served as professor of practical theology at Union Theological Seminary. From there he went to the newly built First Presbyterian Church, New York—a post from which he resigned after refusing to sign the Westminster Confession of Faith. In practical terms, Fosdick's "God of grace and God of glory" sings better than Hine's translation, principally because the former possesses a smoother rhythm—or perhaps a smoother transition. At any rate, Fosdick created some rather fresh images—for instance, "Crown Thine ancient Church's story, / Bring her bud to glorious flower"—and he seemed to have known the value of careful repetition, particularly when he introduced the refrain for each stanza with "Grant us wisdom, / Grant us courage." Add to those devices John Hughes's stirring Welsh tune "Cwm Rhondda" (composed in 1907 for the anniversary at Chapel Rhondda, Pontypridd, Wales), and congregational hymnody in the United States has most certainly been blessed with a truly timeless piece. Fifty, perhaps even one hundred years from now, American worshipers will still be asking God to "Cure Thy children's warring madness; / Bend our pride to Thy control."

From World War II on, the stages of American hymnody become increasingly smaller—which means that the hymns themselves increase in number and in variety. Thus, approximately forty-six years of congregational song may be divided into four fairly distinct periods: 1941 to 1959; 1960 to 1969; 1970 to 1974; and 1975 to the present. Table 33 considers the first of those stages and the representative hymnodists and compositions that appear in the subsequent discussion.

Table 33. American Hymnody, 1941–1959

Date	Hymnodist	Opening Lines
1941	Francis Bland Tucker	Our Father, by whose name All fatherhood is known
1946	Almer T. Pennewell	So lowly doth the Savior ride A paltry borrowed beast
1948	Rowland W. Schloerb	O God, whose will is life and peace For all the sons of men
1950	Robert W. McClellan	God our Father, you our Maker, We your people heed your sovereign call
1952	Ernest K. Emurian	We dedicate this temple, Father, unto Thee
1952	Sarah E. Taylor	O God of light, Your word, a lamp unfailing, Shine through the darkness of our earthly way
1952	Frank Von Christierson	Break forth, O living light of God, Upon the world's dark hour!
1953	Georgia Harkness	Hope of the world, Thou Christ of great compassion, Speak to our fearful hearts by conflict rent
1953	Frederick B. Morley	O Church of God united To serve one common Lord
1953	John Edgar Park	O Christ whose love has sought us out Alone and lost in desert ways
1953	Charles Parkin	See the morning sun ascending, Radiant in the eastern sky
1954	H. Glen Lanier	O Master, who in days of youth
1954	Bradford G. Webster	O Jesus Christ, to You may hymns be rising, In every city for your love and care
1956	Elisabeth Burrowes	God of the ages, by whose hand Through years long past our lives were led

Date	Hymnodist	Opening Lines
1956	Orien Johnson	In God's green pastures feeding, by His cool waters lie, Soft in the evening walk my Lord and I
1957	Barbara J. Owen	We ask no greater joy, O Lord, Than to respond when Thou dost call
1958	William Watkins Reid, Jr.	O God of every nation, Of every race and land

The discussion of American hymnody of the 1940s and 1950s begins with a familiar voice—a transition figure from the 1940 Episcopal *Hymnal*—Francis Bland Tucker and his poem on God the Father. The hymnodist addresses, respectively, "Our Father," Christ the child, and "O Spirit who can bind / Our hearts in unity." At the same time, he holds firm to the idea of love as seen in its various dimensions: love of God for God's family; love of all human beings; and that form of love within the heart that becomes "the dwelling place of peace." Robert McClellan also calls to "God our Father," and similarly takes some time to reinforce the idea of godly love claiming a rightful niche within the hearts of all human beings. The real strength of his piece, however, lies in the hymnodist's willingness to consider the future in a positive vein and to rely upon the Church as the substance which faith can truly stand.

> Church of Jesus, church with vision,
> Built with living faith and hope to stand;
> May your people now rejoicing
> Raise your song of praise throughout the land.

McClellan enlarges upon the image of that strength by stockpiling an abundance of epithets: God as Father, Maker, Lord of all; Christ as leader, Lord, Savior, teacher, Master; the Holy Spirit as companion, guide, Light of God,

comforter, friend. All of these references assume roles as
ever-present symbols pointing in the direction of the
ever-presence of God.

The distance from God the Father to God the
instrument that directs all of the world's nations proves but
a short step for the contemporary American hymnodist.
Elisabeth Burrowes, for instance, praises a "God of the
ages," a past and present God who extends the bold and
visible hand of courage toward a "New faith to find the
paths ahead." In similar fashion, William Watkins Reid, Jr.,
in his "O God of every nation," depicts the mighty hand of
God stretched forth in love and mercy to "heal our
strife-torn world." However, he homes with extreme
sharpness on the extremes of universal ugliness—upon
hate, fear, threat, and greed; upon pride, lust, and avarice;
upon a perverted "trust in bombs that shower /
Destruction through the night." Reid does not engage in
metrical politics; his universal prayer serves simply to
announce the dawn of "the morning glorious / When
brotherhood shall reign." Schloerb also waits for peace, for
a God "whose will is life and peace." His prayer rises to seek
a pardon for "our narrowness of mind"; that same attack
against human lust for greed and human thirst to satisfy
false pride which reverberates through Reid's lines seeps
into Schloerb's hymn, which meets and parries such
human weaknesses with a universal goodness, with a God
clothed in deliverance and with a Prince of Peace creating
in all "the will to build each day / The family of God."

Another theme that attracts the attention of the
hymnodist of this period concerns God as giver of light and
life, an obvious outgrowth from the pastoral motif of the
Old Testament psalmodists. Thus Orien Johnson, in the
poetic syntax of his times—

> In God's green pastures feeding, by His cool waters lie
> Soft in the evening walk my Lord and I;
> All the sheep of His pasture fare so wond'rously fine,
> His sheep am I.

Johnson never extends that single setting, never develops more than that single dramatic instant from the Hebrew psalm. In true folk-hymnodic style, he allows his music to weave a mood around the loose bits and pieces of his poetic phrases—which, as indicated, exist as imaginative fragments. More conventional, and thus perhaps more representative of the God-as-light-and-life theme, Frank Von Christierson's "Break forth, O living light of God" anchors itself to the traditional idea of God as eternal guide in the midst of the "world's dark hour." The hymnodist directs congregational worshipers to seek God's aid in the restoration of truth and in the removal of what he terms "the veil of ancient words, / With message long obscure." Von Christierson's beacon casts an obvious light toward that which is, for the majority of twentieth-century worshipers, an equally obvious appeal for harmony among people and nations.

Two additional pieces on this same theme merit examination: Sarah Taylor's "O God of light, Your word a lamp unfailing" and Charles Parkin's "See the morning sun ascending." The latter serves as a simple expression of congregational praise, a hymn that fits naturally into the opening segments of the worship service. Parkin's angelic choir blends into the radiance of the eastern sky at the same time that "we, in lowly station, / Join the choristers above" in praise of creation and of the love of God. Although Sarah Taylor's images seem equally familiar, she writes a better poem than Parkin. The congregational singer may observe, for example, the word of God in the form of "a lamp unfailing" that "Shines through the darkness of our earthly way"; that message, "Undimmed by time," reveals God's peace, compassion, healing, and wonder as they affect human thoughts and actions. As with Parkin, Taylor does not forget the congregation that must eventually sing her hymn, an "anthem blending" set forth by "myriad tongues."

Light and life can, with ease and justification, stand

aside for a few moments in favor of their thematic
companions, hope and joy. Thus, at least five American
hymnodists who wrote during the 1950s considered such
elements. Bradford Webster, in "O Jesus Christ, to you
may hymns be rising," imagines the text of God's mercy as
a "glad surprising / That your blest Spirit brings men
everywhere," but most particularly for those who search
the cities for heavenly love and care. For John Edgar Park,
the love of Christ serves as an active agent functioning
beyond the outer reaches of the human mind; as worshipers and as human beings, "We cannot understand; we
love." Our joy and adoration of God and His Son come
from the basic instinct of our faith: we trust! In her "Hope
of the world," Georgia Harkness universalizes the sentiments of Webster and Park:

> Hope of the world, God's gift from highest heaven,
>   Bringing to hungry souls the bread of life;
> Still let Thy spirit unto us be given
>   To heal earth's wounds and end her bitter strife.

Georgia Harkness's lines demonstrate clearly the
proximity of hope to joy, as well as the thesis set forth by
Barbara Owen, who finds joy in the talents of human
beings—their actions, their courage, and their strength.
The hope rising from such joy attaches itself to faith, to
human intellects that "seek Thy will / Our hearts to love
Thee and obey." The fifth among the hope-and-joy
hymnodists, Almer Pennewell, recreates the New Testament messianic hope-love concept. Inspired by the gran-
deur of Christ's grace (joy), those on earth—those of
relatively low degree—"Exalt and usher in the day / Of
peace we long to see." For Pennewell, human joy translates
to a form of hope that ultimately will bear fruit in the form
of inner peace and overall contentment.

The final theme to be considered for American
hymnodists of the 1950s concerns the Church. Such a
theme would begin with the hymn as a dedicatory exercise,

then move on to praise of the universality of the Church as an institution. Ernest Emurian's piece is, at the outset, a rhetorical exercise in introductory expression. Each of his four stanzas begins with the clause "We dedicate this temple"; the recipient of the dedication appears as, respectively, God the Father, Christ the Lord, the high Spirit, and (as the climax)—

> To Father, Son, and Spirit
> Whose temple ever stands
> In hearts that learn to love Thee,
> And minds that comprehend;
> In will empowered to witness
> Thy kingdom without end!

The Morley poem, "O Church of God united," appears usual in terms of church goals and priorities—at least until the singer arrives at the third stanza. At that point the hymnodist concentrates upon a variety of doctrine and language, concluding with an idea that emerged, during the 1950s, with increasing consistency.

> Though creeds and tongues may differ,
> They speak, O Christ, of Thee;
> And in Thy loving Spirit
> We shall one people be.

Both Emurian and Morley sound notes of ecumenism that may well have been beyond the reach and the desire of their contemporary Christians. Nonetheless, the two hymnodists seem to have seen with acuteness the ends to which congregational song would eventually direct itself.

Those goals, as they are now known—both theological and hymnological—became clearer for American hymnodists as the twentieth century entered its sixth decade. Gone—both in actuality and in influence—were the prominent figures from the periods that both preceded and immediately followed World War I; a new cadre of names—often totally unfamiliar as hymnodic poets—arose to take their places upon the pages of congregational hymnals. However, the substitutions represent the natural passage of time; in no way does a predominantly new listing of authors and titles imply a dominance in quality and even in popularity of one era over another. Hymnody has always been—and certainly will continue to be—highly traditional in substance and in form. Table 34 considers some writers and works that came to the fore between 1960 and 1969.

Table 34. American Hymnody, 1960–1969

Date	Hymnodist	Opening Lines
1960	Ruth Elliott	Glorious is your name, Most Holy, God and Father of us all
1960	J. Clifford Evers	Where charity and love prevail, There God is ever found
1960	Olive Wise Spannaus	Lord of all nations, grant me grace To love all men of every race
1960	Frank Von Christierson	As men of old their first fruits brought Of orchard, flock, and field
1961	Elinor Lennin	Within the shelter of our walls, Be present, Lord, to guide
1962	Mildred C. Luckhardt	Great Ruler over time and space, Who holdest galaxies in place
1964	Ewald Bash	By the Babylonian rivers We sat down in grief and wept
1965	Frances Martha Hibbert	Cradled in a manger, On the fragrant hay
1965	Louise Marshall McDowell	For perfect love so freely spent, For fellowship restored
1965	William Watkins Reid	God of earth and planets Ranging outer space
1965	Miriam Therese Winter	God gives His people strength. If we believe in His way

Date	Hymnodist	Opening Lines
1966	James Boeringer	Give to the Lord, as He has blest thee, Even when He seems far away
1966	Henry L. Lettermann	When Christ comes to die on Calvary, Created things all hold their breath
1966	Elton Trueblood	Thou whose purpose is to kindle, Now ignite us with Thy fire
1967	W. F. Jabusch	Open your ears, O Christian people, Open your ears and hear good news
1967	Sebastian Temple	Sing praises to the living God, Glory, hallelujah
1968	Herbert Brokering	Earth and all stars, Loud rushing planets
1968	David N. Johnson	Lovely child, holy child, Gentle, mild, undefiled
1968	Paul Quinlan	It's a brand new day, everything is fine. Though it may be gray, I want you to know that the sun's gonna shine
1969	Francis Scott Brenner	Descend, O Spirit, purging flame, Brand us this day with Jesus' name!
1969	Carlton C. Buck	O Lord, the maze of earthly ways Confuses our intent
1969	Elisabeth Burrowes	O God, send men whose purpose will not falter, Who dare to walk where Christ has set His feet
1969	Miriam Drury	Walk tall, Christian, Walk tall and have no fear
1969	Miriam Drury	Within the Church's hallowed walls, Thy glory's habitation
1969	Ernest K. Emurian	Bless Thou the astronauts who face The vast immensities of space
1969	Martin Franzmann	O God, O Lord of heaven and earth, Thy living finger never wrote
1969	Herbert Grieb	May I, a pilgrim, hope to tread The path the Savior trod?
1969	Carrie Hitt Hardcastle	O God, Thy Church eternal Has meaning for this hour

Date	Hymnodist	Opening Lines
1969	Florence Jansson	A bird, a lovely butterfly, A fleecy cloud up in the sky
1969	Henry Lyle Lambdin	To worship, work, and witness, The good news spread abroad
1969	William Watkins Reid	Lord, wake your Church from self-concern, From worship of its ancient good
1969	William Watkins Reid	O God, ere history began, Or man forsook the cave
1969	William Watkins Reid, Jr.	The city is above, O God, With sound of hustling feet
1969	E. Leslie Wood	O Thou who givest the good earth, With soil and seed to grow our grain
1969	Robert Newell Zearfoss	Let Christ be born of hope this day, O friends in fields of night

A number of hymnodists from earlier decades remained active during the 1960s—a sign that, despite the wide cultural and especially political differences that emerged during the period, American hymnody maintained some degree of thematic and rhetorical consistency. Frank Von Christierson's stewardship hymn, "As men of old their first fruits brought," begins on a note of material affluence, with references to "bounteous yield" and "wealth of this good land." The hymnodist sounds an air of sharp contrast in the second stanza, however, in which the congregation sings of a world in need that "summons us / To labor, love, and give" as an equally sharp reminder that the same world needs to be "redeemed by Christ-like love."

From a rural context I turn, by way of the contemporary imagery of W. W. Reid, Jr., upon a city alive

> With the sound of hustling feet,
> With flashing lights and rapid change
> That pulse through every street.

But as does Von Christierson, Reid thrusts alarming opposites against the well-oiled mechanism of progress's Sandburgian strength. Reid's city presents a "bright facade," obscuring for the moment "empty men with hungry hearts," all of whom "Cry out for help, O God." Borne upon the winds of peace and justice, the Church, in Reid's hymnodic scheme, penetrates the density of poverty and crime and lust, serving the weak as well as the strong. Inspired by God, the Church of the middle and late twentieth century performs a mission "to share her dream, / To give the world her song!"

The elder William Watkins Reid has given to the twentieth century three hymns that serve as clear reverberations of the historical and social environments in which he composed them. His hymn for missions, "Lord, wake your Church from self-concern," introduces a thesis describing such work as "Christ-envisioned brotherhood" intended to "stir the sluggish minds and wills, / Of us who raise faint words of prayer." On a broader scale, the elder Reid casts his hymnodic net over the entire universe, addressing an all-encompassing God, a God of earth, planets, worlds, atoms, flowers, oceans, fragrance, beauty, power, home, family, and parents. The piece appears as an exercise in piling epithets upon one another until the congregational singer comes to realize that each of the five stanzas represents a separate sphere of human comprehension, each controlled by God as master, friend, and guide. Finally, Reid's covenant hymn, "O God, ere history began," provides some fresh phrasing for a fairly traditional theme and setting. Our "flick'ring light" of unsteady commitment requires renewed faith; silently we ask God to "Teach us to search Thy word of truth, / To plumb its wells of peace." Although certainly not the most original poet among contemporary hymnodists, Reid does pay strict attention to the present moment, while remaining equally attentive to hymnodic conventionalism. After all, such phrases as "To plumb its wells of peace" evidence a degree of freshness not always noticeable among hymnodic trendsetters.

During the decade of the 1960s, women contributed significantly, both in quality and in numbers, to the development of American hymnody. Those sisters of sacred song do not necessarily present a feminist point of view; rather, they reflect the expanding roles of women in the life of the American Church during the middle and late twentieth century. For example, Elisabeth Burrowes, who was discussed earlier, asks God to "send men" to the ministry—"men in whom Thy heart rejoices, / Men who have heard the call that makes us free." Miriam Drury, in her hymn for missions ("Within the Church's hallowed walls") asks God to "Direct the Church's mission: / To live the Gospel, heal and preach, / And better man's condition." On the other hand, she avoids the obvious issue of generic distinction in confronting the matter of the Christian's broader ministry; she addresses her lines to *all* Christians, commanding them, as it were, to "Walk proud . . . / As Christ's ambassador." Her clear imperatives receive sharp emphasis from the repetitions at the outset of each stanza, as the universal Christian walks "tall," "true," "free," and "proud." Another instance of careful and controlled repetition occurs in Miriam Winter's "God gives His people strength," a piece that achieves unity through its obvious symmetry. Each of her four stanzas opens and concludes with "God loves His people," the objects being strength, hope, love and peace—in that order.

The other women hymnodists—Olive Wise Spannaus and Mildred Luckhardt—demonstrate the degrees to which American hymnodists of the period expanded the substance of their pieces, reaching out beyond their own national boundaries. Spannaus addresses the "Lord of all nations," envisioning God's love for persons of all races within the "bonds of Christian brotherhood." Her singer-worshiper will seek to "Break down the wall that would divide / Your children, Lord, on every side," replacing that barrier with human courage, love, and forgiveness. Mildred Luckhardt develops her theme far beyond the limited political divisions of states and nations. Her "Great Ruler over time and space" extends dominions over time, space, and galaxies, being—in terms of the context of present faith and moral commitment—the "Great Source of every hope of man, / Creator of vast worlds unknown." Appropriately, in terms of the decade in which she wrote the piece, Luckhardt appears caught up in technological progress, and thus she envisions God as the "Kind Father of each airborne man," as a "Source of power for wheels and wings," as a "Key to understanding things." Nevertheless, despite the unknown qualities surrounding twentieth-century technology, the sanity of the world—the balance of the universe—remains apparent. From Luckhardt's vantage, that sanity exists principally because what people do and think continues to be "harmonious" with God's grand scheme for all: "In future years, on paths untrod, / We would walk close to Thee, our God."

Through the efforts of two other female hymnodists—Frances Hibbert and Florence Jansson—one may observe both the form and the substance of children's hymnody in the United States during the 1960s. The Jansson piece, "A bird, lovely butterfly," directs the attentions of young worshipers to the specific and certainly most fundamental objects within the natural order of God's created universe. Indeed, the hymn constitutes a listing of those objects, a veritable roster of clouds, mountains, flowers, plants, and other natural elements that speak, by their very being, directly of God. At the same time, however, those objects inhabit Jansson's hymn as the essences of a child's comprehension of God, the substance of "all the beauty that we know." Frances Hibbert's hymn, on the other hand, is one more contribution to the Christmas Nativity genre. Certainly, her "Cradled in a manger" deserves consideration because it proceeds from the child's point of view; unfortunately, it contains little in terms of thought or of language to distinguish it from scores of nineteenth-century British and American hymns and carols on the same topic. Most assuredly, Hibbert produces a tender vision of the Christ child sleeping "On the fragrant hay"; but aside from that opening image, the hymn provides congregations with little that they—as children or adults—have not sung previously for that occasion.

For instances of pure poetic quality, one of the best hymnodic efforts to come from the period of the 1960s may well be Martin Franzmann's "O God, O Lord of heaven and earth," a piece intended to elevate the spirits of those caught in the grip of a terribly hard and negative world. Franzmann tries especially hard to direct people away from life as "an aimless note, / A deathward drift from futile birth" to simply "The road that leads us back to God." Rather than circle the worn path of generally abstract images representing redemption and restoration, he practically forces one to unwrap what he terms "Thy wondrous gift of liberty," a charm that reveals to our dark and dreary eyes a new but exceedingly clear and simple image: "How beautiful the feet that ran / To bring the great good news to man." Life, for Franzmann, becomes one long statement of praise, a "high doxology" that turns hearts and minds from the gloom and the confusion of the present, that cleanses—through Christ—the "poisoned air" of dark despair. The sharpness of Franzmann's imagery and structure may, at certain moments, deter singers from his lines, for they are not always pleasant to sing. However, he forces worshipers to think, which appears reason enough to include this piece in the worship service on more than an occasional basis.

Three folk hymnodists have brought serious sentiment and quality of expression to congregational song, as well as captured the rhythm and the energy that characterizes their form. The Reverend W. F. Jabusch adapts an Israeli folk song to what he labels a song for good news. More importantly, he asks Christians to open their ears and their hearts to the idea that "God has spoken to His people . . . / And His words are words of wisdom, alleluia!" Sebastian Temple poses essentially the same question before singers and worshipers, although he relies more heavily than does Jabusch upon internal end refrains. Not only does he punctuate each phrase with "Glory, hallelujah," he ends each of the three stanzas with this version of the Gloria:

> Glory to the Trinity,
> The undivided Unity,
> The Father, Son, and Spirit one,
> For whom all life and goodness come, come, come.

Perhaps the most sensitive of the three folk hymnodists, Paul Quinlan, proves to congregational singers that the combination of fresh, active imagery and clear, simple language can serve the needs of American congregational song.

> And the morning will see the rolling sun as
>   he happily rises o'er the land;
> A messenger on his daily run bring news of
>   a Father's guiding hand.

The opening lines of that passage set the overall tone for Quinlan's apparent happiness; he imagines a "brand new day" wherein the sunlight of God's grace will light and warm even the darkest and the coldest aspects of human pessimism. In other words, behind the "time of wind and rain" there stands, ready for all to enjoy, "the sun of future days."

One may now turn to the shortest time span in the discussion of twentieth-century American hymnody, 1970 to 1974. However, the reader will immediately discover that the five years under consideration in Table 35 provide sufficient hymnodic production to allow them to compete favorably with the larger periods that have preceded.

Table 35. American Hymnody, 1970–1974

Date	Hymnodist	Opening Lines
1970	Carlton C. Buck	O God of youth, we come to you for leading, Our minds to guide, our spirits to set free
1970	Carlton C. Buck	We want to know, Lord, touch our minds; We want to see, so touch our eyes
1970	Chester E. Custer	Eternal God, in whom we live and move, Who from our birth has kept us in Thy love
1970	Chester E. Custer	The earth, O Lord, belongs to Thee: The fertile land, the sky, the sea
1970	Miriam Drury	Become to us the living bread By which the Christian life is spread
1970	Miriam Drury	Give us to share a dream, The one-world justice dream
1970	Franklin P. Frye	Tune me in, O God, To your holy will
1970	Bryan Jeffery Leech	Through all the world let ev'ry nation sing to God the King, As Lord may Christ preside where now He is defied
1970	Barbara J. Owen	God of the green earth, Singing with growing
1970	Marion James Price	The Church of Christ has work to do Around this earthly sphere
1970	Thad Roberts, Jr.	God of earth and outer space, God of love and God of grace
1970	Robert Newell Zearfoss	There is enough To feed this world
1971	Ernest K. Emurian	Our hope is in the living God Within whose love our fathers trod
1971	Martin Franzmann	Weary of all trumpeting, Weary of all killing
1971	Wade Alexander Mansur	We gather at Thy table, Lord, To fellowship with Thee
1971	Charles Parkin	Lord, when the way we see cannot see, And troubles burden every heart

Date	Hymnodist	Opening Lines
1971	William Watkins Reid	My hope is not in self To change my grief to song
1971	William Watkins Reid	Where lies the Christian's hope when fear and hate And battles rage
1971	Frank Von Christierson	Christ is risen! raise your voices Jubilant with joy and praise
1972	Frank A. Brooks, Jr.	The day of Pentecost arrived, To one place many came
1972	Chester E. Custer	O Christ, my Lord, create in me The person I am meant to be
1972	David A. Robb	Thou Lord of music, Author of true song, To Thee the lyrics of our life belong
1972	Byron Edward Underwood	O mighty God! when I all-wonder stricken Survey the universe your work ordain'd
1972	Frank Von Christierson	Shout God's Easter triumph: "Christ is risen indeed!"
1972	Frank Von Christierson	Upon a wintry night there came A song of joy and peace
1973	Charles B. Foelsch	Little Jesus, holy Child, Lying in the manger
1973	David C. Norling	Go tell it in the suburb, City, and town, and everywhere
1973	William Watkins Reid, Jr.	God of our common life, Strength of our time and strife
1973	Frances E. Weir	O, we who love our land And sing of her in praise
1973	David Yantis	Turn it over to Jesus, He'll more than meet your needs
1974	Evelyn Kimball Bartelt	Your Church shall stand as it's always stood, Jesus mighty Saviour!

Of the twenty-three hymnodists listed, fourteen may be categorized as new names—as individuals whose hymnodic poetry has not yet, in this discussion of twentieth-century

American congregational song, been mentioned. For example, Marion Price focuses upon the work of the contemporary Church. She describes a social mission that extends "Through alleys, ghettoes, slums"; it incorporates the problems of the blind and the aged, and it devotes considerable attention to particular material and spiritual places

> Where prejudice has locked the gates
> On real estate and school,
> She pulls down walls of racial hates,
> And posts the Golden Rule.

Operating in spheres similar to those of Price, David Norling expends his hymnodic energies on a paraphrase of the black spiritual, "Go tell it on the mountain." Instead he produces, under the refrain of "Go tell it in the suburb," thirty-six lines of contemporary sentiment. For Norling, Christ "died to prove forgiveness, / He rose to energize"; thus, we all need to rush outside and exuberantly inform our brothers and sisters,

> Go tell it in the office,
>   Kitchen, and mall, and everywhere;
> Go tell the news in our world,
>   That Jesus Christ brings life!

A number of people may have difficulty expressing such imagery during a worship service, especially in the midst of gothic stone and stained glass. However, no one ought to experience difficulty perceiving the total dimension of Norling's 1970-model mountain.

As with the majority of American hymnodists who published in the decades following World War II and the Korean conflict, as well as those who endured our national involvements in Southeast Asia, the writers of the 1970s continued to look beyond the shores and the borders of this nation. They continued to consider the relationship between God and the creatures who inhabit all parts of the universe. Thus, Brian Leech begins and ends three of his four stanzas with "Through all the world" (the final verse simply substitutes "If" and "Then" for "Through"). Leech stresses the concept of every nation, every person, and every part; he requests, in the middle of the piece, that "Christ now be the norm to which all men conform." Although very much concerned with the same world, R. N. Zearfoss looks to his own life—even to his own guilt—as a resident of this earth, and he poses a number of extremely serious considerations.

> There is enough
>   To feed this world,
> Oh, yes, enough
>   To let all live;
> So now we strive
> To feed this world,
> So now we strive
> To hate no more.

At a first reading, Thad Roberts's hymn for the space age appears only to advance an extremely contemporary relationship between God, who would "Fling the module through the air," and those astronauts who "soar in lunar flight." However, Roberts knows, as do Leech and Zearfoss, the exact limits of human responsibilities in a God-created, God-directed universe. As humans walk in space, God in turn will teach them how to "walk in grace"; as those same humans leave the perimeters of earth, God will launch them "from complacency to a world in need of Thee." And so Roberts concludes not on a technological note, but upon the strains of love and human understanding, upon the idea of an endeavor that proposes to "Guide the lives of seeking youth in their search for heav'nly truth."

The concrete relationships between musical and religious expression come forward clearly in certain hymns by David Robb and by Martin Franzmann. Although Robb wrote his "Thou Lord of Music" for the fiftieth anniversary

of the Hymn Society of America (now located at Texas
Christian University, Fort Worth), the piece manages easily
to transcend the occasion. In essence, Robb's lines constitute a general tribute to hymnody and to the "Author of
true song," the ultimate composer "Whose verse becomes
the poet's guiding goal, / Who sings a song within the
hymnist's soul." He asks for inspiration and direction for
new hymns reflective of new ages and representative of
human "dissonance and roar," of "wholesome discontent."
Martin Franzmann also asks for new songs, but his motives
differ drastically from those of the Reverend Mr. Robb.
The former's hymn begins with a tone fairly close to
outright disgust.

> Weary of all trumpeting,
> Weary of all killing,
> Weary of all songs that sing
> Promise, non-fulfilling.

He seeks, instead, a single song that he describes as "great
music, pure and strong / Wherewith heaven is singing."
Franzmann's hymn becomes an appeal for an end to all loss
and all suffering—for a surrender of "the foolish sword"
and an embracing of the spirit and the splendor of Christ.
The "trumpeting" of the opening stanza gives way, then, to
a "trumpet with your Spirit's breath / Through each
height and hollow."

During the first half of the 1970s, the folk hymn
continued its popularity among those worshipers impatient with traditional modes and forms. Franklin Frye's
"Tune me in, O God" relies heavily upon simplicity and a
strong sense of idiom to declare an extremely concise and
deeply personal message.

> Let me not drop out of your company;
> Let me not cop out
> Of plans you have for me.

Nonetheless, the substance of the hymn remains fairly conventional, for Frye's narrator-singer tunes the heart and mind to God's will, God's love, and the peace and the power of Christ—those being the ideals to which Christian thought aspires. The notion of "tuning in" to God assumes, for David Yantis, a similar phrase—"Turn it over to Jesus"—implying that Christ will meet the needs, bear the guilt, and take hold of the burdens of all. Yantis adopts that form of hymnodic symmetry familiar among those caught up with the folk-hymn movement. Each of his three stanzas begins and ends with "Turn it over to Jesus," while as a type of denouement, Yantis inserts (at the very end of the stanza) the simple declaration, "He cares." Between those refrains, the hymnodist asks his singers to express their concern over the usual human deficiencies—their frailties, their burdens, and (upon occasion) their lack of humanity.

To the listing of new names that introduced this discussion of American hymnody between 1970 and 1974, a number of familiar hymnodists, who have contributed significantly to the form, may be added. Continuing his concentration upon the major festivals of the year, Frank Von Christierson provides a Christmas hymn (set to "Amazing Grace"), "Upon a wintry night there came," as well as two pieces for Easter: "Christ is risen! raise your voices" and "Shout God's Easter triumph." As usual, he lends fresh imagery to his lines, creating a sense of hope and promise to the faithful within the contemporary world. Thus, the Easter celebration not only proclaims the risen Christ and the defeat of sin and death, it also introduces "the cross of promise / For a hopeless world" that ultimately directs all humanity toward "Life anew—eternal." He extends the thread of the hope-faith relationship by directing the congregational singers' collective attention to the life that God has given them through Christ, an existence that brings new hope and new worth as long as people "Trust this joyful sacred Word."

In his Christmas hymn, Von Christierson declares the occasion of Christ's birth to be "A song of joy and peace" for a spiritually depressed twentieth century. Again, hope emerges as a prevalent quality, for the song of joy and peace is "A song of hope for all mankind, / Of freedom and release." Once more, worshipers must trust to the "living Word / Of love, forgiveness, peace, and hope." Criticism of Von Christierson's hymns as being unnecessarily repetitious in content and in language may be quickly countered by the singer's realization that these very points require emphasis; the consciences of those within the pews need to be prodded continually, lest they forget their moral and spiritual obligations to one another and to God. If a contemporary hymnodic conscience can be said to exist, Von Christierson stands as a prime candidate for that office.

At the risk of belaboring the subject, the issue of hope needs more consideration, for that theme certainly does control the thoughts of a number of American hymnodists during this period. William Watkins Reid, for instance, looks to the matter of personal hope, concluding that the most obvious materialistic objectives of hope—self, action, money, weapons, and even opportunity—come forth as utterly worthless. Only faith and the love for God

> Assures the human breast
> That hopes and aspirations high
> By You are known and blest.

Further, the hope of the entire world appears threatened by hate, fratricide, starvation, terror, and war; thus Reid's title question, "Where lies the Christian's hope?" remains imbedded securely in "The purpose of our God," in His having "fashioned man for role above the brute." In Charles Parkin's imagination, hope takes the form of the grand vision for the new world, "a dream that will not fade," while Ernest Emurian looks directly at the Pauline epistle and declares, with utmost confidence,

> Our hope is in the living God
> Within whose love our Fathers trod,
> And who, throughout His vast domain,
> Doth still in love forever reign.
> Face we the future unafraid,
> On the foundation He has laid.

Both Chester Custer and Barbara Owen prove to congregational singers the effectiveness of hymnody as a contribution to the ongoing debate on the environment. Owen addresses "God of the green earth," asking that human inhabitants acquire wisdom, learn respect, develop love, and practice restraint in their dealings with those creatures "Born at creation / When planets danced and / Morning stars sang." She neither obscures her purpose nor veils her language, choosing, instead, to parade the elements of nature directly before the congregation.

> Wildcat and beaver,
> Bee and brown sparrow
> Have earned equal right to
> This earthly state.

Custer may appear more general and therefore less metrically abrasive than Barbara Owen, but his thesis does not differ radically from hers: "O give us wisdom in our age, / To hold in trust their heritage." He views the environment in terms of its actuality, as all-encompassing. For that hymnodist, "In city street and country side, / May beauty, life, and health abide"—certainly not a complex idea. Beneath everything, however, Custer views the restoration of God's nature on earth in a manner not unlike the Second Coming; he builds on that parallel in the last two lines of stanzas two and three: "From streams defiled we shall reclaim / A cup of water in Thy name"; and "Behold the sun, the distant shore, / And breathe the breath of life once more." Then, in the final stanza occurs the ultimate transition, as "all the wastelands of our earth / Await the day of second birth." The hymns by Owen and

Custer reveal the creative personalities of their authors: the ecologist as hymnodist, the hymnodist as environmentalist.

In 1970 the Hymn Society of America published ten new congregational odes (without music) under the title *Hymns for the '70's*. The committee that solicited the poems hoped to appeal to "the young people of the churches" with ideas "that would be expressed in 'modern idioms' used by the youth of the 1970s; yet would be suitable . . . in a church service by a general congregation." In responding to that purpose, Miriam Drury wrote a prayer hymn for young people, asking God for a dream to share, a "one-world justice dream, / The peace and brotherhood dream / Of Christendom." The dream, when fulfilled, will erase hunger, hate, suffering, and poverty; in actuality, the "dream" becomes a specific aim. Thus, the hymn itself is a prayer for the real rather than for the often nebulous ideal.

Those youth and young adults who sing the first of Carlton Buck's two hymns in the small Hymn Society collection not only express their desire for an intellectual perception of God, they also ask that God touch their hearts, forgive their hesitation and indecision, and inspire their lives. In his second piece, Buck addresses the "God of youth" and alludes to problems not always easily identified.

> The stress is great and absolutes are bending.
> We cannot find our way without your care;
> It seems the search goes ever forth unending,
> And fainting hearts cry out, O Master, where?

Buck identifies the potential insecurity and helplessness among certain individuals—both the young and the old— and thus he attempts, in that hymn, to indicate a route toward the truth and the love of God. Although providing no quick answers, Buck at least strives to shape what he believes to be the proper questions for the youth of that period.

Moving to the final stage in this discussion of American hymnody, Table 36 notes hymnodists and certain of their pieces composed from 1975 through 1986.

Table 36. American Hymnody, 1975–1986

Date	Hymnodist	Opening Lines
1975	Ford L. Battles	The Church of Christ is one: Many are the rays of the sun
1975	Benjamin Caulfield	O God, wise Creator, Sustainer, and Guide Of planets, of nations, of continents wide
1975	Carrie Hitt Hardcastle	Dear God of all creation, May we Thy people be
1975	H. Glen Lanier	God, 'neath whose hand our fathers crossed the sea, Seeking a land of peace and liberty
1975	H. Glen Lanier	Lord of nations, God eternal, Lift we songs of praise to Thee
1975	Brian Jeffery Leech	Let your heart be broken For a world in need
1975	William Nelson	The mountains rise in ranges far and high Above the walls men throw against the sky
1975	Joe Pinson	We see God in His people ev'rywhere We see God in His people ev'rywhere
1975	William Watkins Reid, Jr.	America, how great the dream Your patriot fathers dreamed of old
1975	Gilbert Taverner	God of surging seas and oceans, Of the sun-warmed sandy shores
1975	Anastasia Van Burkalow	Almighty God, who made all things, We thank you for our native land
1976	Louise M. Armitage	The sun is setting in our lives, And we are grateful, God
1976	Gertrude M. Boling	God, our Father now as ever, Guide us through each passing day
1976	Ernest K. Emurian	God of the past, the present and the future, God of all men and nations yet to be

Date	Hymnodist	Opening Lines
1976	H. Glen Lanier	O God, Thy constant care and love Are shed upon us from above
1976	David C. Norling	When Christ the Lord came marching in, When Christ the Lord came marching in
1976	William Watkins Reid, Jr.	Eternal Christ, who, kneeling When earthly tasks were done
1976	William Watkins Reid, Jr.	Mountain brook with gushing waters, Eagle perched in lofty tree
1976	Gilbert Taverner	We bring the little children To this Your Church, O God
1976	Frank Von Christierson	Good news! great joy to all the earth!— The Prince of Peace is born!
1976	James R. Webb	Lord, give me strength for golden years Lived in the sunset glow
1976	Frances E. Weir	O we, who love our land And sing of her in praise
1976	Omer Westendorf	You satisfy the hungry heart With gift of finest wheat
1977	Jane Parker Huber	Creator God, creating still By will and word and deed
1978	Jackson Hill	O Lord of love, who once did speak from heaven To Saul of Tarsus whom all Christians feared
1978	Jane Parker Huber	Christ's partners are we, Alleluia! Amen! In mission joyfully, Alleluia! Amen!
1978	Norman Olsen	When seed falls on good soil, It's born through quiet toil
1978	Joe Pinson	Blessed be our Father God forever; Sing a song of praise to the Lord on high
1980	Jane Parker Huber	Called by Christ to love each other, Called by Christ to seek the lost
1981	Jane Parker Huber	As trees from tiny seeds can grow, As yeast expands the lifeless dough
1981	Daniel Schutte	Only this I want: but to know the Lord, And to bear His cross, so to wear the crown He wore

Date	Hymnodist	Opening Lines
1982	Jane Parker Huber	God, give us eyes and heart to see Signs of Your reign and victory
1983	Jane Parker Huber	Join hearts and voices as we lift Our gratitude for ev'ry gift
1983	Harmon B. Ramsay	Praise be to Christ the Lord of life! Through Him all worlds were framed
1983	David A. Robb	Creative life, when you spoke forth Great power surged on high
1984	Thomas H. Troeger	"Silence, frenzied, unclean spirit," Cried God's healing, Holy One
1985	John H. Dallas	O God of love, grant us your peace within each restless mind
1985	Gracia Grindal (trans. from Sven Ellingsen)	Filled with gladness as we pour this water now we stand before you with our new born
1985	Thomas H. Troeger	Fierce the force that curled Cain's fist— Would he master it or yield?
1986	Hal M. Helms	Let heav'n rejoice before the anthems raise; Let all creation sing its song of praise
1986	Miriam Therese Putzer	Great God, we lift our hearts in praise for blessings without measure
1986	Thomas H. Troeger	Before the fruit is ripened by the sun, Before the petals of the leaves uncoil
1986	Thomas H. Troeger	Forever in the heart there springs a hunger never touched by things
1986	Thomas H. Troeger	These things did Thomas count as real: the warmth of blood, the chill of steel
1986	Thomas H. Troeger	View the present through the promise Christ will come again

Although the hymns and hymnodists of this most contemporary period of American congregational song, because of chronological incompleteness, seem infinite in

form and substance, two themes should catch the immediate attention of congregational singers—one historical, the
other social, and both offering a sense of timelessness. The
observance of the Bicentennial of the United States
naturally promoted a number of church poets not only to
reflect upon the past, but to contemplate the future as well.
Thus, William Watkins Reid, Jr., in "America, how great
the dream," characterizes the nation within the context of
a grand vision, one shared by the patriot fathers in their
search for freedom and political equality. He not only
declares the greatness of that dream, but asks for mainte-
nance, repetition, renewal, and enlargement on the part of
those who currently participate in this nation under God.
For Anastasia Van Burkalow, celebration signals the
opportunity to ask for forgiveness on behalf of those who
have been "Unfaithful stewards of your gifts." Her three
stanzas set forth, respectively, thanks for God-given
beauty, wealth, and freedom. In general terms, she
confesses having bespoiled those gifts, while begging
forgiveness and seeking help "to make earth whole again,
/ And freedom's light more pure and bright." Although
Glen Lanier essentially sees the celebration of the nation's
two-hundredth year in a context parallel to those of Reid
and Van Burkalow, he does take the time (in "God, 'neath
whose hand") to remind Americans not to lose sight of
their priorities.

> May we be great in more than armaments;
> Our vict'ry more than skill in battlements;
> May truth and justice be our mighty sword,
> And brotherhood be more than spoken word.

No doubt that the Bicentennial reminded Americans
of a number of important issues. For example, in 1975 the
Hymn Society of America, in league with the American
Association of Retired Persons, issued a call for new hymns
celebrating aging and the later years of life. From more

than twelve hundred submissions, a panel of judges selected for publication in 1976 *Ten Hymns on Aging and the Later Years*. Although not always rising to high levels of poetic quality, the pieces identify with considerable accuracy, the needs and concerns of American senior citizens.

Louise Armitage, for example, sees life as one significant lesson and asks "That others through our lives may learn / To give Thee grateful praise," while Gertrude Boling fills the void between life's beginning and its end with "God unchanging, ever faithful." Viewing the later years as a new beginning, James Webb—in "Lord, give me strength for golden years"—promotes faith, which he identifies as "my spirit bright." Faith compensates amply for the waning physical powers, and places with ease and clarity the Hebrew psalmodist's ancient vision in a late-twentieth-century context.

> Though I may walk with falt'ring tread
> The path I dimly see,
> Let Thy strong hand be ever near
> To guide and comfort me.

One must never forget that the hymns in the Hymn Society's small collection sound, with undeniable harmony, the notes of hope and strength for the elderly. They do not peal forth the negative reverberations of dejection and dependency that all too often stereotypes the aged.

The Bicentennial and senior citizenry were not the only topics of concern for hymn writers of the mid-1970s. A number of poets from preceding decades continued to remind worshipers of the world's fragile state and to suggest options that might lead to eventual repair and strengthening of traditional American values. Proclaiming joy and peace as God's prescriptions for fear and conflict, Frank Von Christierson demands that congregational singers "Rise up for peace! let every life / Respond with heart and hand." David Norling, on the other hand, rides the vibrant waves of an all-too-familiar hymn tune ("O when the saints") as he challenges Americans to confront the process of decision.

> For you and me what will it be?
> For you and me what will it be?
> Just empty words or Jesus' bold action?
> For you and me what will it be?

On a softer but no less enthusiastic strain, William Watkins Reid, Jr., points to the specific objects in God's world— mountain brook, eagle, flowers, deer, water, wheat, cattle, apples, trees—and proclaims "Beauty, beauty all around us, / Jubilate! Sing for joy!" Reid does more than simply gape in awe at those objects, however; he observes human beings engaged in partnership with God, and therefore prays, "Help us, God, preserve earth's splendor / For tomorrow's world to see."

In the hearts and the minds of contemporary hymno-dists in the United States, the needs of the world at large become the focal point for earthly mission. Therefore, they all seem to grasp the essence of Reid's partnership between human beings and their Creator, although certain poets come forth in more direct terms than others. In "Let your heart be broken," Bryan Leech commands congregations to feed the hungry mouths, soothe the wounds of the injured, apply the principles of love—in a word, "Be the hands of Jesus serving in His stead." Leech wants worship-ers to form a "partnership" with God. The image shifts, somewhat, in Norman Olsen's "When seed falls on good soil"; the word of God (the "seed") descends to find "in human-kind / The fertile soil in heart and mind." The so-called partnership becomes a grand conception and then a birth within the heart and the soul of the human being, an ideal that translates to faith in the Word.

On a slightly more practical level, but obviously within the same partnership vein, Ford Battles shifts the focus to

"The Church of Christ" and simply lays the idea of unity atop that of partnership.

> The branches of the Church
> Are spread through all the earth, and still
> The body of the Church remains,
> Whole, unbroken, one.

Such unity, of course, acquires light and life only from the sun of God, "the one parent light," the "undying light" that spreads over the entire earth and envelops the Church of Christ. Classicists will recognize the imagery of Battles's piece, for it is a translation from the *De Unitate* of Cyprian of Carthage (c. A.D. 252). Nevertheless, Battles speaks directly to his twentieth-century audience in terms of its own understanding of and its place within the natural world of God and the spiritual kingdom of Christ.

One contemporary hymn writer requires special mention for a number of reasons, principally because of his work in the area of what has come to be known as collaborative hymnody. Thomas H. Troeger, an associate professor of preaching and parish ministry at a truly collaborative institution (Colgate Rochester Divinity School/Bexley Hall/Crozer Theological Seminary) works carefully and imaginatively with the sound and the sense of language. Relying heavily upon the Germanic and Anglo-Saxon origins of English, he produces texts that combine strong rhythm with linguistic conciseness.

> These things did Thomas count as real:
> the warmth of blood, the chill of steel,
> the grain of wood, the heft of stone,
> the last frail twitch of flesh and bone.

Thomas's view of reality comes in harsh, striking tones, made possible by the piling on of equally reverberative images. Singers cannot possibly escape from feeling what they read and sing. In addition, of the thirty-one words in this cited stanza, only one—the proper noun *Thomas*—contains more than a single syllable. This is not to accuse Troeger of overreliance on monosyllabic words; he knows and employs rhythmic balance and variety as well as anyone (as in the third stanza of "These things did Thomas count as real"):

> His reasoned certainties denied,
>   that one could live when one had died,
> until his fingers read like Braille
>   the marking of the spear and nail.

The first line yields eight beats from four words; the second, eight from eight words—all monosyllabic; the third and fourth lines, eight beats each from six words. And as in the opening stanza, such images as "his fingers read like Braille / the marking of the spear and nail" attack singers' senses.

In terms of singing such pieces, Troeger has the advantage—or, more accurately, has seized the initiative—of working with his own organist. Carol Doran teaches church music and directs community worship at the same conglomerate institution as Troeger. They compose hymns together—music and text in conjunction with each other—and even conduct seminars wherein they consult with ministers and congregational worshipers about criteria for hymnodic composition and selection. Rather than repeat what has already been written for public consumption, it is suggested that one consult two published essays—required reading, if you will—by and about the Doran/Troeger collaboration:

1. Carol Doran and Thomas H. Troeger. "Writing Hymns as a Theologically Informed Artistic Discipline." *Hymn* 36 (April 1985): 7–11.
2. Brian Wren. "Praise God and Pound the Typewriter: A Critical Appreciation of Thomas Troeger." *Hymn* 37 (July 1986): 13–19. A review

essay of *New Hymns for the Lectionary: To Glorify the Maker's Name*. Music by Carol Doran; words by Thomas Troeger. New York: Oxford University Press, 1986 (a volume that should also be added to the required reading list).

Before turning from contemporary American hymnody, it is necessary to consider the inseparable problems of subject, language, and music as they affect recent trends and practices of congregational poets. Individuals may accept and even embrace the hymn tunes of fifty, seventy-five, or one hundred years ago; however, those same singers and worshipers may as quickly reject certain social or theological concerns as being too limited, certain language patterns and preferences as being too restrictive or too exclusive. Thus, practically all congregational singers have begun to witness the practice of composing new words for old hymn tunes. For example, Gilbert Taverner's "God of surging seas and oceans" may now be sung to "Beecher" (associated traditionally with "Love divine, all love excelling"), "Austria" (known long as the accompaniment to "Glorious things of Thee are spoken"), or the "Hymn to Joy" ("Joyful, joyful we adore Thee"). Another Taverner piece, "We bring the little children," fits easily and intentionally to "Lancashire" (associated with "Lead on, O King eternal") or "Hankey" ("I love to tell the story"). Similarly, the words of Jane Parker Huber have been consciously shaped into pieces to fit easily recognizable hymn tunes: "Creator God, creating still" may be sung to "Saint Anne"—a tune long associated with Isaac Watts's "Our God, our help in ages past"; "As trees from tiny seeds can grow" fits "Federal Street" (associated with "Come dearest Lord, descend and dwell"); and "Christ's partners all are we" has been set to "Madrid," a tune long known to accompany "Come, Christians join to sing").

The matter of the poetic quality of the most recent hymn texts will, of course, continue to cause debate and controversy—especially among those concerned with the relationship between poetry and hymnody. Nevertheless, among singers whose commitment to both the words and the music of traditional hymnody remains strong, there exists the opportunity for a reasonable transition from the old to the new. After all (and to repeat what has appeared on several occasions throughout this discussion), consideration of both traditional and contemporary fashions appears, to the majority of congregational singers and worshipers, preferable to total surrender on the part of one or the other. As the hymnody of the United States approaches the end of yet another century, such a consideration, such a compromise, will indeed become dominant for poets, musicians, and singers. In the end, the last word belongs to the most noted of twentieth-century hymnologists, Erik Routley—a Briton who practiced his scholarly art in this nation as much as he did in his own. In 1981, Routley declared:

> What is for people who are neither literary connoisseurs nor cultivated musicians, and what is designed to become part of their religious lives, must contain something which is already theirs, and something which is newly given.... The composer of tomorrow's hymnody must equally love the tradition and have his or her own comment to make on it—or, if they prefer the expression, rebel against it. But no—it is not the bitterness and contempt of rebellion that we want. It is the developing counterpoint of good conversation. It is a conversation which will continue for a long time yet.
>
> (quoted in *Hymn* 34 [January 1983]:19)

The middle road proves not always the easiest one upon which to travel, but in the context of twentieth-century American hymnody, it can be the only road—for hymnodists as well as for those who express themselves through congregational song.

For Further Reading
WORKS CITED AND CONSULTED

Adey, Lionel. *Hymns and the Christian "Myth."* Vancouver: University of British Columbia Press, 1986.

Barkley, John M., editor. *Handbook to the Church Hymnary.* 3d edition. London: Oxford University Press, 1979.

Benson, Louis Fitzgerald. *The English Hymn: Its Development in Use and Worship.* 1915. Reprint. Richmond, Va.: John Knox Press, 1962.

———. *The Hymnody of the Christian Church.* New York: George H. Doran Company, 1927.

Bickersteth, Edward Henry, editor. *The Hymnal Companion to the Book of Common Prayer.* 3d edition, revised and enlarged. London: Longmans, Green and Company, 1890.

Brown, Ray F. Introduction and Appendix. In *The Oxford American Psalter.* New York: Oxford University Press, 1949. Pages ix–xiv, 231–238.

Carlyle, Thomas. "On Heroes, Hero-Worship, and the Heroic in History." 1941. In *English Prose of the Victorian Era,* edited by Charles Frederick Harrold and William D. Templeman, 169–182. New York: Oxford University Press, 1938.

Claghorn, Gene. *Women Composers and Hymnists: A Concise Biographical Dictionary.* Metuchen, N.J.: Scarecrow Press, 1984.

Dixon, Christa K. *Negro Spirituals: From Bible to Folksong.* Philadelphia: Fortress Press, 1976.

Ellinwood, Leonard, editor. *Dictionary of American Hymnology: First-Line Index.* New York: University Music Editions, 1983. On microfilm.

———, and Elizabeth Lockwood. *Bibliography of American Hymnals.* New York: University Music Editions, 1983. On microfiche.

Foote, Henry Wilder. *Three Centuries of American Hymnody.* 1940. Reprint. New York: Archon Books, 1968.

Goldhawk, Norman P. *On Hymns and Hymn Books*. London: Epworth Press, 1979.

Hughes, Anselm, editor. *Early Medieval Music up to 1300*. London: Oxford University Press, 1955. Volume 2 of *The New Oxford History of Music*.

The Hymn: A Journal of Congregational Song. Vols. 1–38. Fort Worth, Tex. Hymn Society of America, 1949–1987.

Hymns for the '70's. Springfield, Ohio: Hymn Society of America, 1970.

Julian, John, editor. *A Dictionary of Hymnology: Setting Forth the Origin and History of Christian Hymns of All Ages and Nations*. 2d revised edition, with new supplement, 2 vols. 1907. Reprint. New York: Dover Publications, 1957.

Klepper, Robert. *In Search of a Song: A Concordance of Hymn Themes*. Bella Vista, Ariz.: United Church of Christ, 1985.

Leupold, Ulrich, S., and Helmut T. Lehmann, editors. *Luther's Works*. Vol 53. Philadelphia, Fortress Press, 1965.

Lovelace, Austin C. *The Anatomy of Hymnody*. 1965. Reprint. Chicago: GIA Publications, 1983.

———. *The Organist and Hymn Playing*. Revised edition. Carol Stream, Ill.: Hope Publishing Company, 1981.

Mac Donald, George. *Exotics: A Translation of the Spiritual Songs of Novalis, the Hymn-Book of Luther, and Other Poems from the German and Italian*. London: Strahan and Company, 1876.

Neale, John Mason. *Hymns, Chiefly Medieval, on the Joys and Glories of Paradise*. London: J. H. Parker, 1865.

Northcott, Cecil. *Hymns in Christian Worship: The Use of Hymns in the Life of the Christian Church*. Richmond, Va.: John Knox Press, 1964.

Patrick, Millar. *The Story of the Church's Song*. Revised edition, edited by James Rawlings Sydnor. Richmond, Va.: John Knox Press, 1962.

Phillips, C. S. *Hymnody Past and Present*. London: SPCK, 1937.

Ramsey, Dale. E. *Sing Praises! Management of Church Hymns*. Fort Worth, Tex.: Hymn Society of America, 1981.

Reynolds, William Jensen. *A Survey of Christian Hymnody*. New York: Holt, Rinehart and Winston, 1963.

———, and Milburn Price. *A Joyful Sound: Christian Hymnody*. 2d edition. New York: Holt, Rinehart, and Winston, 1978.

Rogal, Samuel J. *The Children's Jubilee: A Bibliographical Survey of Hymnals for Infants, Youth, and Sunday Schools Published in Britain and America, 1655–1900*. Westport, Conn.: Greenwood Press, 1983.

———. *Sisters of Sacred Song: A Selected Listing of Women*

Hymnodists in Great Britain and America. New York: Garland Publishing, 1981.

Routley, Erik. *Christian Hymns Observed: When in Our Music God Is Glorified.* Princeton, N.J.: Prestige Publications, 1982.

―――. *Church Music and the Christian Faith.* Carol Stream, Ill.: Hope Publishing Company, 1978.

―――. *A Panorama of Christian Hymnody.* Collegeville, Minn.: Liturgical Press, 1979.

―――. *Rejoice in the Lord: A Hymn Companion to the Scriptures.* Grand Rapids, Mich.: William B. Eerdmans Publishing Company, 1985.

Sizer, Sandra S. *Gospel Hymns and Social Religion: The Rhetoric of Nineteenth-Century Revivalism.* Philadelphia: Temple University Press, 1978.

Studwell, William, and David A. Hamilton. *Christmas Carols: A Reference Guide.* New York: Garland Publishing, 1985.

Sydnor, James Rawlings. *Hymns: A Congregational Study.* Carol Stream, Ill.: Hope Publishing Company, 1984.

―――. *Hymns and Their Uses.* Carol Stream, Ill.: Hope Publishing Company, 1982.

Taylor, Cyril. *Hymns for Today Discussed: A Commentary on Hymns Ancient and Modern.* Norwich and Croydon: Canterbury Press and the Royal School of Church Music, 1984.

Ten Hymns on Aging and the Later Years. Springfield, Ohio: Hymn Society of America, 1976.

Warrington, James. *Short Titles of Books Relating to or Illustrating the History and Practice of Psalmody in the United States, 1620–1820.* 1898. Reprint. Pittsburgh, Pittsburgh Theological Seminary, 1970.

Watts, Isaac. *The Psalms of David: Imitated in the Language of the New Testament, and Applied to the Christian State of Worship.* London: John Clark, 1719.

Webster, Donald. *Our Hymn Tunes: Their Choice and Performance.* Edinburgh: St. Andrew Press, 1983.

Woklgemuth, Paul W. *Rethinking Church Music.* Revised edition. Carol Stream, Ill.: Hope Publishing Company, 1981.

Zimmerman, Heinz Werner. *Five Hymns.* St. Louis: Concordia Publishing House, 1973.

INDEX TO NAMES, HYMNS, HYMN COLLECTIONS, AND TUNES

279